THE
CORPORATE
STEEPLECHASE

THE CORPORATE STEEPLECHASE

PREDICTABLE CRISES IN A BUSINESS CAREER

· BY ·

Dr. Srully Blotnick

Facts On File · New York

The Corporate Steeplechase: Predictable Crises in a Business Career

Library of Congress Cataloging in Publication Data

Blotnick, Srully.
  The corporate steeplechase.

  Includes index.
  1. Executives—Psychology.   2. Businessmen—Psychology.
3. Success in business.   I. Title.
HF5500.2.B56   1984   658.4′09   83-27454
ISBN 0-87196-840-1

Published by Facts On File, Inc., 460 Park Avenue South,
New York, N.Y. 10016

PRINTED IN THE UNITED STATES OF AMERICA
10 9 8 7 6 5 4 3 2 1

ACKNOWLEDGMENTS

Among the hundreds of people who assisted in this effort, one stands out: Professor Robert Bush, Chairman of the Psychology Department of Columbia University, who shared time, funding and office space when all three were in short supply. In the course of nearly 100 conversations in the last five years, *Forbes'* Editor, James W. Michaels, has provided some important insights. Others who provided valuable suggestions and guidance, statistical and survey assistance, computer facilities and services include: Robert Anderson, Valentine Bargmann, Hugo Beigel, Richard Christie, William Feller, John Graham, Jacob Hartstein, Judith Luscher, Rick Miller, Bernard Newton, Stanley Schachter, Richard Thomas, Robert Vargas and Steve Weinstein.

Also at *Forbes*, Helen Fleming, Betty Franklin, Vera Hayden, Delores Lataniotis, Harriett Miller and John Nolan helped keep track of a seemingly endless quantity of reports, books, papers, data, messages, cassettes, disks, disk packs and meetings. During the publication process, assistance was received from David Abrams, Alan Prescott, Lynn Stern, James Weeks and, above all, John Thornton, whose diligence, high standards and honesty improved the final product significantly.

Contents

CHAPTER
1

Introduction

SOME IDEAS ARE SO appealing we accept them without really questioning their validity; for instance, the notion that each person has one, and only one, profession to which he or she is best suited. The concept certainly isn't new. For centuries, it was widely believed that certain people had a calling. Deciding what the calling was might require painful self-scrutiny and a few false starts, but once the right path was found, everything else would fall into place. One's entire self could then be poured into the pursuit. Exhilaration accompanied the initial discovery; although it remained, in the form of self-assurance, in time it gave way to calm dedication to the profession. Singlemindedness produced peace, not the frenzy we associate with it today.

Eventually the idea was democratized. Instead of the Lord issuing the call, and only a select handful of wealthy young men receiving it, everyone was able to participate in the uplifting process. Men and women, rich and poor, could now obtain this invaluable information from a new, inner source: themselves. The social sciences were called upon in the twentieth century to embody, and therefore legitimize, a secular version of the concept. It was labeled, naturally enough, the Psychology of Professions.

To the modern ear, the label sounds as natural as rain, and by the 1950s the concept was very much in vogue. If people had trouble looking inside themselves and reading the message that described their one right-and-true profession, psychologists would help. Using a variety of pencil-and-paper tests, the direction that previously came from the Almighty could be prodded to the surface scientifically. Then, the path would be clear. Only the technique for discovering it had changed, not the basic concept or the end result.

Thanks to the ease with which the new version could be applied, help from professionals was unnecessary in most cases. Millions of young adults in the post–World War II period used the new self-

I

discovery techniques to set themselves in motion occupationally. Since the marching orders seemed to be coming from within, resisting them would have been self-defeating. Each person insisted that he was merely following the guideline "To thine own self be true."

Be that as it may, the concept that each of us has one and only one profession that best suits us is flawed right to its core. At the very least, it overlooks what has been an essential component of the work world for more than 150 years; namely, that the nature of work keeps changing. Professions rise and fall in pay and prestige; new ones are continually being created, while others are rendered obsolete. Anyone who claims to be able to divine which profession is best for each young adult would do well to realize that not only is this the equivalent of firing the youngster at a moving target, a large part of the target hasn't even come into view yet.

As it turns out, the notion of a psychology of professions, as well as the older concept of a calling, is based on an extremely static world view, one that leaves little if any room for either (1) personality changes throughout one's 40-year work life, or (2) changes in market demand for various types of professionals, much less (3) both factors operating simultaneously.

The conceptual flaws would be merely of academic interest were it not for the fact that people have swallowed this argument whole, in its modern dress. They unwittingly use it to criticize themselves roundly even when they have already made the decision to change professions. If they were being true to themselves before but are now making a major switch, they must therefore be acting in a manner that is at odds with who and what they really are. Something has to give, and most people, acting pragmatically, let it be their perspective instead of their new position. They make the change and worry about explaining it to others, as well as themselves, later. They are the same, they insist when asked; only what they do for a living has changed.

After 25 years of studying the topic intensively, we feel safe in asserting that, even if they are exactly the same as they've been for the decade since their first day on the job, the new position itself will produce unique changes in them as the years pass. We didn't know that when, a quarter of a century ago, we began selecting a sample to study long-term. Instead, we assumed that the large majority would choose a line of work and remain with it. After all, by the time they were in their late teen years, weren't they already well-formed proto-professionals of one kind or another, lacking only the necessary technical training to be fully what they essentially were? In retrospect, the assumption was naive, yet it seemed reasonable in the late 1950s, a period characterized by concern about security and stability. Actually, there was a great deal of occupational instability during that decade as well as this one. Abrupt career changes were common. But the intellectual climate of the time caused a great deal of such behavior to be viewed as eccentric or deviant, an anomaly in any event, not actions in which mainstream men and women would typically participate.

Then and now, one piece of evidence about our work lives seems more revealing than all the rest combined: people in different professions think, speak, look, and act differently. Even within any given profession, veterans in that field confidently claim to be able to tell one subgroup from another. For instance, physicians tell us that they can instantly distinguish orthopedic surgeons (outgoing, hard, and jock-like) from internists (quiet and thoughtful, the most bookish doctors). Similarly, attorneys who've been in practice for many years report that they can immediately spot a trial lawyer (showy and aggressive, with a flair for dramatics; likely to be casually dressed when not in court), as opposed to one who handles legal matters in-house as corporate counsel (inhibited and detail-oriented; wears a tie even when taking a shower). Every profession, it would seem, can not only identify its own members almost on sight; it can also pigeonhole them precisely in a subspecialty.

Why, then, shouldn't psychologists, both amateur and professional, be able to do the same—and do it *before* the person in question enters the field for which he or she is allegedly predestined anyway? Part of the answer, and it is an important finding, is this: Most of the people who will eventually join a profession don't look or act like its current members. Later they will, because the profession will help substantially to shape what they become.

That is especially true of people who enter the business arena after college. Few freshmen eagerly look forward to that day, and it shows in the subjects they choose to study in school. In the 1950s, business-related courses were much less often selected than they are today; in fact they were considered near the bottom of the ladder in prestige. The large majority of students we surveyed in the late 1950s felt that the liberal arts offered the best route to the intellectual acclaim they were seeking. Becoming another Arnold Toynbee or Edmund Wilson seemed a more worthwhile goal by far than running General Motors.

Nevertheless, it was clear to us from the start that most of these ambitious young adults would wind up in the business world, whether they liked it or not, since no other sphere of activity is large enough to house them all professionally. The antibusiness sentiments many were espousing openly (and most voiced in one form or another) were likely to cause trouble eventually. Our question was: In what way would they do so? For instance, would these employees feel too good to be working for a commercial firm, "above it," in some sense? A related question was: Would these workers get over it, and if so, how many years would that take?

Students who were avidly embracing liberal arts or natural or social science majors, yet who would later wind up in the business world, were destined to put the one-profession-per-person view to a severe test. There could be no question that many were trying hard to adopt the attitudes and approach of their chosen field, whether it was history, biochemistry, sociology, English literature, or mathematics. Instead of a mere major, these students had found a new culture to inhabit, one that was as different from the others as the various countries of Europe. To them, the idea of a calling was anything but dead, since they felt that they had found theirs.

What, then, would happen to these dedicated individuals when they graduated and, in essence, had to start over? Would they cling to their old "calling" or eventually find another? If each person really has only one true profession in a lifetime, then perhaps they'd already had theirs and would spend the rest of their lives searching vainly for a new one. In that case, we could expect to find over the years a sizable number of educated and intelligent adults who felt estranged from their employers and everyday work, regardless of their conscious desire to become caught up in it, caught up in *something*, as they had once been in school.

Alienation was a very popular word among adolescents in the late 1950s and, especially, early 1960s. But if the only-one-profession-in-a-lifetime hypothesis were valid, these individuals would experience as adults a degree of alienation that far exceeded anything they had known in their late teen years. Worse still, at that time many wanted to feel it so they could show it off to friends. ("Man, I'm *so* alienated, you know what I mean?") Later, they'd not want it to be there, since among other things, there would no longer be an in-crowd to whom they could brag about it. Yet it would persist, without their even being able to label correctly the chronic discomfort it was causing them. The occupational alienation seemed certain to affect not only their daily moods and sense of accomplishment, but also the stability of their marriages.

The more we thought about the changes that students' lives would of necessity undergo after graduation, the more convinced we became that answers to a wide variety of questions about people and professions could be determined through a study of work-related hopes versus realities as the years went by. Monitoring a large sample of individuals—those who had studied business and finance, as well as those who'd chosen arts or science majors—seemed a good idea, but not good enough. Families too had to be included in the study, since they have an important direct and indirect impact on the outcome. Parents must feel that the money they spend on their children's higher education is a worthwhile investment or, in many cases, college students may drop out or not attend at all. Also, the educational and socioeconomic achievements of the parents create an atmosphere that influences how children see their own future. At the very least, they want to take for granted what their parents have and go on from there.

Rounding up a suitable group to study long-term is never easy, and this one was to prove no exception. Learning from the difficulties other researchers had reported, we decided that it would be highly desirable to be introduced to at least one member of each family that would constitute the sample—and yet, the sample had to be randomly chosen. The combination began to seem as available as the pot of gold at the end of the rainbow until, thanks to a newspaper advertisement, we realized there was one person in a position to arrange that both requirements be met: our friendly neighborhood stockbroker or, more accurately, a number of them working at firms both large and small.

What made stockbrokers especially valuable as intermediaries were the large and growing number of customers seeking them out in the late Fifties. Although it is commonly observed that people spend less during tight times, in fact the reverse is so. Since their incomes decline during a recessionary period, they end up spending relatively more of what they have at their disposal. For instance, during the depths of the Depression, Americans spent 102 percent of their disposable income (the additional 2 percent coming from savings and loans). On the other hand, during World War II the opposite occurred. Personal consumption expenditures fell to a record low of 75 percent of disposable income. The 20–25 percent savings rates seen during 1942–45 in the United States are more typical of what one encounters in postwar Germany or, especially, Japan, but are three to four times the rate that has normally prevailed here since then. Nevertheless, the rapid growth of the U.S. economy in the late Forties and throughout the Fifties allowed net personal savings to nearly triple, rising to $27.5 billion by 1963. In short, by the end of the 1950s, millions of Americans had a sufficient amount of surplus capital in the form of cash, and the needed confidence as well, to want to invest in the stock market. The number of investors jumped from four million to more than twenty million.

Putting money into the stock market instead of the bank, however, is much more of a switch than it seems at first glance. Making a deposit is a rather impersonal transaction; the bank knows remarkably little about each depositor besides address and social security number. Stockbrokers, on the other hand, are required to find out more under a prudent know-your-customer rule; among other things, this is to prevent the limited capital of widows and orphans from being frivolously invested in "hot" stocks that suddenly grow cold, wiping out their owners.

There is also a psychological factor at work here that plays a major role. Quite apart from the detailed questions that brokers must ask and bankers do not, customers at a brokerage firm have an important incentive to befriend their broker. They are convinced that this stock market professional can produce substantial profits for them and might even make them rich. However, since the broker is unlikely to bestow his munificence on all customers equally, each investor wants to be among the select few who do especially well. Currying favor, something customers do for the most part subconsciously, takes a form seen in any pair of people who are fast becoming friends: an exchange of personal and even intimate stories. The specific tales are less important than what their mere presence signifies. The message they implicitly send is, "I'm telling you all about my life, not because I'm a blooming egotist, but because I want you to know that I like you." The unspoken implication in this case is, "Therefore you should like me too, my stockbroker friend, and make me a fortune, even if your other customers break even at best." The magical trade-off, then, is that customers reveal more of themselves to their brokers than they do to many of their everyday friends; and in exchange, the broker is supposed to give them an inside story of a different sort, a hot tip on a stock. That the broker possesses no such magical ability to make his customers rich is irrelevant.

What was striking to us was that people who, under ordinary circumstances, would have been extremely reluctant to discuss their personal lives with a stranger, particularly the details of their financial lives, happily did so in this setting. It was too good to pass up. The amount of valuable information that people were willing to volunteer "in the name of science" was miniscule relative to the amount with which they gladly parted "in the name of greed."

Finding cooperative brokers was easy since each knew at least one other who was willing to be of assistance. However, even having brokers introduce us or a member of our staff to a randomly selected sample (the technical details of the selection process are described in the Appendix on Methodology and the more important people who helped with the study are gratefully mentioned in the Acknowledgments) did not remove every obstacle, because a large percentage of the investors who were contacted (more than 80 percent) were willing to answer a single set of questions but did not want to be part of a long-term study. Nevertheless, persistence produced a sample of the desired size (2,000 individuals), though it took nearly 17 months to assemble. Each broker and investor was told the same thing; namely, that we wanted to see who made money over the long term in the stock market, who lost, and why. The subject seemed to fascinate almost everyone with whom we spoke, even people who refused to participate. It intrigued them that while we are all allegedly created equal, it is clear that not everyone who is interested in making money is equally talented at doing so. What reward could we offer those who allowed us to question them regularly? Only the fruits of our labors in this area, though someone's ability to make money in the market was only the tip of the iceberg that constituted our overall study. The material we gathered on this particular subject therefore had to be published first, and was.[1]

Instead of limiting the study just to adults, we made a determined effort to include the teenage (and older) children of these families as well. Once again, the rationale offered was that we wanted to see (1) which ones eventually developed an interest in investing, and (2) whether the other activities in which they later engaged (professions and hobbies) helped or hindered, not only their investment success, but also their general ability to prosper financially. This turned out to be just about as safe—by which we mean, harmless—a probe as it is possible to use. Teenagers who don't want to learn about the world of finance and investing simply don't. The academic setting they inhabit at the time apparently insulates them to an extent that makes it very easy for them to brush off business and financial queries and tell us what interests them instead, which was music to our ears. In fact, such questions quite often served as the most effective way to elicit information of a more personal sort.

The second sample, consisting of 1,518 children over the age of 13 in the investor families, not only served to lower the median age of the overall sample, it also helped us accomplish two important goals. Keeping track of the members of the sample is half the battle in a long-term study and is often impossible. People may not know where their old friends, classmates, and co-workers are now, but they normally know the location of their nearest relatives and what they are currently doing. They are kept informed of this news via the family grapevine, even if they aren't interested in hearing it. *We* certainly were, and it saved us a considerable amount of effort and expense that would otherwise have been consumed in the tracking process. Furthermore, it gave

---

[1]McGraw–Hill chose a decade-long period and the results drawn from 1,103 relatively active investors, and published the book in 1979 as *WINNING: The Psychology of Successful Investing.*

us an unbeatable conversation opener. Sentences such as, "Your brother Larry says you're thinking of going to law school," allowed us to cut through a host of empty formalities and get down to basics before the respondent's patience ran out, even when Larry didn't quite have the facts straight (which was usually the case). Later, questions about the person's firm or immediate superior were used for the same purpose, this information having generally been offered us in prior conversations as part of a complaint.

There are statistical disadvantages to having two samples drawn from the same set of families; for instance, family members influence one another. Also, while we were very interested in studying the children of upper-middle-class parents, since many seemed likely to end up in influential positions, we sought out children who'd been offered fewer advantages too, since they would be compelled to achieve more on their own. We therefore chose a third and final sample, of a size comparable to the second, that had nothing to do with the world of investing: 1,500 students were selected at random from 16 colleges and universities that represented a cross section of institutions of higher education in the U.S. during the academic year 1958–59. As with the other two samples, we used a safe probe as our ostensible reason for doing the study: we wanted to know which professions paid well, which paid poorly, and how that affected the way in which one was able to live. Many students, particularly those majoring in teaching, art, or the liberal arts, told us to count them out since, as one put it, "My work isn't *ever* going to make me rich." Our reply was, "Fine, but we're still interested in knowing just how little it does pay you, year after year." Fortunately for us, the respondents themselves were usually the ones to switch the topic to the other side of the coin in subsequent conversation, preferring to discuss their personal involvement with what they were doing, or lack of it.

Interestingly, they actually became more responsive to our queries as the years passed, primarily because they hoped we would discover a quick way that they could use to become rich. They said that after using it, then they'd do what they really wanted to. These people too deserved to be thanked for their cooperation. The results connected with the ostensible reason for our research therefore had to be published prior to this work, and were.[2]

The present book is different from the previous two, not only in drawing its conclusions from the full sample, but also in exploring a topic of much broader scope. It could have been published a decade ago but, as mentioned, we felt it was appropriate for the other two

---

[2]Doubleday and Co. called the book summarizing this facet of the study *Getting Rich Your Own Way*, and published it in 1980.

works to come first and, far more important, we wanted to be certain that the results stated in the forthcoming chapters are correct. There have been hundreds of books published in recent years about crises of all sorts, connected with any and every age, decade, and profession. However, to warn people about the wrong crisis is worse than not warning them at all. For they prepare themselves for the allegedly predictable ill that is about to befall them, only to be hit by a setback they had no reason to anticipate. The poor advice they received did little more than set them up to be blind-sided.

We deliberately chose a sample large enough, and studied its members for a sufficiently long period of time, to see what serious problems people could reasonably expect to encounter, decade by decade, in the course of a business career. Nevertheless, the reader may not find the main ups and downs of his or her business life captured in these pages. There were only so many people we could monitor, and the group we finally did settle upon had a decidedly middle- and upper-middle-class character. The median age in 1959 of the 5,018 sample members was 23, and the median household income (in constant 1982 dollars) was nearly $53,000, versus approximately $20,200 for the United States as a whole. Minorities, particularly Hispanics, are underrepresented (147, or 3 percent) only because they were underrepresented at the time in the populations from which we drew our samples. That would be much less the case today. On the other hand, the 2,107 women in the overall sample (42 percent) would have been present in far fewer numbers had we accepted at face value the statements many made to the effect that they intended to have little or nothing to do with business. That was easy to say in the late 1950s, for the young men as well as women in this group, but it seemed to us more a hope than a likelihood. We should also mention that people involved in illegal activities (for instance, drug dealing) were excluded because the main crisis they seemed likely to face was with the law.

It would have been impossible to conduct this study without making extensive use of modern data-processing equipment. Each time we seemed on the verge of drowning in the rapidly expanding sea of data we had collected, an advance in computer hardware and/or software saved our skin. For that reason, it became every bit as essential to keep up with innovations in the computer field as with the movements of sample members. One made the other more of a pleasure to monitor. As a result, a book on computers by the author is being published simultaneously[3] with this work.

The reader will soon notice that we interpret the word "business"

---

[3]It is entitled *Computers Made (Ridiculously) Easy*, and is published by McGraw-Hill, New York, 1984.

to encompass a much wider variety of professional activities than is usually implied by the term. For instance, while an attorney who grows tired of practicing law and opens an art gallery instead may feel that he has switched, in his words, "from the business to the cultural field," we view both as examples of commerce. Similarly, physicians, physicists, and fiction writers who told us that their work was basically "public spirited" nevertheless were rarely able to overlook for long the business dimensions of their activities, and neither did we. In short, while people spending their entire work lives in civil service, teaching, or the military can legitimately claim exemption, we feel that the phrase "business career" covers the large majority of civilian occupations in the United States. The fact that these workers insist on more flattering labels for what they do is normal and even appropriate, but it mustn't blind us to the many similarities that exist among the long-term experiences of people in quite disparate fields.

Two final notes: we have tried to let the people whose case histories are presented in the book tell their own stories, using what in most instances are transcriptions of tape-recorded quotes (from which expletives and dated, therefore silly-sounding, slang have been removed). In addition to their comments, we have spelled out their rationalizations for what they were doing during important periods. Second, none of these figures is a composite; each represents himself or herself alone, although the cases were selected because they are characteristic of the experiences of group members of that particular age. The names of the people being discussed have been changed, for obvious reasons, but the dates, locations, and details of the events have been left largely intact.

I

THE TWENTIES

THE THEATRICAL AGE

CHAPTER 2

Finding the Right Public Stance

WHEN WE FIRST began interviewing workers who were then in their twenties, it was clear that each was making an unconscious decision to emphasize either the present or the future. Some would say, "Right now I'm working on...," while others gave greater weight to, "I'm planning to do...." We therefore made it a practice to ask each worker first to discuss current activities and then his or her plans for the future.

Confining their comments to the present tense caused a different split to emerge. While some described at length their work and any problems they were having with it, others spoke about the work hardly at all and devoted most of the time to observations about co-workers. When the same pattern was seen in subsequent interviews with many members of the group, we began to suspect that a major factor we hadn't foreseen was in operation in these people's work lives. We didn't know it then, but we do now: people in their twenties have a secret weapon. Their actual job skills are backed up by an entirely separate set of talents. When the former don't get them what they want, most don't hesitate to call out the reserves.

Few members of our sample consciously think of their personality as an instrument that can be used to further their career goals. Yet in their twenties, that is exactly how they employ it at work. Sometimes this helps them get where they want to go; other times, after apparent effectiveness, it leads to serious trouble—years later.

The Chameleon's Climb

Howard Taylor was good in math in high school, and that led him to choose electrical engineering as a college major. President Kennedy's speech stating that "the shortage of PhDs [in science and engineering] constitutes our most critical national problem," which accompanied the expanding demand for engineers at the time, helped confirm Howard's decision. But it wouldn't have mattered what major he'd chosen, because he intended to enter management at the earliest opportunity, not remain a practicing engineer. Friendly and outgoing, more sure of himself and his direction than most of his classmates, he wanted to be actively involved with people in a business setting instead of, as he put it during his junior year in college, "spending all my time setting up and solving difficult equations." True to his plan, Howard graduated with good grades and landed a job as a management trainee at a major metals and mining firm. "The program is a piece of cake for me, after all the tough courses I took in college," he commented four months after starting, "but if this is what they want us to do, it's okay with me. I know it'll take me where I want to go. They're grooming us for bigger and better things, that's for sure."

Howard made a serious effort to look presentable at work and seemed not to have minded spending whatever time it took to shop for suits, shoes, and shirts. His wife, Emily, an elementary school teacher, usually bought his ties and socks. In spite of the effort, he always looked slightly disheveled, as though his clothes were one size too large. Howard is 5'11" and 165 pounds, with brown, wavy hair and a long face that often makes it appear that he is peering slightly downward even when he is staring straight ahead. At work, Howard gave a convincing portrayal of a man eager to move up, yet in no mad rush to do so. "Walk softly and carry a big stick," Teddy Roosevelt's motto, was Howard's main guideline in business. He didn't want anyone to think that he was ruthless and power-hungry, prepared to do almost anything imaginable to get to the top quickly. Nonetheless, only someone with towering ambitions would have tried so hard year in and year out to hide them. "I like—I try—to be unflappable," he said proudly, near the end of his first year on the job. "I want people to know that I can roll with the punches."

It is par for the course for a 23-year-old to attempt to appear much calmer than he actually is. There are usually a host of uncertainties in the air, and trying to muffle the anxieties they generate is an expected part of coping with a new, non-school environment. "The situation is very fluid here," Howard pointed out with a nervous laugh. It was indicative of his particular approach to business, however, that he wouldn't have minded if it became more fluid still. "I'm confident of my abilities," Howard said repeatedly during the decade, and he meant it. His confidence led him to believe that in the midst of a commotion he would always manage to somehow emerge a hero. A well-organized firm, with all worthwhile posts filled by quiet and competent workers, therefore worried Howard far more than corporate disorder did. He was certain that mild chaos offered him a much better opportunity to reveal his true worth. That inclination had important consequences for the amount of chaos he himself unwittingly created as the years went by.

Although Howard found the training program a breeze since he had taken finance and management courses throughout the four years of his engineering major, he still made a point of absorbing every relevant piece of information the program contained. He had been a diligent student in school, and the habits established there were serving him well now in an academically less demanding setting. "I'm giving it everything I've got," he said on a number of occasions, "though to tell you the truth, it doesn't take a whole lot." The ability and background that Howard brought to the job were quite likely to bear results sooner or later. The trouble was that he wanted it sooner—tomorrow at the latest—and the world seemed to be conspiring to make it later, at the earliest. "I think I'm overqualified for this position," Howard said during his second year and again in his third. The pace of progress up the corporate ladder struck him as agonizingly slow.

"I think I could move up more quickly if I were somewhere else," he finally said in his fourth year at the firm. A classmate who was a chemical engineer was working at another company in the same industry. As Howard put it, "It's really illuminating to compare notes with him every few months or thereabouts." After a few such conversations, during which Howard expressed a strong desire to leave, the friend arranged an interview with his company, and Howard was hired. Howard's new boss, Ben, a large, soft-spoken man, was very pleased with his new find. "That fellow is going places," he told Howard's friend a few days after Howard accepted the job offer.

Personality is less tangible than height, weight, and mathematical ability; it needs the right setting if it is to fully emerge. In a threatening environment most people withdraw into themselves and play it safe, hoping for better days to come. At the new firm, with a boss who made no secret of expecting a fine future for him, Howard visibly began to do the reverse: he felt secure and became more expansive. "I'm more relaxed here," he said at 26. "And more eager to go places too."

It would be nice to be able to report that this educated and energetic young man rose smoothly and rapidly at the new firm, but nothing of the kind happened. In many ways the situation slowly grew worse, for although Howard's hopes had clearly been raised by the job change, he was promoted as slowly at the new firm as at the old. There was a big difference between the two places, though, and Howard subconsciously began to exploit it. When he said that he felt more relaxed here, he was unwittingly communicating the fact this his personality was more fully in evidence. Now, he began to use it. "Ben's jokes aren't funny," he said a month before his 27th birthday, "but I laugh at them anyway. Someone has to." For him, it was a quite uncharacteristic remark.

Howard was no phony and would have been rightly offended if someone had called him one. Nevertheless, he was determined to get where he wanted to go. Since he was already doing everything he could with his current job skills, and not getting ahead as fast as he wanted to, he decided to use an alternative approach.

Slowly but surely he became more outgoing and friendly. In his mind, that was merely a consequence of the greater comfort he felt in the new setting with its brighter prospects for advancement. As he put it, "I have more of a proprietary air about this place, if you know what I mean, than I did when I was at [the previous place]." Saying hello to a wider variety of people; spending more time in hallway, men's room, water fountain, and coffee machine conversations; being more expressive in his feelings about everything from political and social topics to the color of the carpeting and walls—all these actions were part of a transformed Howard that he wanted one and all to see.

None of it was conscious, and it would have been far less effective had it been. Nor was Howard bending his emotions into pretzel shape in order to please the people around him. He was still largely and recognizably himself. And that's the key point here. His rationalization for what he was doing—namely, that his heightened sociability was nothing more than a reflection of his having "settled in" at the firm at last—was undoubtedly true in part.

Also, he was still at an age in which his personality could change shape dramatically in order to match the requirements of his surroundings. In his teen years, it would have been even easier for him to adopt a different demeanor and appearance on cue, much like a chameleon, but in his twenties, it was only a little more difficult. "I'm still being myself," Howard would rightly have claimed, if we had challenged him. At 26, his personality's plasticity remained sufficiently great so that none of the things he said could be labeled an outright fraud. They were within the range of what was real for him.

"It Must Be My Charisma"

Odd as it may sound, Howard's job skills were the greatest smoke screen at his disposal. If people are faking it totally and are completely undeserving of the positions they hold, it is easy enough to see through them. Encouraging them to rattle on, first about one work-related subject, then another, and watching them at work on a variety of projects will make the truth known. Their limitations and inadequacies eventually begin to surface.

Paradoxically, the more competent people are, the more capable they are of fooling their employer if they so choose. And Howard, subconsciously at least, had clearly chosen to do just that, as we were later to learn. Why wasn't that noticed immediately? The answer tells us much about how certain people in business get themselves into deep trouble. Most examples of deception that one reads about in fiction (particularly detective and spy stories) or sees in the movies involve people pretending to be something that they're not, and getting away with it. The fakery is total and, in that sense, very bold. If nothing else, the daring charade creates tension in the reader or viewer, which is exactly what the storyteller wants.

However, that is not what turned up in our studies of attempted deception by corporate climbers. Much to our surprise, in the large majority of such instances, it was talented and well-trained individuals who decided to stretch the truth a little to get where they wanted to go *faster*. Far from being outright frauds, these people possessed much of the ability to do the jobs they were after. Since they were in an extreme hurry to advance their careers, they'd already managed to convince themselves that they had all the preparation necessary, and then some, to go to the top immediately. What was stopping them, then? Only an inability to convince others. As far as they were concerned, this was one obstacle that needed separate and intense attention. "I can't understand why they don't just turn me loose," Howard said at 26. "I know I could do wonders for this place. Boy, they'd make money so fast, they wouldn't know what to do with it all."

Look at the situation from Howard's point of view for a moment. Here was a basically honest, decent, gifted, and well-educated individual who felt that he had everything required to do twice as much high-powered work as he was being given to do. Two revealing comments he made, at ages 26 and 27 respectively, were, "Why do I have to spend so much time on trivial, low-level crap?" and, "If I were still in school and were this far ahead of where I am now, they'd skip me. They'd probably move me up three or four grades to get me to where I belong."

As far as Howard could see, he wasn't looking to deceive, since he felt qualified to do great things right then. He was only seeking justice, in letting other people know of his state of readiness. Once he had that view of himself firmly implanted in his mind, all things became permissible. Deceit, any time it did prove necessary, was nothing more than a small part of his quest for justice, not an end in itself. It was a slightly immoral act in a highly moral cause.

"Ben's an old fogey," Howard said of his 47-year-old boss. "I've got to find a way around him. Maybe over him. The guy is a turtle; never moves fast—on anything."

"What are you thinking of doing?" we asked.

"Whatever it takes," he replied, repeating one of his favorite refrains.

In the middle of his 28th year, after what seemed to him decades of waiting, Howard was given the opportunity he had sought. Everywhere he went in the firm, he had intentionally been filling the air around him with a cheerful and seemingly forthright manner. Hollywood could not have manufactured a more appropriate persona for him to portray. Of great interest to us, though, was the fact that it was conspicuously absent when we visited him at home in the evening or on weekends, or when there was no one connected with his work nearby. It was a facade that he put on with his suit in the morning, though he never noticed himself donning it. The jacket and tie were a concession to things as they were; the self-assured manner was an appeal for things to instantly become what he wanted them to be. "I want to knock 'em dead wherever I go," he said three days before the offer came.

Gil, one of the people who found Howard's veneer credible, was a 51-year-old colleague of Ben at the firm. He was in charge of finance. The company had decided to make an acquisition; although small, outside firms (called "finders"), and a number of large stockbrokerage firms as well, were suggesting candidates regularly, Gil wanted to conduct an in-house review of his own. "You realize, don't you," he rhetorically asked Ben, "that we can *buy* the assets of the business [into which we want to go] for maybe half of what it would cost us to *build* them?"

That wasn't news to Ben. But he wanted to proceed cautiously just to make certain that the available cash and bank credit lines that the firm had were spent on the right target. "It costs too much money and management time to fix a mistake [in this area]," he told us. "I'd rather get a good one the first time out." A few days later, Gil suggested that Howard be included in the team that was to search for the review acquisition candidates.

Ben wasn't thrilled with the idea, since he saw it as a detour off the road that he had in mind for Howard's eventual move into management. "How many people go from being VP in charge of acquisitions, say, to president and chief executive officer? Not many, I'd wager," Ben said. Howard, though, was very excited when he heard about the proposal, because he felt it would give him the broad exposure he had long wanted. Remember his secret hope: given the large number of new faces he knew he'd encounter, not to mention the disorder and drama involved in the acquisition process, he expected to emerge a star. In chaos there was opportunity. "This thing is really open-ended," he told us enthusiastically.

"In what way?" we inquired.

"If I find a smashing good outfit, they just might put me in charge of it once it's ours. Stranger things have happened, you know."

One thing that puzzled us was Gil's request that Howard be included on the acquisition team to begin with, so we asked, "How come?" Howard shrugged his shoulders and replied, "It must be my charisma, my winning smile." Then, trying to sound more earnest, he said, "I mean, we've never worked together. Gil doesn't even know if I can add."

Gil, however, told him that he felt Howard was perfect for the job. "You look like a real get-up-and-go type," he said. It was the first of what were to be many victories for Howard's one-two punch of a smiling and aggressive manner. Just as he had anticipated, calling out the reserves and filling the air with his personality had finally worked. Operating on its own, as an independent factor, it had helped create the openings he wanted to fill.

Better still, since it was more intangible and less specific than his job skills, it opened doors that the front-line troops couldn't. In its vagueness lay its strength. Different people could see in it exactly what they wanted to see. An abstract sculpture was wandering the halls, pleasing everyone. The shift in emphasis from job skills to personality was working wonders in his own mind and in that of co-workers as well. The vision of vastly expanded career possibilities made Howard's head swim. "I want them to know that they can call on me for *anything*," he said that same day.

Manager or Promoter?

For the next four years, Howard was happily caught up in his dusty travels on the acquisition trail. "I feel like a modern day prospector, panning for gold," he said in a calculatedly laid-back manner, at 30. All that was missing from the Western image he was trying to project was a drawl, a 10-gallon hat and cowboy boots, and a mule standing where he used to park his car in the company garage.

The possibilities that his personality had created for him led to still more of the same. He was occupying a slot that freed him from many restraints he would have had to live with in a line position. Howard realized this to some extent; at 31, he thoroughly enjoyed the double meaning in his sentence, "Where I am now [in this firm], I don't have to stay in line."

There was no question that Howard had found a shortcut, but the key question in our minds was where the shortcut was taking him. He hoped it would be a direct route to a top managerial position. That seemed unlikely. To see why, it is worthwhile to look at the general pattern of behavior exhibited by bright, energetic, and ambitious people in their twenties who subsequently became successful in business.

For most such people, the decade was broken into two parts. During their first three years after college, typically their 22nd through 24th years, they were in a hyperreactive phase. Their emotional response to any demand made upon them was intense. In the balance between job skills and personality, they interpreted any slowdowns or setbacks to be a consequence of the latter not the former, since, like Howard, they thought themselves overqualified for the position.

Under the circumstances, it was only to be expected that they'd try monkeying with their personality profile in order to speed up their rise. Thwarted on one front, they tried to make progress on another. A cynic might say that they had decided to use deceit as a climbing tool, since their more immediately work-related skills weren't taking them anywhere. However, that overlooks the enormously fluid character of the personalities of men and women this age when subjected to persistent inner and outer pressures to get ahead. To put the matter in its extreme form: if one's personality has no inherent structure of its own, then any shape it takes is equally real. None is fake.

Although there is indeed some personality structure present in each case, it is much less than people commonly imagine. They want to feel that they "know" their friends and co-workers, and therefore they assume that what they see is more brittle than it actually is. Nevertheless, with different people, and in different settings, what they think is fixed changes.

So that they might continue to recognize their friends, they hope that others will stay "as is." They themselves, on the other hand, assume a wide variety of emotional configurations to fit the circumstances, and do so without usually realizing it. In short, the three-year period from 22 through 24 was a theatrical one for the vast majority— for those who ultimately prospered as well as for those who fared poorly over the years. It was a time to try on faces, as well as radiate charm, intelligence, class, and assertiveness—a hoped for picture of success.

If future winners and losers both were doing this, what distinguished the two groups? The key factor that set the upward bound apart from those who did not do well in subsequent decades emerged most clearly in the five-year period from 25 through 29. The extreme fluidity of the earlier three-year period lessened substantially in the eventually-to-be-successful. Having draped themselves in a wide range of cloaks, they found one, or at most a few, that fit. That was of critical importance because it allowed them to get on with other things, instead of dwelling endlessly on flaws in their makeup. Rather than concentrate on whether they had adopted the right personality profile to unlock the door to the executive suite, they devoted more attention to developing the job skills they'd need once they got there.

Some readers may feel that we are making too much of the distinction. Intellectual and physical abilities, on the one hand, and personality, on the other, should work together effortlessly to help one achieve. In theory, they are merely parts of a whole and under ideal conditions would mesh seamlessly. However, in practice they frequently clash, and for a very good reason: they lead people down two entirely separate career paths in business. For instance, if Howard had continued to give top priority to sharpening his job skills, he would most likely have moved toward production and management. As it was, with his growing fascination with personality, he had unwittingly set himself on a different road altogether, one that heads toward sales and promotion.

That he didn't realize what card he was playing at the office makes no difference. He was playing one anyway, and people were responding to it. Instead of wanting his work to be applauded, after a wait during which it was carefully assessed, he wanted his personality to bring him attention immediately. It wasn't until Howard was 31 that he gave voice to the feelings that had increasingly been guiding his behavior during the prior eight years. "I want to be loved for myself," he remarked casually.

Everyone feels that way to some extent, but men and women who major in science or engineering usually hold a different view. They are willing to have their professional attainments, not personality, serve as the instrument of their progress. In fact, they feel they have cheated both the system and themselves if favoritism gets them what their work wasn't good enough to. That strikes them more as charity than as a victory. The sentence they use most frequently to embody their approach is, "I'll let my work speak for itself," meaning, "You look at it objectively and decide on its merits; I think you'll be pleased and perhaps even impressed." That is quite a contrast to Howard's "I want to be loved for myself." His work was no longer even in the picture. Just Howard and his imaginary audience.

Had he realized the direction in which he was moving, Howard might have tried to slow or halt what he was doing. Certainly he'd have had to come to terms one way or another with the gap that was developing in his business life. After all, he had been trained as an engineer and still accepted the validity of its approach: that only results count, not charm and good intentions. On some level he recognized that, although we all want to be loved for ourselves alone and must find that in our personal lives if we are to find it at all, the work world demands that we put forth something concrete by which it can judge us. Nevertheless, his personal predilections, in combination with a demand for instant results, were pushing Howard ever more rapidly down a different road. He still claimed that he wanted to be a manager,

yet he was well on the way toward being a skilled salesman and promoter.

Some insight on Howard's part into the powerful forces in operation
here could have made a substantial difference. As it was, time was
running out. *People who think they are using a product- or work-
oriented approach to get ahead, when in fact they are using the exact
opposite, a personality-oriented approach, almost invariably experience a predictable crisis during their business careers.* In fact many
of the more moderate setbacks that they suffer as well can be traced
directly to their confusion over this issue. When Howard was 34, the
abyss he had long been straddling finally claimed him.

But Will Charm Keep on Working?

With Howard's help, his firm made not one acquisition but six.
Having seen how easy it was, and how much publicity it generated,
the executives at the company repeated the process with glee. After
four years of being involved in this area, however, Howard had had
enough. "What is it that you want to do instead?" we asked him shortly
after his 32nd birthday. There wasn't a moment's hesitation as he
replied, "I want to be active in management again."

Ben was able to help him do just that. The two had had much less
contact than they'd otherwise have had during the four years, so Ben
still liked and respected him. More important, as he put it when Howard asked for his aid, "I want to see you get back on the right track."
Ben was seeing what he wanted to see. If Howard had been working
directly for him during the four years, Ben perhaps would have realized
in this case (as he had in others during the period) what the young
man's strengths and weaknesses were. Ben's picture of Howard was
full of high hopes that hadn't yet been dashed. "I can't do much for
you here," Ben commented. "It's slow going up the ladder at a firm
this size, but I do know a smaller company that's closer to consumer
markets and is looking for a president." As Howard later commented,
"When I heard that, I nearly leaped out of my chair and cheered."
Howard desperately wanted the job.

His personable and persuasive manner were an enormous asset in
landing him the position. As Howard put it at the time (without realizing the significance of what he was saying), "I interview well. I
really do. Too bad I can't do it for a living." The two people who
interviewed him liked him but had a few reservations. One told Ben,
"He hasn't had much management experience. No real track record,
to speak of." Ben proceeded to set their minds at ease completely.

Repeating the words he'd heard many times before from Howard, he replied, "He can do wonders for you." From Ben, that was an uncharacteristic remark and high praise indeed. They hired Howard the next day.

For the next two years, Howard's life was a whirlwind of excitement and nonstop motion. "I want to fire up this company," he said three weeks after starting. Product lines were broadened, more salesmen were hired, the advertising and publicity budget was increased tenfold, and Howard began planning a series of new ventures. He used one term continually to describe his strategy: *growth.* In retrospect, it is clear that the philosophy he put into effect at the new firm would be better described as, "We have to have something, some product or service, that will please almost every conceivable customer." The company spent the next 26 months under Howard's direction being pulled in almost every imaginable direction, much to the dismay of the finance and production people at the firm in particular. "They're nitwits," Howard told us irritably during his second year there. "They can't see beyond the end of their pencils. They have no *vision.*"

At the end of the period, with the economy again becoming caught in the grip of a recession, the firm was running out of money fast. "All these ventures will pay off soon, you'll see," he said, feeling cornered. He'd even made a small acquisition. "I'm proud of that," he said, smiling. "They could never have done that without me. It was a steal." But the money the firm had to borrow to finance the purchase (it was for cash) only added to the heavy load of debt already being carried. At the next regularly scheduled meeting of the board of directors, the usually friendly atmosphere vanished and animosity replaced it. Howard was fired and a decision was reluctantly made to file for bankruptcy. "You're not an administrator," the chairman of the board told him loudly in front of the others. "You're an undertaker." Howard was crushed. "You can't do this to me," he told them. "I'm the only hope you have." Howard's power to persuade apparently failed him in the face of a sea of red ink. "They just laughed," he said a few days later.

It has been more than a decade since that meeting, but Howard still hasn't gotten over the damage it did to his self-esteem. What is worse, he drew the wrong conclusions from the disaster and, hence, has been compounding the mistakes to this day. As he put it glumly at the time, "That's the last time I'll associate myself with a company that doesn't have the money to try something really big."

The fact that Howard was in his mid-thirties when tragedy struck must not be allowed to obscure the roots of the problem, which are to be found in events that took place during his twenties. He experimented much less with public aspects of his personality profile than did most of his peers during the three-year period from age 22 through 24. That is par for the course for students who major in technically oriented fields. Time and subject matter—that is, the length and difficulty of the program and the attitude of the discipline—help cause a delay. Howard became more theatrical at the very time that most of his peers were moving on to phase two of the decade, adopting a specific public-professional picture of themselves and trying to make it stick.

Not only did Howard arrive at his theatrical stage late, once there, he stayed far too long. In many ways, he has never left. Apparently, his demanding technical education not only stunted his sociosexual maturity ("There were plenty of times that I studied when my friends played"); it also prevented him from trying on enough faces to find the few that truly fit. As a result, he had—and still has—one foot planted firmly in each of the opposing camps: job skills and personality. His interest in his field wasn't sufficiently strong to make him want to do creative or even production work. On the other hand, he hadn't yet become a sufficiently scintillating personality to pursue an acting career or push products on the broadcast media for a living. What typically happens to others in Howard's position happened to him as well. *Those who straddle the two approaches slowly wind up becoming more promotion-oriented, by default, and eventually become devoted exclusively to self-promotion.*

"Well, That's Show Biz"

People who have received a scientific or technical education often possess a large measure of promotional and sales skill that can be invaluable at times in business. Unfortunately, they usually don't know it. Science and engineering are dedicated to the idea that everything can and should be made as objective as possible. Good salesmen, however, rightly insist that "You have to be liked by everybody in order to do really well," a requirement that is impossible since preferences are subjective. What one person likes in another, someone else might not. Ignoring the theatrical dimension while they were in college may have assisted students majoring in a technical subject to concentrate on their studies. Nevertheless, once these students graduate and enter the work world full-time, the dimension becomes hard to ignore.

The key point here is this: people in business who are naturally gifted with promotional abilities need to know about, and be comfortable with, that fact—even if they decide never to use them. Thanks to the roadblocks that they, as well as everyone else, will inevitably encounter at work, they may find these talents being mobilized automatically. Their lobbying skills—their power to persuade and even awe adversaries—may emerge spontaneously. That is particularly likely to happen if they are repeatedly stymied in their efforts to advance themselves solely on the basis of objective, job-related performance, a distressing but nevertheless very common occurrence.

Failure to realize that the mobilization of promotional skills is taking place, or already has, can lead to tragedy. Temporarily abandoning one's work focus in order to hurdle a human obstacle or accelerate the rate of progress does no harm. Brief detours aren't the problem. But ambitious people who unwittingly undertake *prolonged* journeys on the pitchman's path eventually sink themselves. Instead of temporarily abandoning their work, such people lose sight of it altogether. Then, and this is the crucial point, they have no choice but to stay on the road they find themselves traveling.

Perhaps they were interested in sales and promotion all along? one might inquire, as did we. There are many people for whom a shift into the world of marketing and public relations is no accident. That may well be where they belong. There is nothing wrong with that, though in many cases they clearly think there is. They are inclined to sneer at such activities, convinced that these fields lack prestige. Be that as it may, the economic world needs promotional skills as well as those devoted to management and product development. Someone has to sell the enormous quantity of goods and services the nation produces each year or the whole system would collapse under its own weight.

In short, the serious difficulties people like Howard ultimately found themselves in were a result of two forces. First, they didn't know where their real talents lay, given their hunger for instant acclaim. Second, had they known, they might not have liked it. Howard, for example, had been trained as an engineer and had adopted fully the values of the field along with its technical content. Above all, he wanted to use his education as a basis for becoming a top manager. For him to discover that what he proudly called his "vision" was mainly his ability to inspire others to see things his way would have upset him greatly. Yet one of the people who'd worked closely with him during the two years that he was the firm's president commented, "Howie is very bright and innovative. It's just that everywhere he goes, he leaves a messy trail. He doesn't *think through* his plans, just blurts them out. The guy ought to get himself a manager." Howard was appalled when he overheard that. He wanted to be one, not need one.

To people who majored in the arts, humanities, or social sciences in college, the human element in each person's progress is nothing new. Interestingly, the behavior of some of the drama majors in our sample who had entered the business world helped deepen our understanding of the factors responsible for Howard's plight. Since these individuals were beginning their careers at exactly the opposite end of the spectrum, they tried hard in many instances to develop a repertoire of business skills that were concrete and useful, ones that could readily be judged on an objective basis by outside observers. At first, we interpreted such behavior as an attempt by trained actors to appear to be more real than the real thing. Indeed, they seemed to be trying to beat veteran business people at their own game. The interpretation not only turned out to be too cynical; it also overlooked their subconscious realization that, in the business world, good theater is not enough. They'd done that already, and now were seeking something more tangible to use as instruments to help them win pay raises and promotions.

Take Douglas Baker, for example. On paper, in terms of resumes, Doug and Howard are a study in contrasts. Yet, at one point in their late twenties, it is fair to say that their careers crossed paths. We don't mean that they met, only that they passed one another occupationally while traveling in opposite directions. Both are the same age and, like Howard, Doug is nearly 6' tall, has brown hair, and a medium build. If anything, his face is less expressive than Howard's ordinarily is. Also, his skin isn't as good, having many large pores and some pockmarks. "Sometimes I think I got interested in acting so I could cover up my acne scars with grease paint when it really counted, when the spotlight was on me," he said reflectively at 23. When we watched Doug on stage however it was clear that, under the right circumstances, he could radiate enough emotion on cue to affect the feelings of hundreds of theatergoers at a single clip. That was precisely what Doug did not want to do at work, once he decided to make a go of it in the business world, two frustrating years after graduating from college. "Life in the theater is too competitive," he said at 24, one month before accepting a full-time job at a financial services firm. "Too many aspiring actors trying to land a handful of choice parts. It's very harsh."

The point at which he and Howard crossed career paths came when both were 29. Doug had spent nearly five years learning how to buy products economically for his firm. He had landed a position in the purchasing department and, by sheer dedication, had managed to find the cheapest supplier for hundreds of products his firm usually bought in bulk. Doug didn't have a technical background but, then again, in this position he rarely needed one. Others in various departments decided what to buy; Doug merely made the decision as to where. An added bonus was that the savings he produced were often plain for all to see. At 29, during the first year he was placed in charge of buying approximately one-third of the products and services the firm used regularly, he saved his employer more than $800,000. Upon hearing that, the executive vice-president of the company gave Doug a raise. The two never became friends, and they had little daily contact, but the combination of diligence on Doug's part and the approval of a top officer led Doug, at 36, to be made a vice-president, a position that in 1983 earned him in excess of $100,000.

The irony here is that to this day Doug uses a number of technical terms incorrectly, terms that Howard could more accurately define and use in a conversation. It was precisely such malapropisms that made us initially consider Doug a phony, a theatrical imitation; only later did we realize that he was making a determined attempt to come up with a product-oriented skill that his employers would have to declare worthwhile. We will return to this topic in a later chapter, but for now let us simply note that, although Doug's literally nuts-and-bolts approach is neither feasible nor suitable for everyone in business, in this case, and many others, it was undeniably effective.

Summing up, an early fork in the road that has a decisive impact on one's long-term prospects in business concerns job versus dramatic skills. People who are gifted in one area but think their real strengths lie in the other are likely to find themselves straddling an ever-widening abyss as the years pass. There are people who can manage to keep one foot in each camp as the two drift apart, but not many. In one's twenties, some experimentation to determine one's relative abilities in each area may well result in sizable dividends as the years pass.

The knowledge that one possesses a skill doesn't carry with it the compulsion to use it. Many will find a different direction is more appropriate for them, much like the fellow in our sample who excelled in a particular sport but sacrificed his potential career as a professional athlete to attend medical school. An understanding of one's strengths is critical on the job, particularly in encounters with someone who impedes one's progress. Then, the personality skills one automatically activates to help ease the way won't surprise their owner; more importantly, they won't stay permanently mobilized when one's focus should return to less theatrical matters.

In fact, if one has done one's best to melt or disarm an adversary and didn't succeed, the most effective strategy is usually *not* to keep trying. Instead, it is time to say, "Well, that's show biz," and get back to work.

CHAPTER 3

The First Career Crisis:
No Career

THERE ARE NEARLY one-quarter of a billion Americans now, more than 58 million of whom are in school full- or part-time. Nearly one million students graduated from college alone in the United States in 1983. Judging the academic performance of a group this large requires that a simple system be used to rate each with respect to the rest. Grades have therefore moved into a position of central importance as a convenient, if somewhat dehumanizing, shorthand for assessing the relative merits of the flood of graduates who pour forth from the nation's schools each June.

To many students, particularly those from underprivileged homes, merely getting a passing grade is not only acceptable, it is a cause for celebration. School is the enemy. However, the students in our sample had a markedly different view. Having internalized their parents' hopes for them, they saw education as offering a quick and dirt-free ladder to success. These students often expressed every bit as much antagonism toward school as those from poorer families, but they parted company with the latter group in one critical respect: they valued high grades, highly. A college degree was the equivalent in their minds of a union card, one that guaranteed them job security. Advanced degrees were viewed as even more valuable, offering a ticket of admission to the winner's circle, where prestige and sizable incomes could be taken for granted. Even though the attitude moderated slightly in the seventies, as the relative income of recent college graduates fell significantly with respect to that of high school graduates,[1] education still remained the dominant focus of teenagers; there was, and is, nothing offering a comparable degree of initial advantage to take its place.

---

[1] See R. Freeman, *The Overeducated American* (New York: Academic Press, 1976), p. 14.

Even when the students in our sample played, the pressure to achieve wasn't forgotten; often they played in order to forget. Children in school and soldiers at war live with a comparable kind of tension. Sooner or later a major test will arrive. Some will survive and go on; others won't and will be left behind. In the meantime, in the lull between challenges, a break from the nervousness is needed. Silliness provides it. Having fun makes the time pass more quickly and pleasantly, but the laughter draws much of its energy from the tension in the air.

The focus of our research has been the different phases that people can expect their business lives to pass through. Yet here, long before they have joined the work world, the foundation is being laid for upsetting events that they will experience not once but a number of times after school is finished. The basis for the future turmoil is in learning to ignore the obvious. People do it all the time, usually for good reasons, and can reserve the process whenever they choose. For instance, the parents in our sample have been doing it for decades where thermonuclear weapons are concerned. The threat of nuclear annihilation has been a vivid reality to adults at least since the time of the Cuban missile crisis in 1962, but they ignore it and go about their business as best they can, for the most part forgetting that the subject even exists.

Ambitious students consider the prospect of a failing grade or, even worse, flunking out of school as the equivalent of annihilation, at least of their dreams. Like their parents, they usually learn to ignore it; in fact, they ignore grades altogether when their friends are around. What makes this situation different from their parents' deliberate suppression of thoughts about nuclear war is that few adults are of the opinion that the problem has gone away. It's just that thinking about it strikes them as unproductive, even counterproductive, so they try not to. Students suppress their own concern about grades, at least publicly, for two main reasons: to avoid ridicule and to mask an undemocratic desire to beat out their peers permanently. As we'll soon see, the trouble is that once they've done it long enough, they forget that they are doing it at all.

In short, the point we wish to make in this chapter is that a substantial proportion of the children (approximately 31 percent in our sample) raised in middle- and upper-middle-class families are spending their lives unwittingly trying to be all things to all people. They start out in high school and continue in college publicly suppressing their desire to excel, while privately dreaming of little else. Their calculated indifference to grades, a piece of public theater if ever there was one, and deliberate avoidance of educated speech (no polysyllabic words, complex thoughts, or long sentences, if possible), are two of many indices we used to gauge their fear of becoming openly individualized. Subsequently, these students found themselves unable to make a career decision and stick with it. Settling upon one profession means neglecting the others, a tragedy in their minds, since it implies that they will henceforth be viewed as an outsider by members of the other fields. They want to be everyone's friend, belong to every group of specialists. As a result, they accidentally prevent themselves from ever developing a specialty of their own.

Let's take a look at a few representative examples.

The High Price of Popularity

"I'm not going to drive myself crazy thinking about grades 24 hours a day," Lenore Parry commented at 15. Nor did she. When work was due, it was done. When exams had to be studied for, she studied for them. Otherwise, she made it seem as though school was merely a place to socialize. "What do I like most about my day?" she asked, repeating our question. "Seeing my girlfriends, and my boyfriend." On the other side of the country, Robert Ellis' attitude was much the same. As he put it at 15, "I can get decent grades without killing myself, so I always have plenty of time to do—I don't know, anything I want." Both he and Lenore managed to maintain B-minus averages throughout the four years of high school, and did so largely by being bright enough to absorb in class most of the required material, together with bouts of cramming just before tests.

Lenore was 5'5", thin, and had blonde hair, but it was her blue eyes that one couldn't help but notice. Her skin was light, and the dark eye makeup she used ("They disappear into my head when I'm not wearing any; I look as though I just rolled out of bed") made her eyes appear to have been pasted on, the way they might have been on a doll. Her counterpart, Bob, stood 5' 10" when he wasn't stooping, something he was prone to do. Dabbling in sports kept him from being fat, yet he was 25 pounds overweight and frequently peppered his conversation with promises to get in shape.

These two attractive and intelligent youngsters from first-rate suburban high schools, one in New York, the other in Southern California, had already become supremely skilled at portraying indifference to grades by the time they were high school freshmen. Each could reel off a long list of insulting labels commonly used by their peers to describe students who took school seriously and studied hard: nerd, tool, wimp, mole, creep, weirdo, grind, teacher's pet, and bookworm. Neither Bob nor Lenore had any intention of allowing one of those tags to be pinned on them. There was no fate worse than that. As Bob put it, with the easy laugh he still has, "Once you get it, you can't shake it. You're stuck with it forever."

It wasn't enough just to duck the tag; it was necessary to make absolutely certain that no one hung it on them even in jest. How did they do that? What steps were required to convince classmates that they weren't associated in any way with the ridiculed group? Different things, depending upon whether one was a boy or a girl. The favorite technique among boys Bob's age during the entire 25-year period from 1959–1983 was what we like to call, "scratch and yawn." Here is how it looked: when Bob was trying his hardest to convey the fact that he didn't give a damn about school, he'd scratch himself slowly but continually, first here, then there. One would have thought the kid had suddenly developed fleas. Accompanying his attempts to eradicate a randomly wandering itch were a series of cavernous yawns, as though he was about to nod off at any moment.

Lenore, on the other hand, used the technique most favored among girls her age during the past 25 years: changing the topic. The tactic is simple but effective. It called for her to talk excitedly about a subject—any subject—other than the one she didn't want to discuss. Her heated words were intended to get the message across without actually having to say, "Can't you tell that this is *more* important [than grades]?"

Although vocal, Lenore's approach is actually the more subtle, since it requires an act of interpretation on the part of the listener. Bob's message would have been difficult for anyone to misconstrue. He was unwittingly making use of two of the most powerful ways available to us to tell the people present that we don't care. Persistent scratching, particularly if done lazily and without any urgency which would make it medically forgivable, conveys a high degree of self-involvement. Yawning repeatedly underlines the point, in case there is someone obtuse enough in the audience to miss it.

Bob's physical and Lenore's verbal subterfuge worked. Both knew how to blatantly communicate that their minds were elsewhere, not on the topic under discussion. What needs to be said, though, is that they fooled themselves as well as others with their practiced ability to ignore the obvious. Grades may have been a menace lurking in the background, but they were able to fill the foreground with enough diversionary activity and excited conversation to make the subject seem to vanish. Two things kept bringing it back: tests and parents. Complaining about exams just before they had to be taken was essentially each student's way of telling the others, "We have to drop the pretense that grades don't matter for the moment, don't we? But it's only temporary, till the test is done." Parents were a little harder to dismiss. "My mother is such a drag," said Lenore. "Sometimes I think the only thing she really cares about is my grades." In Bob's case there were two people prodding. "They worry about it," he said shaking his head, "but they don't want to bug me. So they drop a lot of hints."

Still, ignoring the subject was no minor matter. It had to be done, since they risked being ostracized by their peers if they evidenced too much concern (except at test time) about the subject, or worse, broke with the crowd and openly dove into their books for an extended period during the semester. It was a vicious circle: they learned to repudiate the importance of grades in order to be a more integral part of their social circle. And once there, they found it easier to make the subject of good grades seem very remote.

What does all this have to do with the success of their transition from school to the work world? Everything. Because after graduation from college the old social circle was lost. Only the lessons learned within it remained. However, no sooner had their previous friends gone, dispersed to various parts of the country, when a different reward emerged: money.

Initially, Bob and Lenore reacted to the new carrot by trying to ignore it in order to better be a part of their new peer groups at work. This time, it wasn't effective. Paradoxically, they then switched, suddenly becoming interested in talking about little else. Conversations about grades clearly made them anxious while they were in school, but once they were working, conversations about money were much more likely to get them mad. Their forthright approach to the subject seemed to be evidence of an emerging maturity, especially when contrasted with the inhibited and ambivalent attitudes they had previously expressed toward grades. The hypothesis was to prove incorrect.

Listen to Lenore seven months after she had gotten her B.A. in English (again, as in high school, with a B-minus average for the four years) and found a job at a magazine. "All they think about here is money." What did she want instead? "Friends," she replied unhesitatingly. "That's what I need most." No tight, meaningful peer group had yet emerged, nor as it turned out, would it. However, the financial squeeze was on for both her and for Bob, who had majored in political science (and had moved up to a B average for the four years). "I'm barely able to live on what I make now," he said, visibly annoyed at the thought. "Everything is so unbelievably expensive."

No doubt their modest incomes put a damper on the life-style they would have liked to have been enjoying. In spite of supplementary checks which were received sporadically from home, the picture they envisioned of what was appropriate for them materially seemed out of

reach. A number of demographers[2] have stated (and our results tend
to confirm) that this picture is based on what these young adults previously experienced while still living in their parents' home; the gap
can later cause depression if they can't match their parents' income
on their own. Now that school was through, the excuses that Bob and
Lenore had allowed themselves for living at the poverty level as students were no longer acceptable. Frustration about their own financial
position in life slowly set in. It bothered them that they had taken a
substantial step down and weren't likely to reverse it any time soon,
much less move decisively ahead of what their parents had achieved
materially.

Something else rankled them even more about money: there was
no escape from the subject. They had learned how to associate being
sociable with ignoring the obvious goal they and their peers were all
seeking. Now they could no longer overlook it. Grades could easily be
made to seem remote since tests and term papers were a sometime
thing. Money, on the other hand, was a constant need. As Lenore put
it, "You can't go anywhere in this town without some." That made
them soon perceive a new and unpleasant truth: making money is a
painfully lonely pursuit.

"My Job Is a Trap, a Prison"

They could, and did, do something about the loneliness by using
their paychecks. It is impossible to understand the compulsive socializing that Bob and Lenore engaged in for well over a decade after
starting their first jobs unless one keeps in mind what was missing
in their lives. In school they earned grades, which could be ignored
as a way of sidling up next to old friends; at work they earned money,
which couldn't be ignored, but could be spent to sidle up next to
new friends.

Lenore referred to herself jokingly at 26 as a "swingle." Bob often
labeled himself as "available." Were these and many similar comments
merely the remarks of two sexually active young adults continually
on the lookout for bedmates? In part, yes, but only in part. To a much
larger extent, their behavior during leisure hours was an attempt to
make up for the satisfactions their work was failing to provide. Although they were getting paid for their labors now, instead of receiving
just a grade, the amount didn't seem sufficient. Perhaps no amount

---

[2] R. A. Easterlin, *Birth and Fortune: the Impact of Numbers on Personal Welfare* (New
York: Basic Books, 1980).

would have been. If money was the new reward, it wasn't reward enough.

As a result, whatever remained of their paychecks after rent and other essentials were covered, was quickly spent on clothes, movies, clubs, restaurants, travel, records, shares in ski chalets during the winter, and houses near the shore during the summer. Far too much has been made of what they were looking for—allegedly romantic and sexual contentment with the perfect partner. Not nearly enough attention has been given to why their search took on so frenzied and desperate a character during their twenties and thirties, and what connection that had to their work satisfactions and future job problems.

There are many people who contend that they don't need to be thrilled by their occupations, that that is perhaps expecting too much. "All I want is a decent wage and work that isn't too boring," is a common reply in employee surveys. However, college-educated workers, while they are in college and after graduation as well, want more. They aren't seeking just a job; they want a career, a personally fulfilling profession. That is one goal which means quite a bit to them, more in fact than they imagine. When they are unable to obtain it at work, they are forced to look elsewhere for the involvement it would have provided.

They certainly try to find it, often using exercise and hobbies as well as sex, but with marginal results. This is one work-related crisis that has a powerful, hidden effect on their personal lives. *The desire for involvement, instead of being distributed between work and love, falls solely on love. They want a personal relationship to give them all the satisfying absorption they require, rather than merely a part. It simply can't.* Soon the portion it does provide comes to seem paltry relative to the amount they need and are aggressively seeking. Even if they find someone and fall madly in love with the person, the relationship is likely to be temporary. This temple with only one pillar doesn't stand a chance of lasting long.

Removing the extra pressure on personal relationships, therefore enabling them to better survive on their own merits, is essential but isn't our primary focus here. What we want to see for the moment is how this lopsided condition later imperils one's business life.

Bob and Lenore didn't realize that their lack of involvement with their work was feeding their desire to prowl. All they knew was that the hunt wasn't even turning up any exciting one-night stands or long-term lovers, not to mention potential marital partners. In spite of the relentlessness of their pursuit, the results were meager at best. They both eventually concluded that there was nothing else they could do but try harder.

The crisis we are discussing first began to unfold in three seemingly innocent but damaging steps. In step one, both young people began to realize soon after they started working full-time that they needed money to live the way they wanted. That hadn't previously been the case. While they were in school, they did what the vast majority of other students do: manage to get by on whatever amount they have. An income difference between two students doesn't set them apart to the same degree it will later, once they have graduated. Since entertainment and clothes at school are typically inexpensive, and the range of expenditures that would be deemed acceptable to one's peers is limited, few students agree with the statement that having a lot more money would be the best way to improve their social and sex lives. Cash on hand helps, they contend, but not as much as, say, looks.

Once they've entered the work world, that view changes drastically. Within the first two years, they come to believe that they need money most in order to move in the right social circles. As Bob put it in his second year on the job, "My apartment is too plain. It kind of embarrasses me when I think about bringing someone with some class here, but I really can't afford anything better just yet." Lenore agreed. "You know, it costs $25 or $30 just to get into [the most popular dance spots at the time]," she said in her third year after graduating. "You've got to be rich to go skiing nowadays and run into the kind of men you really want to meet."

The quest to find Mr. or Ms. Perfect wasn't going well, but now at least they knew what was defeating them. It wasn't that they spent too little time looking, or didn't have enough interest in finding someone. They were doing whatever they could and were willing to do still more. The culprit, however, was clear: money. They obviously didn't have enough of it. Who was to blame for that? What was preventing them from obtaining the financial wherewithal needed to publicly blossom? Their jobs, naturally. As soon as they pointed a finger at their work as the underlying source of their troubles, they took step two. Now they not only had an identifiable problem; they also knew its cause.

The discovery affected their attitudes toward their employers in a very simple manner: every negative feeling they had toward the firm became magnified. In fact, the most useful way to think of step two is that, during the period, noninvolvement was transformed into animosity. That is, the fact that they found their work uninspiring and unabsorbing was no longer viewed in a neutral light. Instead, they came to see it as an impediment to everything they wanted most in life. Ultimately, that made them hate the place.

In his fourth year at what was now his second job, Bob called his work "a trap, a prison," one that was "stopping me from enjoying myself," both on the job and off. Lenore expressed similar opinions. "What is this job? A nothing. It's no fun and it's taking me nowhere, fast." Interpreting their comments to mean that they merely had the wrong jobs, that switching companies or even changing to another line of work would have made all the difference in the world, misses the point entirely. They did more than their share of switching around from one company to the next—in fact, 60 percent more than their peers in our sample—and averaged 25 months per stay during their first 16 years of employment.

We certainly don't mean to condemn such shifts out of hand. Job changes can be very valuable at times, and we've devoted the whole of Part Three to an examination of the subject. Therefore, it would be premature to discuss the topic now. But, unless we understand the attitude Bob, Lenore, and the many like them had toward jobs in general—and where that attitude came from—it will never be clear why changing jobs proved so fruitless for them. As they well knew, the troubles they were having seemed to follow them no matter how many times they transferred.

The move that Bob and Lenore made in going from step one to step two, from realizing that they had a problem (too little money) to blaming someone for that problem (their employers), may appear minor. Yet in this case it was equivalent to burning their bridges behind them. There was no going back, for they began to despise the only thing that could have remedied what ailed them: their work.

However, people in the grip of step two typically confuse their work and the setting in which they do it. Bob and Lenore thus started to make a steady stream of wisecracks about their firms. "This place wouldn't know quality if it came crashing through the window," Bob commented in his seventh year in the work world. He was explaining what had sapped his motivation to do his best. Four months later, he transferred to another company. Lenore had developed a comparable contempt for her firm. In her eighth year after graduation she said, "My talents are wasted around here. These people are only in business to peddle garbage. I shouldn't even be giving them the right time of day."

In short, she and Bob had begun their work lives uninvolved with their work, and during the intervening years the degree of detachment had slowly grown. They were alienated during the first two years, and have been increasingly irritable ever since. Although both had said initially that they wanted a career, and meant it, after the first few years at work, all they had was a job. In fact, their careers were turning out to be little more than a series of jobs.

"What I Need Is a Promotion"

The first two steps of the work crisis we've been discussing may seem a bit depressing. The third step, however, was nothing if not upbeat and even exhilarating. Bob and Lenore weren't about to walk around just licking their wounds year after year. That would have been too morbid for two such bright and resourceful people. Instead, in a triumph of human ingenuity, both decided to meet the challenge head-on by proceeding to step three: trying to "beat the system."

They found thinking about the goal almost as delightful as doing something to achieve it. "I can *tell* when my boss is coming down the hall," Lenore boasted, "and I always get busy." Then, laughing, she added, "I sometimes dream of putting a mechanical dummy in my chair and faking out [my boss] when he passes. Meanwhile, I'd be at the beach." Bob too had figured out at least one small but exciting way to accomplish the same end. He had a modest T & E (travel and entertainment) account that allowed him to take guests to lunch at nearby restaurants twice each week. The firm expected the guests to be business-related in some way. "Not *one* has been so far this year," Bob said proudly in March. "Nobody checks my T & E voucher. I just write in some [appropriate] names on the American Express slips and hand them in. What a gas."

The behavior may seem like malicious mischief or even spiteful fraud, and to some extent it was both. But there was a perverse kind of logic to what they were doing, and it is worthwhile to spell it out. As far as they were concerned, they had to have money above all to lead the kind of lives they wanted. That was the goal from which they were working backward; that is, since they needed it, they wanted it. Whether they deserved it or not was irrelevant, although they usually were able to convince themselves that they were worth a great deal more than they were getting. Since they weren't being paid the amount they wanted, there was one thing they could do that was equivalent: not work so hard. They may not have been able to increase the quality of pay they were receiving, but they could decrease the quantity of effort they put out. That was in their hands not their employers'. Neither Bob nor Lenore ever wanted to feel that they were being victimized by their firms. Some authority over their lives had to remain in their own hands if they were to feel good about being there. Withholding a portion of their energy and dedication made them see themselves as being in control. "I don't let them push me around," said Lenore in her ninth year in the work world. Bob had a similar attitude at the time. "I'm my own man," he said, straightening his tie. "This place isn't my life."

A concise summary of their thought processes over the years was:

1. "I need more money."
2. "I deserve more money."
3. "They aren't giving me more."
4. "So I'll cut back on the amount of work I do."

All that sounds straightforward enough. And the majority of people we've surveyed consider this sort of logic not only rational but justified. As night follows day, one thought leads to the next in the sequence. The trouble here—and it's a major one—is that this isn't a line of thought. It is a circle, because four leads inevitably to:

5. "Now I need money even more."

That is, once their indifference toward work turns into chronic hostility, they become still more cut off from the emotional satisfactions it could have yielded.

That made Lenore's and Bob's days even more unbalanced than they'd been before. The psychological gap between their careers and their personal lives was growing wider. Work was viewed as an annoying waste of time, one that didn't pay them nearly enough, whereas their nonwork hours were viewed as the only potential source of pleasure. The idea of any of their leisure moments going to waste horrified and depressed them, a telltale sign, since it was exactly the reverse of what we witnessed in the case of workers who were involved with their work and who went on to become outstanding in their fields.

In brief, what Bob and Lenore actually did during their first decade of employment was traverse the loop, one through five, again and again, ending up each time at a higher level of disenchantment with their work lives. Each therefore had to search even more desperately for a satisfying personal life.

The distance they felt from their work (or in their view, the firm) gave them what could have been a useful perspective on it. Unlike people who are totally immersed in what they're doing, perhaps unable therefore to see the forest for the trees, Bob and Lenore felt sufficiently removed from their labors to concentrate continually on the larger picture. "I've got big plans," Bob kept saying. He frequently wrestled with a tactic that he thought would, as he put it, "do wonders for me overnight." Lenore too had no doubt that there was, in her words, "a way to scamper up the corporate ladder more quickly." She was intent upon finding it. Basically, they saw work as a nuisance and, like any nuisance, they wanted it over with as soon as possible. Finding a way to beat the system would, they felt, solve all their problems simultaneously.

They launched their assault on two separate fronts: clothes and management. Bob and Lenore had lost faith in the idea that their work would take them anywhere. "It seems meaningless," is a comment both made repeatedly, not only about their own efforts, but those of the firm as well. "Who would miss this place if it disappeared tomorrow?" Lenore asked caustically about her third employer, and proceeded to answer the question with, "Not me." They were outsiders to their own work, and they saw what outsiders notice most: its purpose. In their eyes, it had none. What they could not see was what people who are absorbed in doing the activity notice most: the pleasure and sometimes pain that results from being absorbed in the doing.

Since the inside didn't matter, only the outside now did, they switched their focus to their clothes. It was a fascinating shift to watch. Our initial assumption had been that people who lost interest in a job would start dressing more slovenly when they were there. That is not what Bob and Lenore did. Paradoxically, the less they came to care about their work, the more attentive they became to how they dressed. In their view it was a hidden key to success. "It's important for me to look the part," Bob said more than once. Lenore made an increasing number of similar remarks.

They certainly looked attractive when neatly dressed, and making a good impression is valuable for anyone. The point here is that Bob and Lenore had little else left to use as a lever. As they readily admitted in private, they were no longer much interested in their everyday activities in the office. Nevertheless, they badly wanted promotions and pay raises. If their work wasn't going to speak for them, their clothes would have to. Bob even learned how to loosen his tie, as he put it, "just the right amount to make it look like I've got my hands full."

As their twenties ended and they entered their early thirties, they began to talk openly about getting themselves appointed to a position in management. "I couldn't ask for it before," said Bob at 32. "I looked too young." Lenore felt that she too was old enough now to start demanding consideration for a managerial post. "I've been around a while, you know," she said, "and that makes me entitled." Their view of the matter was quite simple: time in the work world in and of itself is a credential. They'd both been working for a decade and therefore were qualified for a position in management to the tune of one decade's worth. They had an invisible coupon, one that grew larger every year, and they were now ready to spend it. However, for all the lobbying and external preparation they did, few promotions were to come their way in the subsequent decade. It was a subject they both complained about regularly.

Nonetheless, right in the middle of what appeared to be a continuing defeat for Bob and Lenore was a victory. When they had turned their backs on grades half a lifetime before, they received an increased amount of approval from their peers for doing so. Pretending publicly that the marks they would get in school didn't matter allowed Bob and Lenore to cluster together with classmates at the time. And discuss what? Beating the (school) system. "I had the answers written on my wrist," Bob told his friends with great glee at 15.

Trying to beat the system at work had the same social benefits as trying to beat the system at school. Only now, 10 to 15 years later, it became the main topic of conversation with friends. When we think of people attempting to beat the system, any system, we envision them looking for a trick or formula that increases the chances or speed of a big payoff. But not everything people in the work world do to beat the system is done so consciously. Working less hard, as retaliation for too little pay, was a deliberate act on Bob's and Lenore's part. Dressing well and bucking for a position in management wasn't as calculated a move. Not only did they do it without realizing that they were; they did it without really understanding why. It was a subconscious way of trying to beat the system by moving up fast, a key intermediate goal of both. If it happened, they'd finally have the financial wherewithal and public standing necessary to lead the kinds of lives they wanted. "I can see myself being picked up by a chauffeur-driven limo each morning," said Bob at 34.

When all is said and done, it was a bit bizarre to see so much of their imagination and creativity being funneled into finding ways to beat the work system rather than into the work itself. As they knew only too well, the results of their search were minimal, but not zero. Bob and Lenore had lost in some ways yet won in others. They had suffered what looked to them like a series of career setbacks, but they had reaped a social bonus—something to talk endlessly about with peers and passersby who shared their attitude toward work.

Both on the job and off, they projected the impression that they wanted to project. They seemed ambitious, and thought of themselves that way as well. That was a triumph of sorts. If nothing else, they had sidestepped their share of job-related loneliness by dismissing their work, which might otherwise have had to be pursued diligently at times in isolation. Ironically, the loneliness surfaced during their social hours. That distressed them mightily—"I'm doing all I can *now* [to find good companions]," said Lenore at 33—but it was at least something they could partially remedy: beating the system was a goal that could be, and was, cheerfully discussed for hours on end with co-workers and friends.

Making That Career Decision at Last

Bob and Lenore are representative of the single largest category in our sample and, we believe, in the labor force. By no means are they the only variety of worker, and we'll look at a number of other, distinctly different, categories in the next few chapters. However, since there are so many like them, it is important to see what we can learn from their approach.

Whether we like it or not, work is a major part of our adult lives. While it has much in common with our activities during the school years that precede it, the contrasts are more important than the similarities. It isn't necessarily a tragedy that so many students are indifferent to it (as a group-approval ploy) or merely hope to get by, for two reasons: school in most cases is brief; it is done by the time most people are in their mid-twenties. Second, there is much else happening during the period, everything from physical growth and sexual maturation to the development of social, athletic, and intellectual skills. The internal and public pressures at the time are intense, yet a balance is usually maintained thanks to the socialization forces exerted by parents, teachers, police, and peers.

However, once these students finish school and enter the work world full-time, everyone in essence backs off. They are on their own to a much greater extent than the majority of people we studied seemed to realize. Those whose mothers and fathers were still alive and trying to help felt that the parental umbrella (although it was often resented) would somehow stop them from being harmed. Perhaps in some ways it did, but not occupationally.

Career decisions are postponed for so long by students in the United States, as opposed to what occurs in Europe and Japan, that many really never make one. For better or worse, they enter the work world when school is through, and then they treat it as though they were college freshmen who still had plenty of time to choose a major, much less a profession. Although they are unware of it, ten years into their work lives, many still haven't settled decisively on a direction. All they have concluded thus far is, "I want to be a success."

At what?

To sum up, people who have allowed themselves happily to become an integral part of a profession see the work world primarily as an opportunity to become recognized in their field. On the other hand, those who have spent years shunning a profession so that they might more readily be accepted by the members of every profession see the work world primarily in terms of money. *An excessively social orientation in high school and in college tends to produce an excessively—and frantically—financial orientation on the job. Work, in time, comes to be thought of solely in terms of its monetary rewards, or lack of them.*

CHAPTER
4

Beating the System

PARENTS ARE OFTEN surprised at what their children grow up to be, but relatives who don't live nearby are usually even more surprised. They don't see the youngsters growing day-to-day, and in the intervening months or years between visits enough changes may take place to make it seem as if a different person altogether has emerged.

Doing a long-term study on a group, approximately half of whose members are still in their formative years, is much like being a distant relative who drops in regularly. In many cases, we were not only surprised, but stunned.[1] Teenagers who appeared to others (as well as to us) shy and introverted had undergone a metamorphoses that rendered them confident and assertive. Adolescents who had told us that they spend 26 hours each day thinking about sex lost their giddy, easily distractible manner and became more serious about themselves and the work that would occupy the bulk of their adult lives.

Fortunately, we didn't have to choose which adolescents would turn out to be people whose business careers would unfold in manners opposite to those of, say, Bob and Lenore. We couldn't have or, more accurately, in many cases we would have chosen the wrong teenagers as the most likely candidates to achieve the goals Bob and Lenore set for themselves but never attained. However, in retrospect we now know which young adults became what we initially had every reason to expect these two would become, and we also know why they succeeded where Bob and Lenore failed.

Barry Scott, one of three cases we'll examine, affords us a prime example of the many shifts in attitude and direction that occur in the lives of those making the transition from ages 15 to 30 on their way

---

[1]Daniel Levinson's emphasis in *The Seasons of a Man's Life* (New York: Alfred A.Knopf, 1978) on the term "biography" in reference to the people he studied seems to us appropriate, and even unavoidable.

to productive business careers. The main way in which he differed from the two people discussed previously is this: Bob and Lenore gave the impression of being very ambitious but were actually removed emotionally from their work. Ironically, this distance is what allowed them to appear to be wrestling with it constantly. They did wrestle, too, though only because they wanted to avoid concentrating on it, while still having it take them where they wanted to go. To them, it was little more than a vehicle. On the other hand, once Barry accepted a full-time job and settled in, he related primarily to his work, not the rewards it might one day throw off. As a result, he had much less of a sense of where he was going than did Bob and Lenore, and he thought about the topic significantly less often. Odd as it may sound at first, that made him often appear more flaky and indecisive relative to Bob and Lenore, who seemed nothing if not determined.

As a seemingly separate but in fact related point, Barry applied little pressure to himself during his nonwork hours. By Bob's and Lenore's standards he would have been rated a "leisure slob," since he left the time largely unstructured, realizing on some subconscious level that that was the most effective way for him to recharge and refresh himself for another assault on his work.

Becoming Professionalized

As a 14-year-old high school freshman, Barry didn't seem overly interested in his studies, and he wasn't, as his mediocre marks for the next two years attested. In his junior and especially senior years he buckled down, studied hard, and his grades improved from a B and B-minus average to an A-minus average. Peer pressures to turn his back on grades were certainly present, but Barry had good reason to resist them at this point, both in public and in private. "I want to get into a good college," he said in his junior year. That cost him some friends, and he knew it. "I'm sure some of my classmates think I've turned into a bookworm," he commented, somewhat uneasy at the thought but determined to stay his course anyway. By the time he was in the spring term of his senior year, the opinion of his classmates hardly seemed to matter. He was focusing on a more distant goal.

It was remarkable to see how far he had come in just four years. As a high school sophomore and junior, Barry commented repeatedly that he had trouble keeping his mind off the subject of sex. He had a chance to do more about that than most boys his age in our sample because both his parents worked. Two or three times each week he invited different girls in his school over and they "practiced," as he called it.

"I want to be able to do it *right* when I grow up." One of his bedmates described him in a letter as "a hunk." At 5'9" and 160 pounds, he was more muscular and less awkward in his movements than many of his peers, a result of playing sports all day long during summers spent in camp. His straight, Romanesque nose and curly brown hair highlighted a face that usually revealed the underlying tension he carried. "I like laughing," he often said, and needed to do so as well, to relieve the tension.

Although the college he got into wasn't his first choice, Barry was more than pleased about the prospect of going. "What will you major in?" we asked him shortly before he left. "I haven't the foggiest," he said, and meant it. By the spring of his freshman year, however, he decided upon history. The course he'd taken in the fall semester caught his attention as nothing else had. Barry thought that was a fluke, an event that wasn't likely to be repeated. But he took another history course the following term and found it more captivating still. Why? "It has *movement*," he said enthusiastically. All his other subjects seemed static by comparison. "They're flat, lifeless," he said with an air of finality.

Starting in his sophomore year, Barry not only covered the material that was required in his history courses, he also read a large pile of additional history books each term on his own initiative. "It's fun," he said. "More relaxing than watching television shows," most of which he found irritating instead of soothingly mindless. "I'd rather be doing this," he said emphatically, pointing to a copy of Arthur Schlesinger, Jr.'s, *Age of Jackson.*

By the time Barry was a junior, something happened to him that happened to neither Bob nor Lenore, not in college and not later either. He became professionalized. By that we mean he began to think of himself as an historian. He often imagined himself a full-fledged member of the profession, reading and writing, active and productive. "Sometimes I stop in the middle [of what I'm reading]," he acknowledged a bit sheepishly, while removing a pair of recently acquired wire-rim glasses, "and pretend that I'm the one who wrote it, or a book that's even *better.*" He'd not have been embarrassed at the thought had he realized how normal a facet of the identification process it is. Seeking acclaim from a particular group of professionals is an integral part of what makes young adults like Barry eagerly adopt rather than fight whatever the then prevailing style and conventions of their chosen field happen to be. Without such a step, the people whose approval he was seeking as a professional would view him as alien, too remote to be treated as a member of good standing of the group.

Barry's visions of his future self while he was reading weren't mere fantasies. For he was doing everything possible to give them substance. His knowledge of the field was growing rapidly, thanks to his extensive reading, and the papers he wrote and exams he took earned consistently high grades. That alone would have set him apart from Bob and Lenore, who entertained many similar thoughts over the years about being acclaimed as outstanding in one profession or another. However, for them it was indeed mere fantasy, since their follow-through was minimal in each case. Apparently no picture of themselves as professionals was sufficiently compelling or enduring, and no body of knowledge or activity sufficiently interesting, to make them immerse themselves in the field and happily remain there. "I want to be everything," Bob was still saying at 28.

The first hint that serious trouble was brewing came in the spring semester of Barry's senior year. He had come a long way in just four years. Whereas only one college of the seven he applied to while in high school accepted him, he was accepted at five of the six graduate schools to which he made application, each of which was tougher to get into than any college he applied to in high school. The University of Chicago was his first choice, and he was thrilled when the letter arrived from the admissions committee saying yes.

The thrill didn't last long. Doubts began to creep in less than a month later. The high age at which eminence usually comes to historians weighed upon his mind. "I don't want to be old and gray by the time I become well known," he said, somewhat dispirited at the prospect. "I don't want people saying to me when I'm 40, and just reaching my prime, that 'By the time Mozart was your age, he was dead.' "

However, the factor that seems to have been pivotal in his decision about what to do next, and had made him worry about age in the first place, was that the United States had entered a period of declining college enrollments. The dramatically reduced need for new faculty members made Barry conclude that he was perhaps about to choose the wrong career.[2] Now was the best time to do some hardheaded thinking about the subject. As he put it just before graduating, "The only place that hires lots of historians is universities, and right now they're feeling the pinch." That bothered him greatly because he didn't want to be prevented from doing the work he loved, once he got started doing it.

He wrote Chicago that he'd be coming in September, and he also

---

[2]Figures compiled in annual surveys by the National Academy of Sciences—National Research Council showed that while only 6% of new PhD's seeking jobs had none in 1968, for the class of 1974 the figure had jumped to 26%.

took a full-time job in June, neglecting to tell his employer that he'd be leaving in the fall. "I thought I'd earn some extra money," Barry explained, two weeks after starting work. "Tuition is very expensive, and so is everything else." As reasonable as that sounded, the real explanation for what he was doing lay elsewhere: he was hedging his bets. He wanted very much to see what the work world was like and still have the option of going to graduate school in the fall if he chose. He knew that his first job right after college wasn't likely to be the best position he'd ever hold. Nonetheless, he expected it to give him a realistic taste of what being a part of the world of commerce was like.

"I don't know that I have anything to contribute to a business organization," he said, scratching his head. Although he'd already been on the job in the production department for two weeks, he couldn't have been more estranged from the paper products company for which he was working if he tried. It had nothing to do with the particular firm. It was the work itself and being paid in money. Barry had had part-time jobs before and had worked full-time during the last two summers in high school, but this was different. It was serious. It was supposed to be his life. How did he react? What was he feeling inside? "Queasy," he answered. The terrain he was now inhabiting was so alien to Barry it made him feel a bit nauseous, not from contempt but from the very real disorientation he felt when there. "I feel like a fish out of water here," he said quietly.

Two things struck him repeatedly during the next few months, and he frequently commented on them. He had learned from his studies to view each incident as taking place in a larger context that gave it meaning. He couldn't see any where his work at the office was concerned. As he put it, "It's just absurd what these people do. Absurd." Each act seemed to him divorced of significance, almost random and empty, certainly not a part of a worthy and purposeful whole.

The second observation he often found himself making was related to the first, yet it had even more importance to him. What had attracted him to history as a field right from the start was its dynamism. The sense of movement on a vast scale produced a panorama in his mind that hypnotized him more than any movie could, with its neat beginning and end. "It gets me outside of myself," he said excitedly in his sophomore and again in his junior years in college, "and sweeps me into something *larger* than myself."

Now that came to an abrupt halt. Try as he might, he couldn't escape noticing what he saw as a monumental pettiness to the behavior of the people around him. "They bicker about nonsense," he said with disgust, "and get worked up about *nothing*." The grandeur of history, the epic nature of the events he studied, was gone. In its place were actions that were, to use his favorite term, "trivial."

Much to the surprise of his friends, when the summer ended he did not go to Chicago. "For what?" he asked rhetorically in late September. "To get a PhD that makes me even more unemployable than I am now? I'm better off quitting while I'm ahead. This is how it's going to wind up in the end, anyhow." It is easy for analysts to say that job-market conditions influence career decisions, describing in statistical terms exactly the degree to which that occurs. The studies are interesting and important. But in Barry's life the decision was neither simple nor easy. Nor did the repercussions end once the decision was made. On the contrary, as in most of the instances we monitored, only later did the most serious consequences start to surface.

He had little affection for the firm for which he worked, and he was still reeling from a world that seemed absurd and trivial instead of meaningful and grand. But he eventually concluded that his chances of becoming a successful and satisfied member of the history profession were miniscule. "What I have now [in business]," he said matter of factly, "is probably no worse than I'll find in the future [in academia]." Besides, his queasiness had vanished by September and was superseded merely by mild repugnance. "I can live with it," he said about his job in October. "If everybody else can, so can I."

Settling In

For the next three years Barry remained at the same firm, although he was transferred to a different division as a result of an acquisition of another company by his firm. Subsequently he sought and received a job offer from a competing firm in the paper products field, where he stayed for four years.

It was remarkable to see another instance of someone doing well during his first decade in the work world without having his heart in what he was doing. Anyone who states that a worker can't make good and even rapid progress up the corporate ladder by merely going through the motions well hasn't been closely monitoring the actual development of the business lives of a wide variety of capable individuals. This is a much more common phenomenon than many imagine.

The person's inside and outside can be greatly at odds with one another and still not interfere with the attainment of a steady string of promotions and pay raises. (It is the inner price that is usually high in such cases, a subject we will deal with at length in Chapter Eleven.) After Barry left, and without making reference to him in any way, we interviewed a number of top officials at the firm from which he had resigned. We asked Kurt, the president of the firm, about the phenomenon. He laughed and said: "If we only hired and promoted people who truly loved what they were doing, we'd have just five workers here instead of 500." Since it's too much to ask for, few employers expect it. That allows people who are in the same period of transition as Barry was at this point not only to comfortably escape detection, but to rise as well. That is very important, because they need both the time and the rewards that are coming to them as an aid to making up their minds about happily spending the rest of their lives in the business world.

Interestingly, Barry was one of the few in our sample who came to realize that the work he currently was doing was so removed from his inner emotional life, it might as well have been theater. "There are times when I feel like a bit player in an off-Broadway show," he said in his fifth year. That led to a moment of great insight two years later about his father.

"I never understood how my old man could do it," Barry said at 28. "I'd get up for school, he'd be getting up to go to work. I could tell he didn't love it. But he'd go anyway, every day, and didn't complain. It bothered me because it was so meaningless. I wanted more. [But] I guess I'm doing the same thing now."

The revelation gave Barry a conspicuous measure of relief. Although he never said anything about it to his father, the long-distance sense of parental approval the realization brought him made him more relaxed than we had seen him at any time since he entered the work world. Within the year, he transferred to a much smaller firm, one with 56 as opposed to 500 employees, and has been there ever since.

There have been problems at the firm—or should we say, business problems for the firm. Good times and bad ones have visited the paper products industry during recent years. However, by the time Barry was 31, at least his own personal distance from what he was doing each day in the office was no longer complicating his business life. He'd stopped second-guessing himself continually ("Why am I here? Why am I doing this?") and he finally became absorbed in his work ("I enjoy this," he said surprised at his own words. "I really do.") It had taken nine years.

That was a long and at times upsetting period, yet the math, language, art, or philosophy majors in our sample typically had a still tougher time of it. On the other hand, Barry's experience was significantly more stressful than that of accounting majors, who usually made the easiest transition of the lot. (See Table 1.) As one put it after 14 months on the job, "There really isn't a whole lot of difference between doing this [auditing] for my professor and doing it for the clients."

Table 1: Transition Times

College Major

Accounting (V)	0.5
Nursing (V)	0.7
Pharmacy (V)	0.8
Education (V)	1.2
Apparel Design (V)	1.3
Library Science (V)	1.3
Architecture (V)	1.4
Computer Programming (V)	1.7
Chemistry (A)	1.8
Business Administration (V)	1.9
Journalism (A)	2.0
Engineering (V)	2.2
Biology (A)	2.4
Geology (A)	2.5
Psychology (A)	2.9
Statistics (A)	2.11
Physics (A)	3.1
Economics (A)	3.4
Mathematics (A)	3.10
Anthropology (A)	4.1
Dance (A)	4.1
Sociology (A)	4.7
Art (A)	4.11
Foreign Language and Literature (A)	5.2
Religion (A)	5.3
Political Science (A)	5.7
Music (A)	6.6
History (A)	7.5
English (A)	8.2

Nature of major: A = academic, V = vocational. Transition times are in years and months. Thus, 5.7 = 5 years, 7 months. Figures are medians, not means, a statistical necessity since 22 percent of sample members with a clearly defined "before" (see below) hadn't yet made the transition by 1984, after being out of school for more than two decades.

The figures in the table were calculated using a "before" and "after" that were measured as follows. "Before" is a weighted average of (1) grade point average in the person's major (during sophomore through senior years), not overall gpa; (2) amount of leisure time person devoted voluntarily to further work and/or reading in the field (during the same three-year period); and (3) number of years person was willing to continue to do this kind of work (average of three replies, gathered during spring of sophomore, junior and senior years). The weighting is 35:35:30. Thus, students who did poorly in their major, were unwilling to spend part of their weekends and summers adding to their knowledge of the field without being asked to do so, and finally, who couldn't see themselves devoting many years and perhaps their entire work lives to the field were adjudged not even to have a "before" against which an "after" could subsequently be measured. A score of 80 or higher is required for both.

"After" is a weighted average of (1) degree to which respondents claimed each year to like work they were currently doing (on a 100-point scale); (2) amount of leisure time devoted voluntarily to further work and/or reading in the field; and (3) percentage of pay reduction respondents claimed they would be willing to take in order to continue doing work in that particular field. Weighting is 30:30:40.

What Happens to the Restless?

Bob and Lenore spent the bulk of their time trying to figure out ways to beat the system, but they rarely realized that that was what they were doing. Barry, at the other extreme, wasn't trying to beat it; he wanted to find an interesting place within it, and finally did. Stanley Cooper was more like Bob and Lenore, only he carried the process to its logical conclusion.

"I don't have to put up with this bullshit," Stan told us angrily at 16, about a teacher of his. By any measure, this was a very bright but hostile youngster. Wiry and strong, alert almost to the point of being jumpy, Stan would find himself in scrapes during an incident that other people would have ignored. "I was there first," he said after an elbowing match with another student about which of the two had entered the cafeteria lunch line before the other. "That son-of-a-bitch tried to get ahead of me." Actually, both had gotten there at the same time.

Stan's grades were erratic, the result of doing almost no homework unless it had to be handed in. If he didn't grasp the material immediately in class, it was lost, dismissed as irrelevant. That didn't happen often, but when it did, Stan displayed little willingness to sit down later and fill in the gaps. "Who has the time?" he said, not wanting an answer. More to the point, he was simply too restless.

His impatience was not a problem in his social life. Although he felt he was doing the world a great favor if he spent so much as five minutes looking at a textbook in his leisure time, he could spend five hours with friends doing very little, hardly noticing the time pass. "He's nice," one of his companions commented. "A really fun guy." Said a second, "He's very considerate."

Stan changed very little between his freshman and senior years in high school. He cheated often and readily admitted that he'd have done so even more—"every time," he insisted—if he could have gotten away with it. Only once did he get caught, during a mid-term in French in his junior year, and was instantly given an F. Chagrined but undaunted, he paid more attention in class for the rest of the semester and even studied a bit at home. As a result, he did well enough in the final to get a C in the course.

It was revealing to see that, instead of being pleased, he considered the teacher a fool. In his view the rules were as unyielding as a set of monkey bars, and anyone who bent them on his behalf because of something he did was a weakling and a dupe. Although he fought constantly against any decree that applied to him, he needed its alleged rigidity, for three main reasons: as an adversary against which to define himself; to help impose order on his inner chaos; and to enable him to aim outward the seething hostility he chronically carried. It might otherwise have made him harshly self-critical and even depressed had he held it in. He therefore saw every rule as being far more inflexible than most actually were.

The most obvious change that occurred in high school took place during his junior and senior years. Stan shot up in size, growing from 5'5" to 5'11" during that time, and he added 45 pounds, reaching a solid 175 pounds. Paradoxically, as his height and weight increased, he became more intellectually and much less physically combative. He loved to argue now about such topics as religion and politics, and the comments he made were persuasive and at times profound. The principal thing they lacked were structure and consistency, qualities he considered, as he put it, "the last refuge of small minds." If one lobbed a thought at him, he'd slam it back, hoping for a spectacular score. "I like to win big," he remarked more than once.

The fact that he perceived rules as being totally inflexible allowed him to rail at them boldly and loudly, winning friends all the while; but in college that contributed substantially to his undoing. Suddenly all the decrees that he'd gotten used to making savage fun of in public were gone. Now, no one told him how to dress; he could wear what he wanted. Nor did he have to shave or brush his teeth if he didn't want to, or comb his hair. Or bathe. Whether he kept his room neat or messy was up to him. Here, 800 miles from home, he didn't even have to say hello to his classmates if he didn't feel like it. They certainly didn't care. On a large campus, few noticed one student more or less.

The two things that did occupy a large place in Stan's consciousness were, as he put it, "I can eat what I want—burgers, pizza—all the time," and, "I miss study hall." The three-times-a-week regularly scheduled study periods in high school had been of use to Stan, not to read, but to disrupt. For him, they might as well have been gym classes. "God, I had more fun *there* than anywhere," he said, grinning. The joy of breaking the rules was harder to come by now, for the school left it up to him to study when and where he wanted, just so long as he got the work done.

"I can't do it," he said in his spring term. "I've got ants in my pants, or something." In so unstructured an environment, there were few generally accepted local enemies at which to aim his animosity. That visibly increased his level of anxiety. Stan was having trouble focusing on anything for very long, much less applying himself steadily to his studies. "I think I'm going to flunk out," he said two months before the end of the term, somewhat panicked at the thought. He didn't. With a gut-twisting burst of effort just prior to finals, Stan managed to get a C average for the term. It left him more shaken than elated. "I don't know if I could do it again," he said two weeks later; but he came back the next fall prepared to try. Stan chose business administration as a major when registering for the semester.

The amount of time and energy someone continually devotes to trying to beat the system is one of the key variables we've used over the years to assess how happily caught up that person is in his work. People who like what they are doing usually just do it, whereas those who dislike the task spend significantly more time making it appear that they're doing it (when they're not) or that it is done (when it isn't). Finding a device or trick that enables the person to finish quickly and easily is one solution. In many cases that involves copying someone else's work or making use of a variety of other forms of cheating; for instance, playing sick, looking at the answers, having someone else write the paper or take the test for you.

None of these tactics was good enough for Stan. He used them all when he could, but that wasn't very often. The conspiratorial air among his high school classmates ("It's all of us against the teacher") had weakened considerably in college. "They're real square here," Stan said in October of his sophomore year, after he'd asked a friend for some homework answers and was refused. "Real Little-Goody-Two-Shoes types, afraid of getting caught."

As the semester progressed, Stan fell further and further behind his peers. "I'm losing ground," he said, clearly worried by the first week in November. Since he never felt himself to be an integral part of the educational setting he inhabited, his desire to beat the system was high to begin with. Now, however, the desire soared. People who are doing well in a particular context don't have to come up with a way to edge out the others. They already have. But someone who feels like a loser, or is actually losing, is likely to find that his appetite for ways to compete unfairly has expanded dramatically. He needs a magical device of some kind, not so much to get ahead (although that's what he says he wants it for) as merely to keep up. Stan searched hard but couldn't find one.

Everything changed a few weeks later. In the latter part of November, Stan's thinking underwent a radical transformation that produced exactly what he was looking for. Most of the students he knew were taking school seriously, playing around at times, yet doing their work as well and getting good grades. Instead of seeing them as competitors who were upstaging him, he suddenly began to view them as gullible innocents who'd been deceived by society into believing they were doing the right thing. "They're never going to get anywhere pounding the pages [of their books]," he said, happier than we'd seen him in many months. He was nearly shouting the words. "They've been sucked in."

That was a more important comment than it may appear. He no longer felt compelled to do the same thing they were doing, namely, study. He'd found a perfect way to get the jump on all of them: quit school. Before he dropped out of college, though, he was determined to rub his classmates' noses in the dirt. How? By partying, having a hell of a good time, right in front of them. "They're green with envy, I can tell," he said after coming home stoned at 5:00 A.M. and letting out a cheer that he wanted all of them to hear.

For his purposes, staying up late was almost as good as staying out late, and he delighted in reminding two of his classmates at midnight, "Come, come, boys, don't you have to be up *early* in the morning?" Although he was registered for the same 9:00 A.M. class they were taking, he made a point of sleeping till 11. "Another boring lecture?" he asked offhandedly when they returned. They didn't answer.

It wasn't all a pretense on Stan's part. In spite of his decidedly above-average ability to get people on his side—which had failed him, however, in this case—he himself seemed convinced that his route was the right one. "What a pathetic way to waste your life," he said about his friends when they weren't around. Then, smiling, he added, "I feel *sorry* for these jerks." On December 10, he left, feeling victorious at last.

On the Road to Fame and Fortune

Odd as it may sound, there was no question in Stan's mind that he had achieved one of life's most important goals: he'd beaten the system, and publicly at that. Although he was blissfully unaware of it for the moment, in doing so he had pitched himself right into another system, one that is vastly harder to escape. He didn't have to be concerned about grades anymore, unlike his benighted classmates who were still in school, but now he had to worry about making a living. There was no question in his mind that that would be a breeze. "It's got to be better than *this*," he said, four days before leaving the campus for good.

When we first began our study, we had little reason to doubt Stan's comment. At the time we anticipated that certain people would do better as students, while others did poorly in school but later excelled at making money. That seemed only fair and democratic: those who were outstanding academically would go on to become professors, and those who were good in business would go on to become millionaires. Each would be a success in a different area.

We felt that the vast majority who entered the business arena would make the transition only with difficulty (and that this was an insufficiently explored subject), since school and the work world differ in so many ways. Some culture shock was to be expected. After many years spent in educational institutions where the main measures of progress are grades, some would naturally be expected to have more difficulty than others in adjusting to the world of commerce where pay and promotions are the main measures of progress. As Table 1 indicates, that turned out to be so.

What we did not anticipate was this: the many students like Stan in our sample who dropped out of college because they couldn't "get into it," to use Stan's favorite description, didn't later get into their work either. In switching from school, where they felt uncomfortable, to the work world, which was supposed to have been a far more fertile setting for their talents, they jumped out of the frying pan and into the fire. Instead of flowering, they faded fast. To put it another way, no group of American youngsters was so sure it would make the transition from grades to money more easily than college dropouts, yet no group wound up having a tougher time of it.

Revealingly, when things went wrong at work, or they couldn't get the job they wanted, they immediately concluded that the rejection was based on their lack of a college diploma. In some cases it undoubtedly was. But in the majority of instances the problem had more to do with the goals of the potential employee than the academic degrees demanded by the current or prospective employer. What kind of goals? "I want to make money—piles of it—and soon," Stan said as he hunted for his first job. He eventually found one as a waiter. That didn't sound like the pot of gold at end of the rainbow, but Stan viewed the position in a different light: "In an office, I *know* what I'll be making. Here, who knows?" Since the amount wasn't specified in advance, and certainly wasn't likely to be the same monotonous number each week, Stan could let his imagination puff it up to the point where it interested and even excited him.

After seven months on the job, he was conspicuously less excited. Switching to another restaurant improved his income but not his mood. "I'm still making peanuts," he said, doubly disappointed that the work left him dissatisfied and the pay was no match for his dreams. For fifteen months he supplemented his income by dealing a little in marijuana ("Grass brings in $70, sometimes $100 extra a week"), but when a friend was arrested for doing the same, Stan stopped ("Getting busted isn't for me"). Besides, his supplier was now gone.

He had been out of college for three years when a regular patron of the restaurant offered him a position in the field that he is still in now, twelve years later. "You'd make a good salesman," the well-dressed customer told him. "You know how to handle yourself with people, know how to talk to them. Come see me on Tuesday afternoon at 4:00, if you're interested. Here's my card." Less than a month after that, he was an apparel salesman, selling to stores. "I *like* all the traveling," he said a year later. "Being on the road this much doesn't bother me."

Stan has worked for five employers in the 12 years, and has been married and divorced twice during that time. Every step of the way, what intrigued him about his work, if anything did, was beating the system. For Stan it wasn't so much a goal as an obsession. What allowed him to feel that he was succeeding was that he could rattle off a long list of pluses before we could even finish asking our question: he traveled; most other workers stayed put. He continually ran into new faces; they saw the same ones day after day. Other people got paid a salary; he had a sizable expense account. That allowed him, as he put it, "to play with the numbers and fool IRS *and* my boss. Nobody but me knows how much I really make."

It's not a great deal, that much we've been able to determine. Like quitting college, this too was a mental victory, and continues to be.

Stuck Between School and Work

Lynn Wilson, the last example we'll look at in this chapter, was very different from the people we've already met. Bob and Lenore were unwittingly trying to beat the system. Stan was consciously trying to do the same, whereas Barry wanted above all to sink softly into it and be happily productive. In that sense, Lynn most closely resembles Barry. What makes her case so interesting is that she is representative of the large number of men and women who never fully make the transition from school to the work world because they get stuck somewhere in the middle, straddling the two.

As a 14-year-old high school freshman, Lynn was above average in intelligence and energy, but she was an indifferent student. Her attention span, like Stan's, was close to zero at the time. Unlike Stan, she did her homework, whether it had to be handed in or not (usually while the TV or stereo was playing); as a sophomore she even displayed the remarkable ability to talk to her girlfriends on the phone while rapidly writing papers that were due the next day.

"What would I most like to change about myself?" she said, repeating our question to her during the first month of her junior year. "My frizzy [light brown] hair and my height [she was, and still is, 5'9" but would have preferred to be two or three inches shorter at the time], and I also want to be more popular." That was less conspicuously a problem than her words made it sound. She had many friends, including a core group consisting of three girls and a boy. The topics of their conversation were neither intellectual nor malicious; instead they were an endless number of excited and at times amusing observations about everyone they knew. "Amy's mother had a facelift," Lynn commented to a classmate, "and now when she opens her mouth, her eyes close."

What was not obvious from her easygoing manner and the enormous number of hours spent in lighthearted chatter was her ambition. She was a driven young woman, more so than she realized then or now. When we asked her in the latter part of her junior year what she would choose as a college major, she unhesitatingly replied, "English." Her answer was the same in the fall semester of her senior year. However, during the summer between high school graduation and her first term in college, she read two books that influenced her; George Homans' *The Human Group* and Daniel Lerner's *The Passing of Traditional Society*. She decided to register as a sociology major.

But she didn't find the courses captivating during the first two years, and she was somewhat puzzled at that. "Maybe it's the textbook they're using," was an explanation she offered more than once. She drew a considerable amount of motivation from the supplementary readings she dug up on her own. "I can go into a bookstore," she said in the fall of her sophomore year in college, "and find *ten* paperbacks that are better than this." She held up a book by Talcott Parsons (one that was required reading for the course) as though it were a smelly dead fish. Then she added a comment she'd make again the next year. "Sometimes I think they're trying to kill our interest in the subject."

Lynn wasn't about to let that happen. Although she was somewhat disappointed in her major on the basis of the course content thus far, the outside reading she was doing gave her the inspiration she needed to continue in the field. "I could read about small groups morning, noon, and night," she said in the fall semester of her senior year. Her grades were high, and she was making plans to apply to graduate school. But by the time she sent for and started receiving the applications she'd requested, she had decided not even to fill them out.

That surprised us. During the previous three years we had watched Lynn make a determined effort to find a comfortable place in her chosen profession. There had been plenty of obstacles along the route. Pompous, sterile, and badly written sociology texts bothered her considerably and helped deaden her enthusiasm. But instead of fleeing from her field, or mocking it, she had wanted to make herself part of it. Now suddenly a different factor altogether was guiding her thoughts. "It's a mistake to apply," she said, having already made up her mind. "There's no [academic] job waiting for me when I get out [of graduate school]." Apparently nothing happened during the spring term to change her mind, and she graduated in June with no further educational plans.

For nineteen months after that Lynn worked for one of the nation's largest insurance companies, but she found herself too distant from what she was doing. That alone was sufficient to make her eventually move on. "I don't care about this [claims] work, and that's not good," Lynn commented apologetically ten months after starting. Quite apart from how that made her personally feel, she believed she was cheating her employer. Her second job was at a toy manufacturer, and right from the start Lynn was intent upon making the position more satisfying than the prior one had been.

She threw herself into her work, finding other tasks to attend to as soon as the ones she had been assigned were complete. "There is always so much to do around here," she said harriedly after a year there. "I'm not sure I'll ever catch up." Her diligence stood in sharp contrast to the pace her co-workers usually maintained. One commented, "She works like a demon, always busy." Lynn continued at that clip for a little over three years. "I can't sit here and do nothing," she had said a number of times. "That's just not me."

At the end of the period, however, she could no longer mask the fact that something was wrong. It wasn't her marriage, of that much she seemed certain, and later events proved her right. She had met and married an attorney who had an office in the same building as the company for which she was working, and they now had a two-and-a-half-year-old daughter. "When I'm unhappy [at work], it affects me at home," she said, continuing to search for an answer.

One thing that troubled her deeply was that her education no longer seemed relevant to what she was doing each day. Switching from an insurance to a toy firm excited her initially because she liked spending some of her leisure hours reading serious books about play, whereas essays on the topic of risk left her cold. To that extent, the job change had been all to the good. In time, though, the connection between her everyday work and her academic readings again grew too thin for them to breathe extra life into her work. At 27, she still felt detached occupationally, and she didn't like it.

Lynn then decided to enroll in graduate school. "That's what's missing," she said, relieved to find the alleged answer. She sent away for applications. "I only hope I can still get in. I really should have gone [at the time]." The job market for recent graduates in the field who had masters' and doctoral degrees was even bleaker now than it had been a half-dozen years before, but that didn't seem to bother her. It was the context itself, school, that she was unwittingly seeking, not what it might do for her later on the job.

She was thrilled to be admitted four months later to a large university less than a 30-minute ride from her office. "I'm really going to give it everything I've got," she said and there was little reason to doubt her words. However, within the first few months of being back on campus full-time, her mood had clearly soured. "I feel so old," she said in November, pointing to a handful of young students. Yet what she really meant is that she felt out of place, and it had nothing to do with age.

Although Lynn had had strong opinions as a college student about the curriculum she was required to study, she recognized that, as a novice in the field, she might be wrong. "What do teenagers know?" she remarked at 19, as a way of erasing her derogatory statements of a moment before. Now her attitude was different. The emotional intensity was gone, but in its place was the certainty that comes from a closer, second look with older eyes.

"This is a farce," she said calmly during her spring term. "My professors wouldn't know reality if it hit them on the head." What was it she objected to most? "They drone on and on, talking about abstract theories that mean nothing and have no content. They live such *sheltered* lives. No wonder their comments are so inane." The bulk of her criticism wasn't aimed at them but at herself. "I was under the illusion I could go back," she said the following year, as she was completing her MA in sociology. "There *is* no going back. This place is a business— just like the toy company—only it's much more *petty*."

That should have been the end of it. We had noticed that, when someone expressed so negative an opinion of either school or the work world, later he or she would find it significantly easier to embrace the one not condemned. Lynn had tried both. At 29 she had arrived at a sufficiently hostile view of school to make it almost certain that she'd gladly try to become engrossed in her work, by default if nothing else. That is what the majority of people we studied did and, for a while at least, that is what Lynn did. But by the time she was 32, the old dissatisfaction again began to surface. In spite of the energy she brought to her day's activities in the office, she rarely found them fulfilling, a fact she could hide from everyone but herself. "I'm on the outside looking in," she said, not at all happy about the thought. "Maybe I should be doing something else."

She decided to go for her PhD in sociology. This time, she didn't speak of the program longingly as a return to a comfortable, captivating, and intellectually uplifting world that she had lost. Now she viewed it strictly in terms of the alleged usefulness of the degree as a credential in the work world. That, at least, is what she would have us believe was motivating her. In any event, she decided to go only part-time.

It has been two years. "How much longer do you figure it will take you?" we recently asked her. "Probably another ten," she replied.

While it may be tempting to dismiss Lynn as an isolated example, it is essential to realize that there are an enormous number of men and women like her. Only a small proportion enroll in part-time degree programs, much less quit their jobs to go back to school full-time. Nevertheless, they do think about it. Some merely want another degree, hoping to make use of it professionally or to gain added self-respect. Others like the idea because they've been out of school long enough to cloak it in pleasurable fantasies. They envision an idealized setting that is relaxed, mentally invigorating, and fun. Some perhaps even find it, though a much larger number (Lynn included) do not. Unfortunately, the majority take no decisive action in either direction—and that is the point. They bounce back and forth in their own minds between the two, trying vainly to embrace one and then, when that fails, the other. Yet, they are unable to come to rest happily in either sphere. Many are spending decades stuck somewhere in the middle, not fully a member of any world in which they can plant some roots, feel at home, and develop themselves in an occupationally relevant way, instead of agonizing endlessly about where they belong.

The Launching Pad

It is time to switch our focus from individual instances to the group as whole. Examining a wide variety of cases allows us to draw some general conclusions about the kinds of trouble that frequently develop during the prolonged psychological transition from school to work, and what can be done about them.

There is a satisfying sense of progress to school, even if one's marks in any given term are nothing to write home about. Each passing year involves yet another conspicuous move up the ladder of educational achievement. The work world seems almost static by comparison, and many years may pass before something even of the magnitude of graduating from the eighth grade and entering the ninth takes place. Worse still, when school is finally finished, students have to do something many find appalling: start over. That is exciting in its own way, but it is a blow to their pride as well, so they subconsciously distort the picture they face at this point to make it a bit more palatable. Since they are young, it is hardly surprising that they do it with an abundance of optimism. That is healthy, since there is little to be gained by yelling and screaming about having to begin again at the bottom of a new hierarchy. All such protests would do is call attention to their lowly positions, something they are uncomfortable about in the first place and will be even more so as their first few years pass. But the great optimism has a number of unhealthy aspects too; the most important of which is the speed with which it makes them think the work world will shower them with whatever rewards it has to offer.

Merely questioning the massive optimism of young workers may strike some readers as the equivalent of attacking mom and apple pie. After all, this seems at first glance to be a national resource of considerable value. Nevertheless, there is good reason for believing that there is more here than meets the eye. Once the expected rewards prove slow in coming, an interesting switch occurs. Reversing the feelings most had while there, college-educated workers in their twenties convince themselves that school is devoted to a satisfying life of the mind, whereas work is merely mercenary. The former is an exalted endeavor, while the latter is crass. Hidden inferiority feelings are the source of this piece of projection: people who are still in their first decade in the business world can use it to claim that they and their present position aren't low; money is. In fact, they haven't really been demoted, only contaminated slightly, especially if they have to handle the green stuff directly. Even then, their purity and innocence, their unwavering dedication to truth and virtue, have been preserved within.

Two key things are wrong with this face-saving rationalization. First, recent college graduates happen to like money, and want it. Regardless of what they say, they have an enormous appetite for the very thing they claim to loathe. Second, it interferes significantly with their ability to come to terms with their permanent new setting. There isn't anything else they can use for the purpose, so, by default, school soon comes to be depicted in their minds as a place of honesty and goodness (at least for purposes of this comparison), while the business world is viewed as a den of deceit and evil. It must be, since they aren't doing nearly as well as they had hoped.

Many feel duped. School was supposed to be a dirt-free launching pad to fame and fortune, yet they are now required to soil their hands in a different way, thanks to money. The solution most seek in order to escape that fate is to try hard to beat the system. The retrospectively glorified view of school is almost forced on them; they need a moral-sounding base for the wholly self-serving and immoral campaign they are about to begin. The *logic* of their case draws support in their minds from the feeling they have that they've acquired something essential in their first arena that will be of major use in the second. They don't want to think of themselves as having arrived at the door to the business world empty-handed.

In the past, "character" and a knowledge of Greek and Latin poets and playwrights were touted as being that precious possession. However, that could be deemed sufficient by students only as long as they came from wealthy families and therefore already had money, not to mention good positions waiting for them in the work world after graduation. Once colleges became something other than private way stations for sons of the rich, character and the Classics stood revealed as pathetically inadequate legacies to carry from the first arena to the second. In fact, it left one pretentious and instantly obsolete in an industrial society that grows more technologically advanced every day.

Since something nebulous would not have been considered acceptable to the post–World War II tidal wave of students from predominantly middle-class families, money was tried. "A college education is worth an extra $100,000 in lifetime earnings," proclaimed the new myth, popular in the early sixties. It worked for a while though, needless to say, it turned out to be false. Even if it had once been true, college students in the seventies and eighties knew it no longer was. They could see the problem here with their own eyes. As one put it in 1983—after just paying a $10,000-per-annum tuition bill and laying out $5,000 more each year for room, food, and expenses—"Think of how much I'd have to make on this investment to make it financially worth it to go to college." The arithmetic is grimmer than he thinks, since he is not only shelling out a large sum; he is also failing to earn a dime during this period.

The huge, automatic financial returns weren't there, as he and his classmates well knew. So it became necessary for them to produce an updated reason to go to, and remain in, college and graduate school. Particularly in light of the strained economic climate of the 1970s and

early 1980s, mere intellectual pleasure seemed a more frivolous justification than ever, unless, in traditional fashion, one had wealthy
parents or was prepared to earn little as an adult. Setting aside for the
moment programs such as law and medicine, which legally require
college attendance and graduate degrees for admission to these professions, what was the new version of the argument? The same as the
old one, except that the promise of financial benefits—right down to
a specific dollar figure—had to be de-emphasized.

The younger students in our sample therefore came to believe that
when they eventually went to work, they would have an edge where
some mixture of pay and promotions was concerned. They might not
be able to make back the full amount they had spent on their education,
when viewed solely as an investment, but it would come back to them
in preferential consideration when management positions became
available. Or so the story went. The old rationalization had obviously
survived largely intact, though it was reshaped by college students who
had a greater job-market awareness than their counterparts in the 1960s.
So promotions, not pay, received top billing.

That annoyed many employers and executives in our sample, who
apparently didn't realize the source of the new demands. A typical
comment, "They've been here for only three months, are fresh out of
school, and already want to be president of this place tomorrow. It's
worse now than ever." True enough, and for good reason. The main
consequence of shattering "the $100,000 myth" was that there was
nothing else for these students to aspire to as instant, external vali-
dation of their worth.

In short, throughout the period of our study, when students graduated, started working, and realized that their education was conferring
no miraculous advantage upon them—not enough pay in the sixties,
and not enough pay and/or promotions in the seventies and eighties—
they took matters into their own hands. If their schooling couldn't
help them beat the system automatically, they would find a way to do
it calculatedly. By no means was this the only reaction, but it was the
most common.

They wanted what was promised them. When they said, "The world
owes me a living" (something many felt and few actually stated), this
was what they really meant; they felt entitled to special consideration—if nothing else, because they'd spent so many years in school—
and they knew they weren't getting it. In trying hard day after day to
leap ahead of their peers, they were mainly seeking to collect what
they believed was their due.

Condemning them for duplicitous behavior on the job shouldn't be
done too hastily since they were merely acting upon the implicit as-

sumption that they had been present all along: school will catapult you into the lead. Their demand was simple enough: "I have done what you asked me to, and I deserve what's mine. Give it to me, if not as pay, then as promotions."

"You Can't Hit a Moving Target"

With so many comparable people clamoring for the same thing, the claims of the individual are soon lost in the general din. However, and this is the central point, the real harm is self-inflicted. Our experience has been that few people who adopt a deceitful approach to their work openly acknowledge that they have done so, even to themselves. Instead, using the very same mechanism that has long been used to justify genocide, they project those feelings onto the world around them. Suddenly, behavior that they previously would have condemned becomes perfectly acceptable. For instance, if they want to lie or cheat, they now have the internal go-ahead that is needed. As one put it, with rare candor, as he was leaving with one of the firm's electric pencil sharpeners, "Of course I hate my boss. I have to. It's hard to steal from someone you like."

Most people with his attitude steal something less tangible: time and dedication. But the theft backfires, for it divorces them still further from a setting in which they need to find a place for themselves, the sooner the better. There is a pressing need for active intervention here; our studies make clear that people who cast themselves in the role of the innocent, and the business world as a den of iniquity, are capable of living that picture for their entire work lives. The damage they do to their self-development would hardly seem to offset any pleasure they might get from walking around happily cloaked in the illusion of their own innocence. Yet, the condition persists—and allows them any degree of duplicity or malice they wish to aim at an employer.

There is an acid test people can use to see whether they are heading for trouble on this front, to prevent the situation from getting out of hand. To describe it, and why it works, we need a bit of background.

A spectrum with the word "absorption" at one end and "fake" at the other can be used to analyze the feelings of the vast majority of workers in their early years on the job. Some are obviously caught up, love what they are doing, and don't have enough hours in each day to devote to that particular activity. At the other extreme are those who can't have done with their work soon enough. They have to do it, so they will. Otherwise, they'd just as soon not. For them, the day usually seems endless. Why not just call these people clockwatchers? Why so

derogatory a word as "fake?" Because, if they have any college education at all, that is how they themselves feel. And the more education
they have, the more fraudulent they are likely to view themselves as
being for holding a full-time job doing work they dislike.

One may object that even the most devoted people sometimes get
tired of their work, and conversely, even the most detached at times
become enthusiastic about it. True enough, but when responses are
collected twice each day, for three weeks each year, for a decade—the
index being the degree to which people are absorbed in what they are
doing—there is less variation here than one might imagine. What most
workers have known for years about their colleagues and didn't need
a statistical analysis to measure has been confirmed: some people are
much more interested in their work than others—and continue to be
so, year in and year out.

Now we can pose the question: Where work is concerned, how much
of each day do people spend feeling like fakes? Asking them only how
absorbing they find their work is not as satisfactory a question, because
the very act of trying to answer it may change the answer. (The same
thing often happens when people are happy. As soon as they say they
are, they may find that they no longer are.)

There is an alternative form to the question that the majority of
people we've studied found easier to relate to. It has to do with fear.
It is this: How much of each day do you spend waiting to get caught?

Much to our surprise, we found that a considerable portion of our
sample, nearly 37 percent acknowledged that they live with this fear
on a regular basis. By the time they were in their late twenties, many
realized that they'd been secretly hoping every year since puberty to
escape detection. "I always prayed that my teachers wouldn't find out
how *little* I really knew," said one. However, that wasn't the end of
it. More than three out of five people who made such comments unwittingly transferred the concern from teachers to bosses after making
the transition from school to the work world. Instead of being free of
the fear, it followed them.

They didn't even know what they were afraid of, so it was experienced as a kind of generalized anxiety. Interestingly, they were subconsciously preventing themselves from making the worry more
specific. For, if they said, as one did, "I have to be careful around my
boss—have to make certain the boss doesn't find out too much about
what I do and how much I know," the next question is automatic:
"Oh? How come? Have you got something to hide?" To avoid being
asked the question, by themselves as well as others, they walked around
with a nameless nervousness, while trying to function as best they
could.

How did they handle it? By moving continually and fast. Almost without exception, people who felt they had something to hide were convinced that their best defense lay in constant motion—physical, verbal, it didn't matter which. Keeping things light made them more mobile. The comment they were most likely to make about the subject was always said in an offhand manner. "You can't hit a moving target."

Stopping, staying in one place for long, could be deadly. "People get to know you after a while," said one, age 29. "Then you're in a fix. You lose your charisma [in this case, image of competence], and no one wants to have anything to do with you. It could cost you your job."

What was common to all these cases was the vicious cycle that slowly developed over the years. These people didn't feel they'd learned enough as youngsters in school, so they were thrilled to be able to graduate or leave with most of their shortcomings undetected. The remedy for the fear was to run. But when they went on to the next step, and entered the work world full-time, they didn't feel even moderately prepared for it. There were cracks in the foundation upon which they were trying to build a public structure. In order to prop up their image of themselves as professionals, new fakery had to be added to the old. Soon the facade was no longer convincing enough (people were beginning to see through it), and another move was needed. So it went, round and round. Gaps in their knowledge and abilities ultimately required a transfer to another setting, which made it all the harder to just sit down, fill the gaps, and be ready for the next step up the ladder, which, alas, they had already persuaded someone to let them take.

The key issue here isn't that they were getting well ahead of themselves. Of far greater importance, they were being prevented, as a result of all the maneuvering, from settling in, never realizing that one area of work-related activity intrigued them more than another, then arranging to do as much of it as they could. Instead of being absorbed in their work, they were at the opposite end of the spectrum, spending an excessive amount of time waiting to be exposed publicly as being less than they had claimed to be.

The question we were therefore interested in answering is: where work is concerned, how much of the day does each person in our sample spend being concerned that he or she will eventually be caught and unmasked? Significant disruptive effects on the development of a career were seen, even in cases where the answer was as little as 15 minutes a day. It took a while for the underlying causes of the damage to emerge. People who are afraid that their level of ability is not what co-workers think it is do two overlapping things that harm the growth of themselves and their careers.

First, they don't make sorely needed repairs in their current reservoir of knowledge. Second, they try to expand their abilities far too little. This is always a risky venture, even if one has a firm foundation from which to make the leap into the unknown. The step was avoided repeatedly because it was adjudged too likely to make their ignorance visible.

The end result was that these individuals had to make it look as though they already possessed the skills they weren't willing to risk developing in public. Odd as it may sound, we noticed that they then sought—indeed, demanded—a promotion. That isn't quite as bizarre as it may seem. Their underlying hope was that they could elevate themselves to positions where they would be "above being questioned."

As they are now discovering, there is no such thing.

II

THE THIRTIES

STANDING OUT IN A CROWD

CHAPTER 5

Is It Independence
or Merely Insubordination?

As STUDENTS go from the fourth to the fifth grade, say, and even more so, from sophomore to junior year, they are increasingly in charge of their own behavior. Each year they are given a little more personal liberty. When they are young, their parents continually remind them to say, "Hello" and "Goodbye," "Please" and "Thank you," and "May I?" Once school begins the matter receives even more attention: they are graded on their conduct. And, at least in their parent's eyes as well as those of the school, getting low marks for being badly behaved is as upsetting a piece of news as doing poorly in spelling.

During junior high school, the material in their texts is given greater emphasis than their decorum, and in high school the shift gathers momentum. Although good or bad behavior can at times affect a grade, it no longer has the same significance it had in elementary school.

Going to college completes the shift. Now, mastery of course content, not conduct, becomes the sole determinant of grades. Stan's reaction in the previous chapter is a common one. Students often are not only thrilled but amazed to be granted so much personal freedom all at once. The narrow nature of what is being demanded from them can best be seen in those who are on the dean's list or in honors programs yet dress as though they live on skid row.

Students in school are asked to subordinate themselves only to a limited extent, mainly in the area of knowledge. They have to learn the material their professors want them to, or fail. On the job, however, good behavior suddenly counts again, more so than it ever did. Parents may chastise their children for an infraction of the rules, but the tie that binds the two sides together remains. Teachers too allow some lattitude in the early years, recognizing that a certain amount of mischief is normal during the period. The boss, on the other hand, isn't likely to condone more than a minimum of misbehavior on the job. In fact, there is an entire code of office conduct that one is expected to adhere to, without even being told.

As Lynn put it, still shocked at the discovery, "I only had to smile for my teacher during class. Here, I have to do it for the bosses all the time." Bob got an even ruder awakening. "I'm back to being seven again," he told us irritably, after being asked to say "good morning" each day as he passed the division manager's desk. In some ways Bob was lucky. We found that supervisors who resented the boorish behavior of an employee were unlikely to tell the person about it; instead they usually mentioned it to one of their own peers or did something about it when the subordinate least expected it. Then they did it in another guise.

In short, there is an anti-democratic dimension to the work world, and it isn't about to go away. If anything, the growing size of many U.S. firms, and the recent tidal wave of corporate takeovers, have combined to magnify the problem. Although Americans intensely dislike the idea, subordination at work is often required and insubordination penalized.

That wouldn't come as news to most of the workers and students we studied, but they were certain they could find a way around it, particularly if they took it into consideration from the start. "If I'd wanted to be in the military," said Henry Burke, "I'd have joined the Army." He didn't. After finishing graduate school, Henry took a job at a small consulting firm instead, where he was able to work on electronics problems in private. "Most days this place is as quiet as a morgue," Henry said happily. As an undergraduate he had majored in engineering physics. This was followed by graduate study to a master's degree, and then some, in electrical engineering.

While most people who graduated college in the late sixties have outgrown their "flower child" ways, Henry's wire-rimmed glasses and long, greasy, fine hair were a definite throwback to a bygone era. His lanky body was frequently covered with slightly soiled T-shirts bearing an assortment of messages and never tucked into faded jeans bagging in the seat.

After four years at the little consulting company, he decided to accept an offer as a systems engineer from a major computer manufacturer to whom his firm had acted as a consultant from time to time. His job was to help in the custom design of VLSI (Very Large Scale Integrated) circuits for in-house use.

His new office was very different from the old. It was three times the size and had a huge photographic blow up of the square circuit that he was working on. There was a more important difference, though it was necessary to step outside Henry's office to see it: people, lots of them. Rather than being at a small firm with ten members, Henry now worked at one that had well over 1,000.

One would never have known it from watching how Henry behaved. He noticed the noise ("It's much louder here, but I close the door if it gets to me"). Other than that, he clearly considered the new firm to be just like the previous one. Actually, in his mind both were like college. As he put it, "What I like about working in the R&D [research and development] area is that you can still be *yourself*. They only care about your results."

In college and graduate school that was certainly so, for Henry as well as other students, and he loved it. Indeed, it is fair to say that Henry became addicted to it, because it allowed him to focus single-mindedly on his work. As he commented in his senior year, "If I don't have to think about how grubby my jeans are, I can concentrate better." Since Henry and the university he was attending were both concerned primarily about his grades, all was well. But that made him leap to a dangerously false conclusion: not only is that the way things are here; it's also the way things will—or at least should—be everywhere. As far as he was concerned, any company that wanted to get the best out of him would have to do as his school did and not worry about how he dressed. That was the unspoken quid pro quo: he'd try his hardest to do good, original work, but only on the condition that they not mention his disheveled appearance.

They didn't either, at least not to him. Henry by this time was an experienced, 30-year-old engineer whose dedication to his field was beyond question. With few exceptions he put in 10 to 20 hours more each week than his employers asked him to, and he did quite a bit of extra work on their behalf that they never even knew about.

However, we wanted to see how well Henry did at the firm over the years. Pay and promotions were important to him, but so was his independence. If preserving it meant that he'd have to accept both a slightly lower level of earnings and be passed over regularly for managerial posts, he'd have been willing to make the trade. But it is crucial to emphasize that Henry didn't expect to have to make any such trade. Remember, one of the reasons he'd chosen to do R&D work in a corporate setting in the first place was that he thought only his "results" would matter.

To some extent, he was right. Yet as the years passed, it became clear that he was not doing as well as comparable colleagues on the staff. In his sixth year at the firm, a co-worker suggested to Henry that he buy himself a suit. "Why?" Henry snapped. "Am I about to be buried?" Within the month, he heard the same message in a different form. He accidentally overheard a supervisor say, "No, I don't want to send Henry [to the customer]. He looks like a hobo. That's not the impression we want to make."

From then on, Henry had no illusions about what the path he'd selected was costing him. Still, he had no intention of changing his ways. The tradition of eminent but shabbily dressed scientists, with Einstein acting as a symbol for them all, was planted firmly in his mind. Less than a year after he overheard his supervisor's comment, Henry said, "No one is going to tell me what to *do*—I mean, how to *dress*." [Italics added.] It was the only time we ever heard him make the slip. But his confusing the two words tells the whole story.

This isn't a book about fashions for the aspiring executive, and although Henry frequently made a fuss about his tattered jeans, they weren't the issue either. The point is that Henry was using his clothes as a declaration of independence. They were taking his stand for him. He appeared cooperative and accommodating in most areas, but here was the place he put his foot down. He perceived the giving of even an inch in this quarter to be a threat to his individuality. "Once I let people start pushing me around, where will it stop?" he asked more than once. This was the terrain he intended to defend, even if it cost him his job.

It didn't. And in some ways, that is too bad. He is still with the firm, but good research scientists in industry who don't eventually move up into management are comparable in certain respects to old baseball players who can't get jobs coaching. In both arenas, younger competitors come along soon enough and displace them. What is more painful in Henry's case is that it is happening before his very eyes: some of his junior co-workers have passed him by and recently been promoted into managerial posts he is convinced he deserves.

Broadcasting One's Distinctiveness

Many of Henry's co-workers were of the opinion that his pay and promotion problems were a result of his clothes. They were wrong. We found a substantial number of men and women who had the same problems Henry did, yet were always dressed nicely. In fact, they'd not have thought of going to the office any other way.

"I *like* to look good," Gail Simmons said, and she did. The time spent buying clothes, shoes, and cosmetics didn't bother her since she accepted it as a normal part of what holding a job meant. Nor did she make a fuss about the matter. If anything, she minimized it. "I plan what I'm going to wear the next day," she said. "It only takes a few minutes. Sometimes I lay out the stuff I'm going to wear, so I can get ready faster in the morning."

Gail worked for a multibillion-dollar communications company, owner of one of the three major TV networks. As an English major in college, her manner and appearance were usually casual. However once she graduated and got a full-time job, both changed. "How come?" we asked. "I want to do well," she replied, "at *some*thing. I don't know what yet."

Gail's height and weight gave meaning to the description "big boned." Not that she was fat. Her 5'8" height balanced her weight, but she was always dieting. In repose, she was an attractive woman, with long lashes, a cupid's bow mouth, and dark curly hair haloing her face, making her look somewhat like a little girl. The image was shattered the minute she opened her mouth, and the loud, machine-gun manner in which she spoke became her most obvious feature.

Gail had three jobs during her first eight years in the work world and disliked each more than the one before. Two factors stuck out in her comments about them. "This place is incredibly disorganized," she said while at her first and third positions; and, "There's no room for growth here," she essentially said at all three. The years may have been distressing for her, but they served their purpose. For she unwittingly made the transition from school to work during that time, at least in terms of ridding herself of what had been a moderate amount of academic snobbery. "It should be a law," she had said in the spring semester of her junior year. "Everyone should have to read a novel [that is a masterpiece] each week."

Now, with that behind her, she was ready to settle in. Gail deliberately chose a large, diversified company that offered a variety of career paths. The production division appealed to her most. "It's the nerve center of the business," she said after accepting the position, one she'd gotten on the strength of her involvement in the field at her last job. "What a difference," she remarked, amazed at the complexity of her new firm. "This makes [the old place] look like a bunch of amateurs operating out of a garage."

Gail had been on the job less than four months when she had the first run-in of the type she'd have again many times in upcoming years. Her boss, an overweight woman named Sally, made a comment about scheduling with which Gail sharply differed. "I told her I thought that was ridiculous," Gail said proudly, adding, "That fat bitch doesn't know anything. She only thinks she knows." Sally didn't take it well, and there was friction between them regularly after that. "Who cares?" Gail said a few weeks later. "They'll let her go soon anyway, if they're smart."

The subtle but chronic state of conflict existing between Gail and Sally started to appear in Gail's other working relationships as well. In some ways that wasn't surprising, since she saw the world in intensely personal terms: it was divided into friends and enemies, with few people in the middle. As her old college roomates had discovered, Gail was very argumentative, and she had become much more so in the intervening years. She happily made certain concessions connected with earning a living, such as being willing to get up early and be at work on time, and to work hard once there. Nevertheless, one area in which she had no intention of budging was in her opinions. "If that's what I feel, that's what I feel," she'd often say. "I know my own mind." And she was only too pleased to give people a piece of it.

That went for co-workers as well as supervisors. Where questions of judgment were concerned, Gail wanted to be able to state her view forcefully and have others take it seriously. She and Amy, who was two years younger and had a job similar to hers, got into a verbal shoving match about who should get the extra administrative assistant that the division was thinking of hiring. "She's an idiot," Gail said irritably later that day. "We do more in a week than her group does in a month."

It is important that we not convey the wrong impression of Gail, who certainly didn't spend all her time at the office fighting. Quite the contrary, she was generally cordial enough, if a bit reserved. Like Henry, she had intentionally placed herself in a corporate context and was willing to be part of it, or so she thought. Yet the key point here is that she was using her opinions to accomplish the same goal that Henry attained with his mode of dress.

At 35, she still insisted upon taking the identical approach she had utilized as a 19-year-old. "It's a sin," she had said at the time, "not to speak out if you believe in what you're saying." That sounds simple enough, yet a careful analysis of her opinions during the previous 15 years shows that either her views change as rapidly as the weather in March, or else she often takes strong (public) stands in order to appear to have strong (private) beliefs.

What is fascinating is that after graduating from college, she spent six weeks in France, her second trip there, and came back with an astute observation. "Frenchmen often adopt a [political or intellectual] position," she said with a smile, "just to sound sophisticated." Nonetheless here she was, a decade later, unaware that she was doing exactly the same thing—in business.

Talking to her about the subject (we didn't, but a few co-workers did) produced the same unreasonable reaction that Henry's friends got when they mentioned his clothes. She took it as an article of faith that people simply weren't individuals unless they broadcast their opinions whenever they were given the chance. More despicable still was to sit silently while someone said something with which one disagreed. As she saw it, the first only compromised one's individuality; the second meant one didn't deserve to have any—and perhaps didn't.

By Gail's standards, then, she was proclaiming her uniqueness regularly, especially when she got into one of the many quiet but heated quarrels she engaged in with co-workers and supervisors. The fact that they were muted disputes, in which neither side took to shouting at the other, masked their two main features: they were tense—and continual. People who annoyed her annoyed her greatly, and the feelings were likely to be there, festering, months later. Although none of the disagreements or pitched battles were deliberately provoked, she'd have insisted that whatever else they accomplished, they also achieved the purpose of communicating her distinctiveness. As she put it at 34, "What are you when you just sit there? You're anonymous, that's what."

Gail's approach may have served her personal goals but it was destructive to her career goals. She has been with the firm for the last 12 years, yet the pace of her progress there has been slower than that of anyone else in the company with comparable credits and experience. "Why?" we asked one of her bosses who had switched to a competing firm on the other side of the country. The reply was: "I, and a couple of others, think she has a personality problem."

This response would have flabberghasted her. As far as Gail is concerned, she is one of the few people at the company that even *has* a personality.

Making One's Presence Felt

John Hart, our third and last example, was very different from Henry and Gail. Unlike Henry, he always dressed neatly, and unlike Gail, he was nothing if not polite. As we'll soon see, that was no accident.

"I need time to think about it," he replied when pressed for an answer, at 20, by one of his classmates. When John made a decision, he made it only after a great deal of thought. People often accused him of moving too slowly ("He takes forever to make up his mind, even about little things," said his girlfriend), but let this be said: no one ever accused him of being reckless or impulsive. Those who didn't like him labeled him mousy or meek. The words didn't physically characterize the man. John was 6'2", slim, and fairly strong, but the insulting description was psychologically accurate in some ways. John would never have started a fight, particularly a fist fight, and would avoid verbal battles as well whenever he could.

Business administration was his choice of a major in college, and it was a subject he found thoroughly enjoyable. "I can see myself putting this material to good use in the future," he said as a junior. Not only was the field interesting to him, John also liked the image of himself that went with it. He had no trouble conceiving of spending the bulk of his business life happily batting about in an office. "That's where the action is," he said as a senior. That was an uncommonly loose way of expressing himself for John, who used colloquial and slang phrases stiffly if at all. Sometimes his attempts to use the current in-phrases on campus made him seem a bit foolish. "He gets the words right," a good friend in college remarked, laughing, "but they sound like a foreigner trying to imitate an American being 'cool.' It just doesn't go well on John." He knew it too, and usually concentrated on speaking precisely instead.

After getting an MBA, he joined a multinational chemicals company and was delighted with the position he had landed. The pay was good and there were opportunities for advancement. "It's nice not to have to start at the bottom," he said about what he viewed as his good fortune. "I expected less." Since John's main area of interest had been management, a subject in which he'd taken every course available to him as an undergraduate and graduate student, he was eager to put some of his ideas into practice. "I think there's a lot for me to do here," he said after his first four months on the job.

It wasn't until John's fifteenth month at the firm, however, that he got a hint of what was to prove a continuing source of trouble. He was invited to be a member of a committee that was being given responsibility for assessing the firm's flow of operational reports. "The [needed] information isn't getting to top management," said John, "and that's the problem." The company was huge, with operations in various parts of the world, so the combined skills of many individuals were required for an effective review.

Unfortunately for John, that gave his bosses a chance to compare how he did relative to the other members of the committee. One thing they couldn't help but notice within the first few weeks of the project was how much slower he was than his peers. "C'mon, John, get a move on," his immediate superior said in a friendly but no-nonsense manner.

Instead of feeling encouraged by the comment, John balked. "Speed," he said with disgust. "That's the only thing that matters here. Everybody wants you to get it done yesterday." The very nature of the assignment the group had been given brought the subject into the spotlight. For, as it turns out, the information being funneled to top management about worldwide operations was indeed getting there. The real problem was that it was arriving too late to be acted upon in a timely manner. Under the circumstances, John's cautious, methodical style stood out like a sore thumb. That prompted one member of the team to quip, "If you've got bad news and want it to travel at a snail's pace, tell it to John."

He survived the episode without much apparent harm, in large part because near the end of the project he moved into high gear and worked as fast as the others. "I can do it when I want to," John said at the time, visibly irked, "but that doesn't mean I have to like it." He received two minor promotions in the next five years. During one of the meetings his boss, after telling him that he was being promoted, said, "Your work is good. Sometimes it's a little slow, but it's always good."

John decided that he stood a better chance of having, as he called it, "an area all my own" at a different chemicals company, and switched. He was 31 and once again wound up with a better position than he had expected to land. "I like it here very much," he said a few months after taking the job. "This place suits me." His co-workers and superiors, however, have spent the last 13 years seeing sides of John they hadn't bargained for and often didn't like.

If a popularity contest had been held within two years of John's arrival at the new firm, he'd have placed dead last. That's not to say he was less competent than his better liked peers. But there can't be any doubt about the fact that the other middle managers and their assistants recognized that John was—well, different.

How? Listen to what the fellow who had the office two doors down the hall from John told us a month after transferring to another firm. "He's infuriating sometimes, he really is. You give him something to read, and that's the end of it. He sits on it, and sits on it. You could develop cobwebs waiting."

Said another, who left a year and a half later, "He's a very stubborn guy. Cold, too. This is one 'John' you're not tempted to call 'Jack.' You know what I think? I think he's an anal retentive."

John's view of what he was doing during the decade was straightforward. "I'm not going to let *anybody* rush me just to suit them," he said, at 32. "I'm not here to be a rubber stamp," he added, at 33. "It's not convenient for me to look at it [this long]?" at 35, he asked someone on the phone, answering with, "Well, that's too bad. They'll wait." And at 38, he said, "I'll do it when I'm good and ready." After pausing for a moment he added a comment he often made, "It's a matter of principle."

Perhaps. But John's "principles" are costing him his career. He's not much further along at 44 than he was at 31. As with Henry and Gail, a number of younger competitors have passed him by easily. As he himself irritably asked us rhetorically four years ago, "What do *they* have that I don't?" It may seem frivolous to compare Henry's baggy pants and Gail's truculent opinions to John's chronic recalcitrance, but there are crucial similarities among all three cases. All along, John has been every bit as determined, for instance, as Gail to make a mark on his company. However, he didn't intend to use charm or personal magnetism to achieve that aim. Unlike Gail, he had an unobtrusive personality; in fact, he was one of the people she'd have pointed a finger at as having none.

No matter, he had another way. John had made good use of it for many years and, in his view, could utilize it to even greater effect as he rose in the corporate ranks. The approach was, as he frequently put it, "I'm going to do my job right." How did he know when that was? The answer would have floored him. "When someone else gets mad at me for the way I'm doing it. Then I know I'm doing it right." He wasn't always the boulder in the path of progress. That would have been too obvious and resulted in his dismissal. He wanted to make his presence felt, not get fired.

So he judiciously selected a number of key projects and made his mark by raising a forest of objections, trying to bring them to grinding halts. But, the reader may be wondering, how did he know which ones to select? That's what was—and still is—so ingenious about the approach. He didn't know, so he left it up to others.

The more impatient they became with him for creating obstacles, the more evidence he had that the project mattered, at least to them. And if they went so far as to become openly angry, he had all the proof he needed that the project was very important. It was then that he usually became stubborn beyond belief. What excuse could he use for such plainly uncooperative behavior? The best: "I intend to make an independent judgment. That's what I get paid for. And I won't be rushed. It's a matter of principle." He even had a response ready in case one person lobbied on behalf of another. "Going along," he would say pompously, "without giving the topic the appropriate consideration, would be terribly irresponsible, don't you agree?"

Gail did essentially the same, only in most cases it was opinions, not projects, that were the target of her attacks. If her co-workers or superiors held one view, she unwittingly felt compelled to take the opposite side. As in John's case, she couldn't afford to do this automatically, contradicting any and every opinion that was offered. That would have been too obvious a technique. Selecting a few was sufficient, but which ones? Those in which other people believed most strongly. The heated, verbal contest that developed was her proof that she was contradicting the right views. Small wonder she detested people with no "personality." They were like smooth, slippery rocks in a stream down which she was rapidly being carried toward a fatal waterfall named Anonymity.

Becoming Distinctive

The problems that plague the business lives of these three, and many others like them, aren't leftovers from college days. To find the source we have to go back to high school, junior high, and even earlier. It is normal for youngsters to seek to call attention to themselves—or be afraid that everyone is watching them, which is just the same desire, wrapped in anxiety instead of joy.

The more common fear, one that grows as the years pass, is of not being distinctive enough to be noticed at all. One of the central concerns of youngsters and young adults therefore is, "How will I stand out in a crowd if I'm not special in any way?" School, the first exposure American youngsters get to life in a mass society, presents them with the challenge in a two-sided manner from the start. On the one hand, since this is their everyday reality, they have to come to terms with it and fit in or risk being continually miserable. On the other hand, merely to vanish into the social soup is acceptable to very few. The desire to individualize themselves in their communal context is powerful and usually well rewarded.

First things first, though, and the number one item on their agenda is to separate themselves from their parents. There are a number of ways to impose distance between one's self and someone to whom one is emotionally connected. The most abrupt and decisive way is through anger. Getting mad at the person with whom one is involved temporarily severs the bond. However it is an exhausting way to achieve the desired result. Truly, it's a young person's technique; it might kill an older one. And once the anger lessens, so does the sense of distance.

Having separated themselves from their parents sufficiently to create an us-versus-them mentality, youngsters tackle the second item on their agenda: becoming distinctive for, and in the midst of, their social circle. Note well the order of things—first a concentration on independence, then a continuing effort to publicly present one's individuality.

It is hardly surprising that so many adolescents combine the two tasks. Each goal is hard enough to accomplish on its own. Achieving both simultaneously is a back-breaking burden for most youngsters. Without realizing it, some fuse the two goals to form one consolidated objective. It is a simple, understandable, but tragic strategy from which many never recover. Decades later they will still be pursuing one goal, or is it the other? They themselves no longer know which.

Henry wants to be different, distinctive, and no one can fault him for that. We all want the same, if not as intensely as we did during adolescence. But the way he goes about it at 34 is more typical of the tactics used by 14-year-olds. At that age, their individuality hasn't flowered to nearly the extent that it will later, and they are more closely tied to their parents as well, whether they like it or not. So they do the best they can, and concentrate on the first goal, independence, by rebelling against their parents. Whatever their parents do—or ask them to do—they do the opposite. If their mothers and fathers dress neatly, then wearing sloppy clothes aids the cause. And if their parents wore hippie or punk gear, the youngsters would probably walk around in suits and ties. The rule they keep repeating to themselves is: *If they act one way, you act the opposite. And if they get mad, then you know you're doing just fine. That's how you know that you're doing something they wouldn't have. That's how you know you're really independent.*

Gail is very verbal and always has been; in fact, she's enormously more articulate that Henry. So what he sought to accomplish mutely with his clothes, she tried to accomplish with words. However, adjusting for that difference, little separates the approach each used in the office. Gail waited until someone stated an opinion, then she stated the opposite. It is worthwhile to repeat the rule which guided her business behavior: "You can create a distinct self for presentation to your audience by disagreeing with that audience, at times vehemently. True, they may not like you for your stand, and you may not disagree with them nearly as much as it appears from all the smoke that is created, but if your main goal is to distinguish yourself, this certainly does it."

John utilized the same device but in a more subtle form. Although he was the quietest and least obtrusive of the three, he could only tell how worthwhile a major action of his was by the nature of the reaction it elicited; namely, it could not be a favorable one. The reason is the same as in the previous two cases. If everyone around Henry were to dress in the same shabby manner he did day after day, he would verge on panic, particularly if the boss had asked them all to wear that particular outfit. If everyone around Gail agreed with the stands she took, as subordinates often tried to do, she would soon be ready to jump out of her skin. And if everyone were to applaud all of John's decisions, he would know he had done something terribly wrong. The decades old terror lingered, ready to seize them as soon as they felt themselves again becoming lost forever in the crowd. The remedy they resorted to was almost always the same: synthesize some uniqueness by flying in the face of someone else's position. Unfortunately, that is all it was—synthetic independence, and temporary at that, since it was doomed to disappear once the person who had served as the anvil on which it had been fashioned was gone. Then the wait would begin anew until someone else arrived who was suitable for the purpose so that the process could be repeated.

What made the unwittingly self-destructive tactic all three were using so unfortunate is that they genuinely liked their work. These weren't cynical deadbeats devoting their lives to ripping off the system while others worked hard and long to make certain it remained intact. They enjoyed their jobs and happily put in many hundreds of hours each year that they needn't have. The key point here is that they might as well not have bothered. Neither their pay nor promotions, not even the degree of personal satisfaction they felt, reflected the talent and dedication they continually brought to their work. For all the fights, loud or silent, the three had with co-workers and supervisors, no one has stunted their careers nearly as much as they themselves have.

Adolescent Anxieties at Work

Although this problem may seem like a deep-rooted psychological matter that requires psychotherapy, in the vast majority of cases that isn't so. What most people need is practice, not a shrink. But before considering exactly what to practice, let us look more closely at a pair of seemingly simple words: independence and individuality.

In the business setting we are discussing, the major differences between the two are clear. Independence means the freedom to come and go as one pleases, the ability to do what one wants. It implies freedom of action. It also entails freedom of thought; that is, an absence of undue influence or coercion, so that one can make up one's own mind about issues large and small.

Individuality, on the other hand, involves being unique and, equally important, being able to express that uniqueness. We will be concentrating more on the latter for an important reason: we found that it was precisely people who *doubted* their own uniqueness who were most insistent on expressing it at every opportunity they could find or create, both on the job and off. Something was gnawing away at these people from within, making them feel that they weren't sufficiently distinct from the people around them to be identifiable. Individuality implies being recognizably different, and they obviously didn't think they were. They therefore seized every chance to proclaim the uniqueness they secretly felt they lacked, a proclivity that eventually annoyed both co-workers and superiors.

There is a close connection between this fragile image of one's own individuality and the concept of independence. To put the matter briefly, those members of our sample who doubted their own uniqueness displayed a chronically heightened concern about threats to their independence. They were excessively fearful, usually subconsciously, about being influenced, swayed. As a result, they worried about having too little emotional distance from their co-workers. What made that so odd in the business settings we're discussing is that, if anything, they had too much distance. While at one time it was common for workers to spend each day laboring in close proximity to family and relatives, that is dramatically less so today. More than 96 percent of the men and women in our sample don't work with, and don't even see, anyone to whom they are related during their business day (though they often talk to them on the phone). They are surrounded instead by strangers and people who've become friends at the office only in recent years. The business distance from relatives is a fact about which, privately, they are rather proud. It is mute testimony to their modern state of self-liberation. But under the circumstances, imposing a sense of mental separation between themselves and their co-workers would, at first glance, seem superfluous.

However, in the United States this is a cultural problem every bit as much as a psychological one, and that magnifies the amount of time normal, as well as troubled, people spend thinking about it. Freedom from influence comes to represent a key goal as well as a major gripe. A typical comment is: "I don't like anyone telling me what to do." As Americans, we bruise quite easily in this department. We want our rights preserved. We want to give our consent voluntarily, not be coerced. Nonetheless, and this is the central point, most people have trouble in this area primarily because they are looking for conflict, though not consciously. To be more specific, they *want* someone to step on their toes or contradict their views, for it is only in such situations that they feel either independent *or* like an individual. As we'll soon see, these are the people most likely to be confused about independence versus individuality, and therefore to be pursuing both at the same time.

Stressing one's independence from the influence of others is easy to overdo, but the bulk of the serious problems that eventually arose at work were associated with the confusion itself. To repeat, individuality means being publicly distinctive in some way. Given the enormous emphasis placed on this attribute in the United States, it is amazing that so few Americans really think they are. What they forget is that it is only people in a foreign country who "all look the same" to us, and we to them. On the other hand, the people we see daily at work are unmistakably unique; we can tell them apart almost without trying. If we so readily discern the individuality of others, there should be little doubt about the ability of others to discern our own. With our colleagues at work, our sensibilities are incredibly refined. The giant radar dishes we each possess may go blank when we think about the inhabitants of a nation on the other side of the globe, but they function very well with our co-workers, alerting us even to the minutest distinctions among them. That shouldn't be surprising. Throughout history, our safety and well-being have always depended on such intense local awareness.

It is clear that a person who remains uncertain about how much of an individual he or she is needs to make a determined effort in his or her early thirties, if not before, to put such doubts to rest, once and for all. Each person is indeed unique. The fact that, in one's own case, one can't see precisely how is irrelevant; everyone else can.

To turn the clock back for a moment, adolescents if anyone have good reason to worry about this topic, because they are still experiencing rapid developmental changes and have no way of knowing whether the process will leave them well or poorly prepared for the lifelong effort to stay afloat financially and occupationally. School, their first taste of what life is like in a crowded world, traumatizes many. After graduation, many acknowledged with a sense of despair that they never became part of the "in-crowd," never became high school heroes or heroines. Decades later these people are still fretting about their ability to broadcast their distinctiveness, this time in a business setting. Not only does the quest destroy their peace of mind, in far too many instances it stunts their careers. This is one adolescent anxiety they would be well advised to be rid of.

In short, to understand why so many people are their own worst enemies in business, it is only necessary to watch what happens to them when their ideas are opposed. They may not evidence it at the time yet, judged by the comments they make in confidence immediately after the incident, one would have to assume they were—and still are—fighting for their lives. Repeatedly activating so basic a survival mechanism is not only exhausting to them; it exhausts superiors as well, who move one step closer with each such episode to saying, "I've had enough of this."

Handling Confrontations Calmly

When people in business are as defensive as these three were inclined to be, it is natural for their associates to leap to the conclusion that the defensive behavior is a self-protective smoke screen created to hide ignorance. While that was unquestionably a valid assumption in other cases, it wasn't accurate here. Henry, Gail, and John knew as much about their respective professions as any person in their positions could be expected to know, and then some. (That is a good part of the reason their cases have been chosen for discussion.) Yet that didn't stop them from acting in a blatantly self-destructive manner.

They were convinced that the only way to "leave your mark," as Henry usually put it; "have your voice heard," in Gail's words; and "make your presence felt," as John was fond of saying, was to take a firm and uncompromising stand. What they really meant, and never said, was: "take a firm and uncompromising stand *opposing* someone else's view."

Whose? Who better than the boss's? No sooner did a superior propose one thing, these three instantly began finding reasons to do the reverse. "I could feel myself building a case against it," Gail said, at 33, when one of the executives with whom she worked was making a suggestion. Ironically, the idea was one Gail herself had proposed only a month before (something the executive did not forget and was later puzzled by).

The three were doing themselves irreversible damage. Years later their bosses, many now at other firms, told us that they still remembered the irritation they felt at the, to use their words, "abrasive," "infantile," "petty," "hysterical," and "obnoxious" treatment the three dished out regularly. As one put it, about Gail, "I'm not her mother. Let her find out the hard way [about being rude]." Said another, about Henry, "Make him a manager? No way. I'd rather give the job to a monkey." What all eleven ex-bosses we interviewed resented most, without wanting to come right out and bluntly say so, was Henry's, Gail's, and John's inability to be deferential. In a democracy, deference is a very touchy subject. But at work, it is expected nonetheless.

Some readers may get the impression that we're picking on these three, asking them to do things people shouldn't have to do in the first place. And now we seem to be adding insult to injury by implying that they should be willing to act like subordinates with their bosses. Nevertheless, we haven't been hinting all along that Henry have his pants destroyed, Gail pretend to have laryngitis, and John start eating prunes. Nor are we now telling them to lick their boss's boots. The attempted manipulation would be noticed and resented by their supervisors even more than the current, basically hostile approach.

It is essential to understand that the confusion in the minds of these three between the concepts of independence and individuality is causing them to be, not only uncooperative, but insubordinate. Being stubborn, or snarling at co-workers, is part of the same problem that makes them unwittingly bite the hand that feeds them. Unfortunately, they think they are acting appropriately, and even ambitiously. As Henry put it recently, "I'm letting them know that I'm an independent individual." However, his actions indicate that he hasn't the foggiest idea what the words really mean.

The behavior we are discussing is so fundamental to success or failure, it is worthwhile to look at the matter from a different angle. Many of the people in our sample attacked the opinions they heard, not because they wanted to offer one of their own, which they had long held; instead, they lashed out at the incoming view because they didn't want to be affected by it. They feared its ability to influence them and, by attacking it with its mirror image concocted on the spot, they hoped to fend it off.

That may seem silly to someone not involved in the interchange, who can dismiss it as "mere words." Yet for thousands of years, words have had the power to heal and, even more so, to harm. In fact, Marcel Mauss was the first to suggest[1] that magic was invented to ward off not only natural disasters, but also the evil curses hurled at us in anger by our neighbors, which under the right circumstances were capable of causing "voodoo deaths."

In a modern business setting, one often sees people who are using their own brand of magic to accomplish the same goal. The guideline they are following is "A good offense is the best defense," and they have been using it at least since their teen years. However, allowances are made for it during this period, especially by adults, so descriptions such as "feisty," "headstrong," "willful," "stubborn," and "argumentative" aren't generally intended to be permanent characterizations. What we discovered is that in many instances they do indeed end up providing an apt, lifelong characterization of the person's business behavior.

What the description omits is the all important question of why. As it turns out, the source of the stubborn or argumentative position is a fear of being overwhelmed by the words of others. Comments and opinions are assailed with a ferocity and immediacy that makes it clear that they are perceived as an overriding threat. Since the words do come from other humans, what is at issue here is the attempt by people to fend off, with words, the influence others might have on them, perhaps through words, perhaps not. The defensive counterattack is likely to be verbal, especially in a business setting, whereas the threat may or may not arrive in verbal form. If it does, all the better, since that makes it concrete and counterable.

It is easy to see why this topic can easily consume someone throughout his or her business life. In the United States, the land of the free

---

[1]Marcel Mauss, *A General Theory of Magic* (New York: W. W. Norton, 1967).

and the home of the brave, independence is so highly valued we aren't even supposed to acknowledge that we might want someone else to relieve us from time to time of the burden of directing all our own actions. Thoughts of Nazi Germany, or row after row of mindless Japanese or Soviet soldiers, keep us alert to the dangers inherent in this proclivity to fall casually in line with the views and direction of another. Nevertheless, Stanley Milgram,[2] among others, has shown that this proclivity exists in the United States; under the right circumstances it may be stronger than we, as freedom-loving Americans, would like to believe.

In short, Henry's, Gail's, and John's business behavior can best be understood as unproductive attempts to maintain their highly valued independence in the face of profound—but unwarranted—beliefs in their inability to do so. This is a desperation defense, a leftover from adolescence. There, at least, it was somewhat appropriate, since one is nothing if not impressionable at that age.

To sum up, *people with a strong sense of their own uniqueness repeatedly demonstrated the ability to better handle on-the-job challenges to their independence.* How can people know that they have finally left adolescence behind, and that it is no longer a threat to their careers? When can they be certain that they are able to distinguish independence from individuality where it counts most, at work? In the course of our study we discovered an unequivocal test: They have finally made the transition from adolescence to maturity when they can pay a co-worker or, especially, a superior a compliment that is deserved, and not feel that they demeaned themselves or lost something in the process.

---

[2]Stanley Milgram, *Obedience to Authority* (New York: Harper & Row, 1973).

CHAPTER
6

The Switch from
Individual to Team Effort

UNTIL RECENTLY, sex was a taboo topic. People did one thing and said another—or said nothing. Euphemisms abounded for everything connected with the subject, including pregnancy. Other topics that were draped in silence were mental illness and death. Circumlocutions and vague references were so commonly used, it was often difficult to tell exactly what had happened to the unfortunate person being discussed.

Now all that has changed. We are totally explicit. Each subject has not only been dragged from the darkness and placed in the spotlight, every detail associated with it is also explored in full view of the audience. We seem to have become a nation of long-winded exhibitionists intent on parading our private lives in public while narrating the performance. "And why not?" many have asked. "We've got nothing to hide. We're open and honest now—about everything."

Everything?

There is a crucial area of our business lives that is rapidly heading in the reverse direction. It is steadily becoming enshrouded in distortions that are deliberately designed to make the underlying reality harder to see. And for a very good reason: where this topic is concerned, most people have plenty to hide.

If one interviews a wide variety of working Americans, they give remarkably similar answers to questions about the subject of teamwork. Since the word "team" calls to mind a group of people participating in an organized manner in a sport, most comments are couched in analogies with the two most popular sports—football and baseball. "I'm the captain of the team," one chief executive told us. Another top official viewed himself in a comparable light. "I quarterback the club."

Fine. Let's take them at their word for the moment, and ignore the many critical differences between a typical business enterprise and an NFL or major league franchise. To play in a team sport requires excellence on two separate fronts. First, one's own unique talents have to be developed to the highest possible degree. Second, and of equal importance, they have to be exercised in perfect harmony with those of your teammates.

The first part is no problem. For most Americans, self-improvement is a continuing passion, and has been so for at least a century.[1] We love to develop our skills and expand our knowledge. The trouble arises where the second part of teamwork is concerned: integrating and co-ordinating our skills and knowledge with those possessed by others. One thing prevents that from happening during the decade of our twenties and a different one in our thirties. The majority of people in our sample, when they were between 20 and 29, and in the work world full-time, wanted above all to have their *personal* efforts recognized. They could rattle off a long list of famous names and, if given a magic lantern and just one wish, they would have wished for their own names to be on the list.

In their thirties, they no longer sought personal glory merely as a goal unto itself. Now they wanted it because they also hoped it would help them obtain a pay raise and a top managerial position. Their pace of progress up the corporate ladder wasn't fast enough to suit them. Most concluded that the only way to find what they were after was to achieve something truly praiseworthy, or at least make it appear as if they had. As one put it, "Just doing my job isn't getting me the notice I need." Said a second, "You have to make people see what you personally can do, or you'll never get anywhere." What sense would it have made for them to submerge themselves into a group? They felt far too anonymous as it was.

In short, teamwork in the United States is little more than a spectator sport. It's all right for others, but not for ourselves. And, our study indicates, nowhere is that more true than at the office. Although Americans may greatly admire a well-executed move made by a team on a playing field, at work different rules apply. Money and promotions are at stake, and only a fool would risk it all by being too cooperative. Nothing is worthwhile if it comes at the expense of one's personal prominence.

Exit Visas

While these attitudes may seem "natural" and in need of no explanation, the fact remains that if people are consistently encouraged to

---

[1] Donald Meyer, *The Positive Thinkers: A Study of the American Quest for Health, Wealth and Personal Power from Mary Baker Eddy to Norman Vincent Peale* (New York: Doubleday & Co, 1965).

shift from an egoistical to a group orientation, they often will. As things now stand, however, there is astonishingly little inducement in American business life to make such a shift. The extremely individualistic attitudes that are bred in school—for instance, students can't pool their knowledge at test time (it's called cheating)—become magnified rather than moderated after entry into the work world. A number of specific features of the business environment in the United States tends to make even dedicated workers solely concerned about their own personal success.

Job changes, for one thing, are very common. And that means getting ready for a switch long before it becomes necessary to make one. The time allotted for preparation may be cut short if one is fired or laid off, but most people assume that they will be leaving their firm sooner or later anyway. The next step, the questions of where to go, is an important consideration. However, an equally important thought is what to take with them that is truly and uniquely theirs.

Not the firm's profits, that's for certain. They stay even if the employee who quits or is fired had a major hand in bringing them in. Nevertheless, for purely selfish reasons most workers want the firm to do well. If the company is prospering, there is less chance that they will be let go and they may even get a raise. Also, that gives them more latitude to leave or retire when and if it suits their purposes.

But back to the original question: what truly belongs to people that they can take with them when they change jobs? At the top of the list is their *profession*. They didn't get it from their employer, and even if they did, it is theirs to take with them when they go. The crucial requirement of portability explains why workers often cling so tightly to their job specifications, and why professions are so important in America. Job descriptions are a key part of anyone's walking papers. Their title is their exit visa.

That usually leaves hardworking and talented workers in an awful bind. They are used to doing far more than they have to, far more than their job description says they do. Without realizing it, they spill over and fill voids left by others. A sentence voiced by the majority of capable, energetic people in our sample—and they meant it—was, "It's very difficult for me to put down on paper precisely what I do."

Try telling that to an executive recruiter. As one placement pro put it, "What am I supposed to do with that? I'm good, but I can't wave my arms and just sell air." As the head of another personnel agency commented, "I hate it when people come in here and say [about themselves], 'I'm very good with people.' That is simply not enough. It's hardly anything for me to work with." In brief, no one who is considering a switch misses the point: the more specifics they have on their resume, the better, the easier to place them.

Readers who like their present employer and aren't thinking of changing jobs may have concluded that the matter we're discussing doesn't apply to them. But it does indeed, if it applies to the people around them. Are the others equally fond of the firm, and do they intend to remain on board, working away happily until retirement? If not, their actions can be counted upon to have a major detrimental impact on one's own position. In the tug-of-war between one person's team orientation, assuming he or she does in fact have one, and the individualistic, glory-oriented quest of co-workers, it shouldn't be hard to guess which approach will ultimately prevail. We were rarely disappointed on this score.

The second thing that workers who are leaving may take with them is *credit*, but it usually is theirs only after a struggle. And a titanic struggle it will be if co-workers are worried about not getting all the approval they feel they need. As far as each is concerned, it is absolutely essential to stand out in a crowd and thus not be passed over when praise is being given.

Paradoxically, the people we studied became more interested in approval and acclaim as the years went by. That surprised us because we had expected that appetite to decrease as the star-struck period of adolescence came to an end. As we saw in the last chapter, in many cases it didn't end. However, there was another powerful factor in operation here: time. When graduating students first entered the work world, they could take hours spelling out for us the many things they planned to accomplish in the upcoming years. Yet once they had been in the labor force for a decade or so, they began to look back as well as forward. They started to examine where they had been in addition to where they hoped to go. It became increasingly difficult for them to escape the question, "What, if anything, have I achieved thus far?" Most could candidly admit that the answer was, "Not much." Instead of making them throw in the towel or want to slow down, the realization made them even hungrier for applause than they previously were. Having been around a while, they thought they deserved some. Few wanted to feel they had merely been taking up space and collecting a paycheck.

The result: in their late twenties and throughout their thirties, the majority of people in our sample spent an extraordinary amount of time mentally and conversationally jostling with one another, each trying to grab the lion's share of any credit being handed out. Like ravenous birds in a nest, they all wanted their share.

The key point is that they were attempting to divide up what cannot be divided. A company's growth is a seamless whole, not a cluster of distinct segments with the name of a different employee neatly written on each. Even the separate projects the firm undertakes represent the joint efforts of many people who usually receive no notice and whose contributions are very easily overlooked.

Henry, Gail, and John were acting in an entirely typical manner in making certain that they weren't among the overlooked. "I was a prime mover," said Gail, about a venture in which she participated. John expressed similar sentiments about a program in which he'd had a hand. "I think it's fair to say I did most of the *important* work." Such comments rarely failed to trigger a characteristic reaction in co-workers. Once one person decides to start seizing a piece of the pie for publicity purposes, the others have to do the same, for self-protection if for no other reason. The situation occurs so frequently, most people in business have become quite adept at using it as an excuse. As Henry put it, when discussing the jockeying frequently engaged in among scientists seeking public esteem, "Around here [as well], you really have to watch your ass. Otherwise, someone else lays claim to what *you* did."

Closet Kings

What is fascinating about such remarks is this: they seem merely self-protective yet are actually part of a highly aggressive tactic. In fact, it is the most widely used personal strategy in American business. Typically adopted by people during the second decade of their careers, it quickly becomes a cornerstone of their work-related thoughts and behavior from then on.

To see how the approach is used in everyday settings, we have selected two representative cases, Jeff Price and Carol Gordon. They are strangers, as are Henry, Gail, and John, but have far fewer of the problems connected with eternal adolescence that plague the careers of the latter three.

Jeff was given to wearing madras ties and khaki suits, the better to offset his blue eyes. Of a slightly stocky build, he wore his sandy hair close-cropped and his face clean-shaven. In more casual clothes, many people told us he could easily have been mistaken for the young golf pro from the nearest country club. Carol, on the other hand, differed from Jeff in both look and personality profile. While no one ever called her beautiful, some people found Carol attractive when she was excited and bubbling over. After they spent more time around her, they usually reported that they found much of the exuberance tiresome and the dancing eyes somewhat affected. Her round face had an upturned nose, generous lips, and smallish brown eyes on which she used little makeup. Her nails were short, and she wore her thick, brown hair off her face, held by two barrettes. She frequently wore neat suits to work decorated only by the printed silk bow tie at her neck, and she always carried a briefcase.

Jeff, at 31, stated that, "Nobody here gives a damn or does really good work, except me." According to Carol, at 30, the other people in her office, including the bosses, are "only interested in their pay envelopes and vacations." These two intelligent people are very involved with their work, and there may well have been times when they labored longer and harder than other workers. Rather than being the end of the story, though, that is only the beginning. For their assertion that others at the firm care much less about their work than these two do *frees* them.

To do what? Praise themselves endlessly. And a special kind of praise it is: their belief that they alone genuinely care about the affairs of the firm allows them to toot their own horns continually—in the name of the firm. There is no question in the minds of either that they are the sole parties who have the best interests of their respective companies at heart.

Having established that much, at least to their own satisfaction, they were able to proceed confidently to the next step. It is a delicious one, in which they get to do two things that are equally satisfying: criticize others (for their alleged laziness and indifference) and aggressively seek to boost their own reputations (as the only rightful heirs to the firm's top position).

Telling them that that is what they are doing (we haven't, but others did) produces a shocked reaction. "What?" Carol replied to someone who called her arrogant and accused her of overstepping her territory. "You think I want to *be* in this position?" Jeff and Carol have created impregnable fortresses for themselves. They never tire of telling themselves that they are acting that way, not because they prefer to, but because they *have* to. They are the firm's valiant, only—and lonely—protectors. Reluctantly, therefore, they have been forced to scrap the concept of teamwork. Mind you, they didn't like doing so, and they aren't pleased about the decision. They're merely trying to make the best of a poor situation. They've been left with no choice but to become exclusively individualistic in their focus. In short, it's not egotism. It is necessity.

The four-step strategy that they and an enormous number of others in business are using can be summarized simply.

First, dismiss the competition. "They are all careless and incompetent."

Second, acclaim yourself. "I'm the only capable and industrious person here."

Third, coronate yourself. "The firm, *c'est moi*. I *am* this firm, by default, since there are no other legitimate candidates for the title."

Fourth, luxuriate in the spoils of victory. "I deserve all the credit, the glory, for carrying this entire kingdom on my shoulders."

To these four many add one more.

Fifth, suffer externally to hide internal exultation. "Heavy is the head upon which sits the crown." "I have to do everything myself." And, "My work here is *never* done."

Jeff and Carol had arranged things so neatly in their minds, it is difficult to imagine them having trouble. But trouble they did have, abundantly. As long as they remained in their mental monarchies, out of contact momentarily with co-workers, all was well.

However, without their knowing it, many of their co-workers were doing exactly the same thing they'd done: turning the firm into an empire and secretly placing themselves at its head. To the casual observer it may have looked as though Jeff or Carol were merely having a tense conversation with one of these similarly self-deluded people. What was really happening, though, was more serious. Two people had somehow become rulers of the same kingdom.

It had to mean war. Neither was prepared to compromise, saying, "I'll take this half of the realm; the other half is yours," because neither was ready to admit to the other that a self-coronation had taken place. The two closet kings thus fought intensely, day after day, without ever once identifying their true (that is, royal) inner selves or acknowledging what the real stakes were in the battle.

At this point it is reasonable to inquire, as we repeatedly did, "How much do Jeff and Carol really differ from Henry, Gail, and John?" They certainly seem to have arrived at the same way of viewing themselves and the people with whom they worked. Nevertheless, there is one extremely important difference. Jeff and Carol never get tired of lecturing people both on the job and off about the virtues and benefits of teamwork.

The first time we heard that they were delivering these hallway and lunchroom sermons at the office, we found it bizarre. They had already told us at length that they considered none of the people around them intelligent or dedicated. Yet here they were, lecturing those very people about the rewards they would all allegedly reap by working together. When we asked the two about it, they had a ready reply. "Why tie a lame horse to a good team?" we inquired. Their instant answer was, "*Somebody* has to do it. Someone has to make these bimbos pull together."

That may have sounded eminently reasonable, but it was miles from their actual motives. Remember, these two didn't see themselves as employees at their firms. Instead, they *were* their firms. So, in asking their co-workers to rally together on behalf of the company, they really meant, "You have to do more for me—as the company. You're not doing enough."

Somehow, without being aware of the specifics, their co-workers sensed that something foul was afoot, that the message they were getting was twisted and fraudulent. They responded accordingly. As one put it, "I get real tired of Jeff's rah-rah crap about team spirit." Said another, about Carol, "She's just trying to win brownie points for herself, that's all." Nevertheless, Jeff and Carol persisted. The opposition, what little of it they heard, was no more than they expected in the first place. What was remarkable to us was that they were able to get away with complaining bitterly to the very people they complained bitterly about in private.

The upshot, we now know, was predictable. Wherever these two tireless advocates of teamwork went, they rapidly destroyed whatever vestiges of teamwork existed before they arrived. They were constantly creating serious hurdles for themselves, ones that appeared to grow even higher the moment they made another seemingly well-intentioned effort to get over them. It upset and frustrated both repeatedly. Jeff, visibly dejected, said at 34, "I spend all my time fighting with people—people I'd much rather be working with than fighting."

Carol too couldn't avoid noticing the nearly complete lack of co-operation from others, but she had a soothing and face-saving explanation for it: moodiness. As far as she could see, most people were subject to major—indeed, huge—mood swings every day, and the fact that they weren't interested in working with her at that moment had nothing to do with her. As she repeatedly put it, "Most of the time he [or she] isn't in a very good mood." We would be the last to dismiss the importance of emotional factors in human behavior. However, people became conspicuously more moody when Jeff or Carol were around. Even some of the most amiable sorts became closed and defensive in their presence. There could be no mistake about the fact that these two were generating, year after year, the uncomfortable working conditions with which they then had to contend.

When we think of a crisis, we envision one terrible event. In most cases the picture is accurate, but not here. The numerous bouts of depression and despair, each tinged with rage, that assaulted Jeff and Carol in their late twenties and thirties, produced far more inner turmoil than any full-scale crisis would have, yet did so over a substantially longer period of time. One acute attack would have been much easier to bear.

Better to Trust No One

It took us a number of years and a wide variety of cases to find the best indicator that trouble is brewing on this front. When we asked Jeff and Carol why they spent so much time snarling at their co-workers, usually from afar, the confidential answer was, "Because I don't trust them." There are few statements one hears in business that sound this simple yet contain so many major implications. The single best indicator that trouble is brewing is precisely this broad lack of trust. The reason it gives rise to problems is that, if people distrust someone they work with—in fact, have serious misgivings about how well the person is able to do his or her job even when motivated—they aren't likely to relax. How can they? They have their own work to worry about—and the other person's too. That is hardly a basis for teamwork.

In short, to say that we distrust someone as a worker is much like distrusting him as a fellow soldier during a time of war. It doesn't merely mean we have reservations about the person's competence or diligence, it implies something more drastic: we don't want him on the team. Well then, what happens if we have the same doubts about everybody in the office? Who is left as candidates for the team?

That is what made the position taken by Jeff and Carol, or by Henry, Gail, and John for that matter, impregnable. Whan a friend of Jeff's labeled him as "ye of little faith," Jeff retorted irritably, "Yeah, and I've got good *reason* to have little faith." He then related episode after episode of errors and mix-ups that were caused by the alleged indifference and ineptness of the people with whom he worked.

Carol, who had a better memory for such events than Jeff, took the matter a step further. Instead of waiting until someone cornered her and wanted to know why she usually held such a negative view of everyone in her office, Carol made her case before they had a chance to strike. The stories she continually reported to friends about co-workers' mistakes were intended to prevent anyone from calling her cynicism unwarranted. At least in one instance that we witnessed, someone did anyway.

"You're awful," an old co-worker, now at another firm, said to her only half-kiddingly. "All you do is criticize." Carol laced into her. "You *must* be joking," she said with a sneer. "How could you say that after everything I've told you about these bumblers? And you haven't heard the half of it."

Jeff and Carol had both mastered the art of using their distrust to demolish anyone who seemed eligible for the team. For example, when

Carol's old co-worker reminded her that there was at least one truly hardworking person at the firm, a fellow named Tom, Carol replied, "That's true. Too bad he's such a dim bulb." Jeff used the same tactic. When he was told that a co-worker of his was generally considered by people in the field to be brilliant, Jeff quickly came back with, "So what? He's lazy." No one was granted both brains and diligence. If they were capable, they were branded as lethargic or indifferent. And if they were undeniably dedicated, they were labeled dullards. As Carol put it about Tom (who was recently made the president of the firm), "He *has* to work that hard just to be average."

In sum, an assessment of whether people who have held a given job for at least six months are really interested in teamwork begins with a simple question. Ask them who, if anyone, at the firm they trust. If there is no one whose abilities and devotion command their respect, either they are at the wrong firm or they couldn't be part of a team if they tried.

There is a vicious circle here, and it is easy to become caught up in it. No one can make people hold their co-workers in high regard if they don't want to. As Jeff and Carol demonstrate, it takes little effort to dismiss someone, for there is always some point about the person that can be used as a fatal flaw. In fact, we noticed that once people became attuned to finding what was wrong instead of right about their co-workers, they were able to find all the additional, corroborating evidence they needed to prove their initial condemnation had been accurate. If anything, they came to believe that they had previously been too kind. "This place is even more of a rat's nest than I'd thought," they both told us at each place of employment, forgetting that they had arrived at that conclusion at the former firms as well.

Not only does it make people feel important to perceive themselves as the only able and interested workers at the firm, an additional motive for this approach is that the confidence they place in others usually comes at the expense of the confidence they have in themselves. Better to trust no one and stay self-assured than to give others respect and feel less than perfect.

Unfortunately, it isn't that simple. Whether they like it or not— and they don't—sooner or later they require the assistance of the very people they have secretly condemned. Then, all the chickens come home to roost. Between the hostility they usually generate within (since they are asking people they view as being beneath them for help) and the anxiety as well (the people in question can't be counted upon to do their jobs), inner discomfort quickly mounts.

People who successfully make the effort to trust at least a few of their more capable co-workers may feel a bit less full of themselves at first, which they may experience as a mild feeling of letdown. Nevertheless, two main improvements in their business lives should more than compensate for their imaginary losses: *peace* and *greater productivity*. Regarding the first, as long as we continue to view the people we have to work with as inadequate at best, we are secretly at war with them. ("I can't let these people have their way. They don't know what they're doing. I, of course, do. I could run the whole place by myself, and should be.") Also, we have to remain apprehensive about them. ("What did I do to deserve such half-wits as colleagues? I had better keep an eye on their every move.") Under the circumstances, tranquility is out of the question. What is especially distressing about the stance is that it wastes most of one's energy, and it overlooks the fact that the mistakes of others can be found and corrected calmly, instead of angrily—long before they are actually made.

As far as the second benefit, greater productivity, there is so much self-congratulatory sniping going on, the majority of workers in our sample have become used to being targets of little but criticism. To trust them, and mean it, is a rare compliment that they aren't likely to forget. Granted, there are many people in each firm who don't deserve the respect. No one is suggesting a promiscuous approach with something this important. Selectivity is crucial. But once a discriminating choice has been made, it still needs time and sincerity to yield the required results.

Although it would upset many members of our sample to hear it, they need other people to help them accomplish anything worthwhile. To put it another way, if all their accomplishments are solitary and portable, how much have they really accomplished? Maybe the best thing they will do in life will be an integral part of something so much larger than themselves that it will have to be left behind them when they go.

Traveling Light and Alone

We've all grown so accustomed to criticizing others as a way of boosting ourselves that, when we stop doing it, we are likely to feel less outstanding. "To be honest," said one person who tried the new approach as part of an experiment, "I thought to myself, 'Maybe I'm not a superstar anymore.'"

That is a lot to give up, though the payoff is well worth it. To avoid making changes, many people are tempted to view griping in an optimistic manner, as being capable of leading to improvements in the firm's operations. When our study first began, we too thought that would be the outcome of some of the complaints. It was, but not very often. More to the point, the self-praise we are discussing goes on largely in private and in a covert form that can't be implemented unless the firm surprises everyone by appointing a new president. Complaining quickly attains a life of its own.

To see how a change in attitude can result in real improvement, consider the typical example of Kirk Strickland. (The lessons we learned from the Jeffs and Carols in our sample, we put to use with other groups who volunteered to give a different approach a try.) Even when Kirk was in a good and generous mood, he still doubted the ability of his co-workers as well as their willingness to use it. Compliments of the kind we discussed in the previous chapter were viewed as ridiculous and false. ("These people deserve to be flogged not praised.") That left it up to him to do things right, as the only competent person around.

Yet Kirk got surprisingly little accomplished, and that small amount required a sizable and continuing struggle. Also, there was usually a high degree of antagonism in the air. That puzzled him since he thought he was giving a rather convincing performance of being casual and cooperative. Nevertheless, he was merely going through the motions, and it showed. The response was predictable: each side quickly dug in, going nowhere but pleased anyway, for it was at least preventing the other side (which it viewed as selfish and self-centered) from making any headway.

Once Kirk became genuinely inclined to give a handful of others the benefit of the doubt, his new attitude produced a less tense and more productive kind of contact with co-workers. Since he had stopped assuming automatically that everyone else in the firm was an idiot, which until then had been his favorite label, he had one less self-imposed obstacle to overcome each time.

Keep in mind that there are many people who have trouble cooperating, no matter how much they are trusted. As we learned in the last chapter, the large number of Henrys, Gails, and Johns in the business world make anything even approaching perfect harmony on this front an unrealistic ideal. These people can be counted upon to throw up opposition to almost anything that is proposed, and they will demand their hastily constucted counterproposal be considered instead. Often, chronic objectors become thought of merely as pessimists, who therefore serve as a useful antidote to unwarranted optimism. That is dangerously inaccurate at times, since their approach is likely to produce inactivity. As we've seen, a better explanation for their behavior is found in terms of a stunted adolescent's rebellious attempt at individuality, and it should go a long way to making clear why they probably aren't going to be on anyone's team.

Making the effort to exclude or work around them in the beginning, if at all possible, has proved very worthwhile. Ironically, once a nucleus of team players has been assembled, the troublemakers typically become eager to join it. Ignoring them initially, and concentrating on more mature and motivated workers, turns out to be the best way to bring self-important, juvenile antagonists around, if anything done on the job can.

Thanks to the tendency of United States workers to spend the bulk of their time trying to come up with something that is exclusively theirs, conflict rather than cooperation is always on the verge of erupting. As a result, many find it difficult during their thirties to avoid the depressing feeling that decades are passing by while they achieve nothing. Changing matters for the better requires a break with the great American tradition of traveling light and alone through life. By constantly attempting to lay claim to what they feel is rightfully theirs—their contributions and the resulting credit—these workers are aggravating their co-workers, who in turn have no choice but to be equally grasping and egotistical in order to protect what they too see as legitimately theirs.

Sooner or later, one of the parties involved in this tug-of-war will move to another firm. In some ways, the war then worsens, because it is frozen at the point where it was interrupted. Both parties are separated now yet still defending themselves against the threat the other once posed. In a services-oriented economy, which the United States increasingly is,[2] a large part of what each person accomplishes over the years resides in the minds of others. Alienating them through credit-wrestling is the business equivalent of undergoing a lobotomy.

To sum up:

1. Teamwork is consciously espoused but unwittingly shunned by most people in business because they are deathly afraid of it. They think it will render them anonymous, invisible.

2. In spite of the huge number of hours Americans spend watching spectator sports, their picture of good teamwork is that of an army, marching in unison, each soldier doing precisely the same thing. That is definitely not the kind of cooperation that success in business requires. What is needed is for each individual to be busy, day after day, doing what he or she does best.

3. People in business are convinced that a team is like quicksand: once one becomes a part of it, there is no graceful way to take one's

---

[2]V. F. Fuchs, *The Service Economy* (New York: National Bureau of Economic Research/Columbia University Press, 1968) and R. K. Shelp, *Beyond Industrialization: Ascendancy of the Global Service Economy* (New York: Praeger, 1981).

leave. However, we found that when it is functioning most effectively in business, teamwork is only a sometime thing.

That was the dead giveaway in Jeff's and Carol's behavior. They wanted people to be team players, morning, noon, and night. *Whenever anyone in an office (as opposed to assembly-line) setting proclaims the virtues of such endless cooperation, they almost always turn out to be egomaniacs seeking to suppress everyone else's ego except their own.* Basically, they are hiding their unwillingness to be part of any team, except the team of one that they are already on.

4. As far as the flip side is concerned, well-meaning people who are spending even a moderate portion of their day worrying about how well they fit into the team, aren't doing their work—the work for which the firm wanted them on the team in the first place.

III

CHANGING JOBS

CHAPTER
7

The Job-Change Checklist

IT IS A rare worker in the United States who graduates from school or college and takes a job at one company for life. While the event is common in Japan,[1] the inducements here to move on in the vast majority of cases eventually outweigh the reasons for staying. The problems we've been discussing certainly play a role, yet the fact remains that job changes are as omnipresent in the U.S. business environment as high-rise office buildings; and they are undertaken by people who are as well adjusted as anyone we've ever seen. From its inception, our study therefore concentrated on the question of who made the changes well, who made them poorly, and why.

The financial health of the companies involved had to be a factor every bit as much as the mental health of the employees making the switch. This didn't strike us as an easy topic to investigate, and it wasn't. However, we had a substantial amount of outside assistance in investigating the soundness of various firms, especially public ones, and that allowed us to focus primarily on the psychological dimensions of the matter. Financial analysts who were assessing these companies for their own purposes (usually on behalf of a brokerage firm or business publication) provided important insights that prevented us repeatedly from jumping to obvious but incorrect conclusions.

For instance, one firm in 1973 had what we believed was the good fortune to be the employer at the time of two of the most talented and hardworking people in our sample. Both left within a four-week period, complaining largely about their respective superiors, not the state of the firm. That surprised us, since the positions they held seemed good ones, and a steady stream of compliments had been coming their way. It wasn't until we talked with three analysts who had been keeping

---

[1]Thomas P. Rohlen, *For Harmony and Strength: Japanese White-Collar Organization in Anthropological Perspective* (Berkeley: University of California Press, 1974).

close tabs on the company, and watched carefully as subsequent statements were released, that we were able to gauge the pressures that had been building up—and were being passed down. Not only was the economy entering a prolonged period of recession, but the firm's position in its major markets was deteriorating, developments that were to lead to earnings losses in the next three quarters as well as substantial layoffs. So, these job changes were timely but, as we were to learn, they involved transfers in both cases to the wrong companies. Still another job switch was required in each case to remedy the error.

This topic of a company's financial health turned out to be important during every decade of one's career and therefore merits detailed discussion of at least our principal findings. We have placed this part here because there is greater risk associated with ill-advised job changes after the age of 40.[2] One thing is now clear: regardless of age, most people who are thinking of changing jobs are so repelled by their present position, they rejoice at the mere thought of having another. That gives them an overly rosy picture of the place they are considering transferring to. *The most critical mistake they make is a failure to figure out what their current company offers them that has helped get them as far as they have gotten.* The aspects they find obnoxious about the present firm blind them to what may be invaluable—and missing— at the new.

After we look at a few representative examples, we will be in a position to discuss general guidelines.

Not-So-Long Division

Roger Burrell graduated at 24 with a master's degree in electrical engineering and accepted a job offer from General Electric. "I had doubts about coming here," he commented three months after starting. "I was worried about it being too big, and all that. Afraid I'd get lost in the shuffle." Then, breaking into a smile, "But it's a friendly place, and you get to know the people in your immediate area pretty fast." Roger had a boyish, oval face, a shape that was easy to see since he was prematurely balding. "I went to a few of those places that swear they could grow hair even on a billiard ball," he said in the pleasant, moderated tones with which he voiced almost everything. "But all they did was give me a further scalping, so to speak."

---

[2]For example, workers between the ages of 55 and 64 tend to be out of work significantly longer than those who are younger—more than 20 weeks (in 1983) as opposed to less than 9 weeks for all age groups as a whole.

For eight years Roger remained with the firm and seemed happy enough. The second year there, he met Ellen, an elementary school teacher, while on a ski trip with co-workers. They were married ten months later, and eventually they had two children, a boy and a girl.

During his seventh year at GE, he began to grow impatient with the slow rate of increase in managerial responsibilities that he was being given. "I'm getting there," he said, his restlessness showing, "but not quickly enough. Maybe I'm expecting too much." It was just a line, a self-calming comment that worked temporarily yet didn't interfere in the least with his emerging determination to move up faster elsewhere.

Almost a year passed before he sent out four resumes in response to ads he had seen one Sunday in the *New York Times*. "I don't know why I procrastinated so long," he said a few days after putting them into the mail. "Ellen and I have made up our minds to leave [this city]."

All four firms replied, and one invited him to be interviewed at an "open house" a few weeks later. "It was held at a Holiday Inn, not one of their plants," he said, amused at the events that had transpired. "There must have been 200 guys like me there, looking for jobs." Roger was usually an optimist, but not this time. "I'll be lucky if they remember my name," he said, shaking his head. "It was like registering for a new semester at college."

They did more than remember it; they sent him a personal letter inviting him to come, at their expense, to their main R&D [research and development] facility and talk to some people working on a project similar to the one that had occupied him for the past two years. Roger was thrilled. "I think they're really interested," he said, waving the letter happily.

That they were. He liked the people he met there, and they apparently liked him. In less than two weeks he received a formal offer that included approximately an 18 percent pay hike. Seven weeks after getting the letter he began at the new firm, one of the nation's largest defense suppliers.

Six months after that he was fired. So were dozens of others. In fact, nearly 20 percent of the staff of his division was let go; scientists, engineers, technicians, draftsmen, clerical and maintenance people all were abruptly dismissed. One of the mechanical engineers who had the office next door commented philosophically while packing up, "Well, that's what happens around here whenever we have an outbreak of peace." Roger was stunned. "Where am I going to go?" he asked, a hint of panic in his voice. "We've already sold our house [near GE], and I'm not going back there, anyway." The problem was more serious than it seemed. "Do you realize there's not another defense contractor within 100 miles of this place?" he asked in utter disbelief. He and

Ellen eventually found other jobs, but it took four full months of frenetic searching and a 2,700-mile move. "I've never been so miserable," Roger remarked when it was over.

From the depths of his despair it was easy for Roger to conclude that the severe and costly troubles that had befallen him were peculiar to the defense industry. They aren't, as will be clear when we look at another example, drawn from a field that could hardly be more different.

Cynthia Marshall knew she wanted to be a fashion designer early in high school but doubted that she would get into a design school. "*Any* of them," she added. One accepted her, though, and she leaped at the opportunity to go. "I'll make it now," she commented during her freshman year there. "This was the hard part."

Her sense of direction was so strong, she was able to see her admission to and attendance at design school as the end, not the beginning, of her trials. It also made her oblivious to the dreams of her classmates who were equally dedicated to one day becoming the newest sensation.

After graduation she found first one job, then another, with small firms. Neither was to her liking, and neither one lasted more than a year. At that point she managed to land a job at a major apparel manufacturer as assistant to a well-known sportswear designer. "I'll take over [here] before you know it," she said in her first year at the firm. "I'll be ready soon."

The study of ballet in her younger years gave Cynthia's long limbs a grace of movement. Her short, straight hair, cut in the latest geometric shape, moved with each motion of her head, sometimes covering her left eye. She preferred to dress monochromatically top to toe, favoring black over all colors. On any given day, her fire red lips and nails were the only bright spots of her ensemble.

Instead of seizing control overnight, she spent the next 11 years battling to keep her job. The firm continued to expand, and it hired three other assistant designers besides Cynthia. "The biggest bunch of no-talents you ever saw," as she described them to us during her third year there. Nevertheless, their presence caused her to realign her sights; whereas previously she had focused almost monomaniacally on ultimately displacing her boss, now she was forced to devote an increasing amount of attention to what her in-house competitors were doing. "They're nowhere," she said in her ninth year at the firm, "but I have to keep an eye on them anyway. They're sneaks, good at politics. That's how they get by."

In her eleventh year there, Cynthia suddenly decided she'd had enough. Her patience vanished less than a week after she heard that

Barbara, one of the other assistant designers, was being promoted and would be doing a line of her own. "I don't believe how stupid [the executives here] are. Barbara hasn't got the brains she was born with."

It took Cynthia almost seven moths of following up on every promising lead to finally locate the position she was seeking. "I think I've been to see everyone in this [apparel] market," she said wearily, near the end of the period. She had received two offers as a result of her search but found both unsatisfactory. "I want a *label*," she said firmly. "It's time for me to make my [fashion] statement. I want the customers to know *I* designed the clothes they're wearing. No more anonymity for me."

The firm to which she transferred agreed to give her not only a label but also "a piece of the action," a share of the profits generated by the division of which she was now the designer. The appearance in *Women's Wear Daily* of the announcement of her appointment delighted her as nothing in her professional life had until then. "Oh God, I'm so excited," she said, barely able to stand still.

For the next ten months she worked feverishly, hiring assistants, seeing textile ("piece goods") salesmen, sketching and approving samples, and having heated conversations with merchandisers, salespeople on the staff, and a handful of department store buyers with whom she'd become friendly over the years.

On a sunny Friday afternoon during the last week of her tenth month on the job, Ken, the head of the firm, came into her office. That wasn't unusual. He often stopped in briefly to ask how things were going. This time, though, he quietly said, "I'd like to talk to you," and closed the door behind him, something he'd never done before. He sat down.

Cynthia could tell from the look on Ken's face that something was wrong. They had spent many hours working together during the year. This was the most troubled she'd ever seen him. "I've been trying to think of a nice, easy way to tell you this," Ken began uncomfortably. "Maybe there is no easy way."

Cynthia could feel herself becoming tense. She suddenly didn't know what to do with her hands. Her mind raced, trying to figure out what was about to hit her. "Did I say something to Helen [the merchandiser] I shouldn't have?" she asked herself, concerned about an argument the two had had that morning. "Did she go to him and complain?"

The minute Ken started speaking again, Cynthia knew it was bigger than that. "We've enjoyed having you here," Ken said, looking at his hands.

"I've enjoyed *being* here," Cynthia blurted out.

"And we hope you'll stay on," Ken continued. "But we have to make some changes. We've decided to close your division, as of today."

"You've what?" Cynthia asked, wanting to jump up and run. "But we haven't even *shipped* anything yet."

"We're not going to, either," he replied. "We haven't been getting enough paper [that is, signed orders]. Now is the time. I'm sorry. It just didn't work out."

Before Ken left he offered to help her find a different position at the firm, one that would allow her to remain there if she chose. Cynthia wasn't interested. "All I could think about was the humiliation," she later said. "By Monday *everyone* in the market was going to know what happened to me." Within the month she took a job at another firm. "I wasn't staying there," she said about the admittedly hasty move. "I don't need their pity."

Traps Awaiting the Highly Motivated

We could cite hundreds of other examples of people who have had experiences similar to Roger's and Cynthia's, but it is revealing to see what these two cases have in common. As it turns out, the mistakes they made are found in the overwhelming majority of other instances.

Three features are conspicuous. The first is that neither Roger nor Cynthia knew anyone at the firms to which they transferred. In Roger's case that was only to be expected. He was on one side of the country and switched to the other. In Cynthia's field, however, a job change often involves a move from one side of the street to the other. Although she'd known someone who had previously been employed there, the person had left nearly a year before she was offered the job. Looking the person up did not seem wise. "I didn't want to tip my hand," she said a year later. "This is a small, closed, gossipy field."

The second feature is that neither knew what the financial practices and economic standing of their prospective employers were. Good securities analysts always want to know not only how much money a public company has, but also what it is inclined to do with it. For instance, is it predisposed to paying it out as dividends; spending it on capital investment in plants and equipment; using it for internal growth through the development of new ventures and divisions; acquiring, with it, other companies in the field; or finally, reacquiring, with it, its own shares in the open market or through tender offers?

Let us call these tendencies an external view of the firm, and the comments made by any friends who work there an internal view. The point is that it isn't necessary to know anyone at the firm personally in order to find out a great deal of information that could prove valuable to someone thinking of transferring there. The material usually isn't difficult to obtain, and later we'll see exactly which parts of it have proved most worthwhile to gather.

The third feature is that neither Roger nor Cynthia had given much, if any, thought to what would happen in case things didn't work out. They simply assumed that everything would, and that was all there was to that.

In short, if "look before you leap" is the best advice people who've changed jobs unsuccessfully can give, it is clear that very few people follow that guideline. They simply go. When? Whenever it suits them. Where? To almost any firm that will have them.

To be specific, the more highly motivated people are, the more likely it is that they will leap at the wrong opportunity. What we've discovered is that, where job changes are concerned, motivation is very easily transformed into impulsiveness. Most ambitious men and women operate in a very simple manner: trusting to intuition and experience, as well as to their ability to adapt to almost any situation, they happily take the plunge if given the chance, hoping that somehow they will land on their feet. Under the circumstances, it is a small miracle that they ever manage to do so. There has to be a better way, particularly since things so often go badly.

What, then, should they be looking at before they take the leap? Number one is the health of the industry itself. What is interesting is that students trying to decide on a major are more likely to pay attention to this question while still in college than they are after they've graduated. The economic incentive to choose a field that is prospering exerts a significant influence on student decisions about occupation. For instance, the glut of elementary and secondary school teachers in the mid–1970s caused the proportion of college freshmen who planned a career in the profession to plummet by two-thirds for both men and women (relative to the levels seen a decade earlier). Similar shifts, in response to job-market conditions, are found in many other fields, such as engineering, physics, mathematics, biology, psychology, philosophy, and law.

Nevertheless, once students have obtained their undergraduate and graduate degrees, and they have entered their chosen profession, they spend little time thinking about the subject. As one put it, "Looking over my shoulder and asking, 'What if?' won't do me any good." Said a second, "It's too late now, I've already made my choice."

It isn't quite that simple. It is possible for people to remain in the same profession, the one in which they received their academic training, and still better their chances of doing well by pursuing it in an industry that is flourishing rather than troubled. Even so, they might decide to stay with the industry in which they are presently employed, regardless of how well or poorly it is faring as a whole. That is what the large majority (more than 60 percent) of the workers we've surveyed say they intend to do, and follow-up surveys indicate that they usually mean it.

In that case, the number two consideration—the particular company they choose to work for within the industry—becomes an especially important decision. Keep in mind that when an industry experiences a prolonged period of economic distress, not every company within it suffers equally. Roger, for example, was laid off by a defense contractor at a time when three other firms in the field were aggressively hiring, one of which became his next employer.

That so few workers (less than 6 percent) in the 20-to-40 age-range make serious inquiries about the financial soundness of their prospective employers is astonishing. Why don't they? The two main reasons they offer are, first, "I won't be taking much money from them, so what difference does it make." That is, they don't see their own monetary drain on the company as substantial enough to affect the firm's overall financial situation—which they view as someone else's (management's) responsibility, not theirs. As a 32-year-old purchasing agent at a paper company put it, "Hey, I can't keep this place afloat *and* do my job."

The second reason they give is, "That kind of information is really of use only to people playing the stock market." The comment is immensely revealing about how people who are in the process of changing jobs actually think and act. Those who are trying to decide whether to invest in a company follow one route, while those who are considering whether or not to work there follow another. That the two routes are so separate is a recipe for disaster.

What is truly puzzling is that people who play the stock market regularly *and* who happen to be considering a job change still keep the two approaches so separate. However, the securities analyst's view seems to them too external, and thus irrelevant. "I might *like* it there, you know," said a 36-year-old veteran investor and airline employee, "even if they're not making a fortune."

After listening for a few minutes to a friend who worked at the company, this fellow accepted a job offer from a firm in which he would never have invested a dime. Why did he do it? Because he'd gotten the allegedly all-important internal view he was looking for.

This is an artificial distinction, one that needs to be erased since the external (economic and financial) view of the firm eventually has a crucial impact on the internal view (what it feels like to work there). We were especially surprised that people playing the stock market ignored that fact, inasmuch as the mistakes they make as investors merely cost them money, whereas transferring to the wrong firm costs them a much more precious and irreplaceable commodity: years of their lives. The terrible irony here is that highly motivated men and women later explained that they made the move so quickly precisely because they were trying to make good use of every second. As one put it, "I wasn't going to let grass grow under my feet while I tried to make up my mind."

The White Knight Syndrome

The third thing people who are thinking of changing jobs need to consider, once they have become knowledgeable about the image and financial strength of the company, is the particular division that they will be working for at the company. One of the most striking differences that emerges from surveying executives at a firm versus the responses given by people who are thinking of transferring there is this: the executives are painfully aware that certain subsidiaries and ventures are doing wonderfully, while others are static, barely holding their own, and that others are slowly dying. The inconsistency is often on their minds and affects many of their day's activities.

Prospective employees, on the other hand, tend to have a monolithic perception of the firm. They see the lines that separate subsidiaries as being no real barrier to the movement of funds, so that the profits of one division naturally overflow to another that is doing less well. Although they are well aware of the concept of personal rivalries between departments, in their view no concrete financial compartments exist at the firm. People compete; money goes where it's needed.

That misperception has a major impact on their willingness to take a job at the company. As long as one division out of as many as even six is doing well, they hastily conclude that they have nothing to worry about. The good ventures and product lines will subsidize the bad ones. If they then proceeded to make certain that they landed a position in the one profitable division, their distorted perception would probably cause them no harm. But that is rarely what they do. The glow that emanates from the sole source of profit colors the entire company. They therefore happily accept a job in one of the least profitable sections of the firm, thanks to their mistaken impression that it doesn't differ in any essential way from the most profitable division.

Faulting management for bringing highly motivated new employees aboard a sinking ship accomplishes nothing, since that in fact may be the place where they are needed most. Paradoxically, the evidence indicates that that is particularly likely to happen to them if they are very capable as well. The booming subsidiary doesn't need new talent nearly as much; it obviously has a number of able individuals already at the helm.

However, unless people explicitly ask whether they are being placed in a sagging division in the hope that they will somehow help shore it up and even turn it around, they shouldn't be surprised if they aren't given that information voluntarily. Even if they ask, they still may not get a straight answer, for two reasons: management may continue to have some genuine optimism left about the operation (otherwise they would close it, rather than throw good money after bad by hiring additional people to staff it). Second, executives who level with an outsider about the fact that it is do-or-die time might scare off the very people the company needs most to attract just then. Usually management is deceiving itself about the prospects for a favorable outcome far more than they are cynically manipulating prospective employees.

Odd as it may sound, approximately one-third (31 percent) of the ambitious men and women we studied are drawn to such situations unasked. Instead of recoiling at the prospect of trying to return a division to profitability, perhaps single-handedly, they rejoice at the idea. "If anybody can rescue it, I can," said a 39-year-old salesman who took a job at a firm that was so close to being on the edge of bankruptcy, no one had to tell him it was teetering. Despite a valiant effort on his part, 14 months later it failed.

In the majority of instances it isn't that obvious. Quite the contrary, the firm seems like a going concern that is merely having trouble turning a profit. This is the type of situation that most members of this group found appealing. They loved the challenge and, in our opinion, deliberately chose to overlook exactly how troubled the firm was. Few asked. Fewer still wanted to know. As one put it, "I don't need the *details*. I'm just going to throw myself into it and see what I can accomplish." In this case, though not in the majority of others we monitored, things eventually worked out well.

Let us call this display of personal altruism in business the White Knight Syndrome. The key point that needs to be made here is that people may find themselves having to play the role of the White Knight even if they don't want to *and* the firm isn't foundering. What combination of circumstances would cast a person in such a role, whether he or she sought it or not? This one: he or she is the only person hired at the time by the firm and is given an important position of responsibility.

The pressures that quickly develop have as much to do with co-workers as with management's high hopes for what might now be achieved. The spotlight is always on any recent arrivals, and for good reason. The employees who are already on the staff, and have been there quite a while, are known entities. No one really expects miracles from them anymore. If they've been on board for a number of years, a good job from each will be deemed more than sufficient. However, the dream of the firm's top officers—that someone will come along in a subordinate capacity and nudge the company into a distinctly higher level of profitability—winds up in the lap of the new employee, by default. No one else there is a candidate any longer for the role. Cynthia, for instance, was saddled right from the start with the task of producing instant results, a near impossibility in her field. Months and years, not minutes and weeks, go into building a solid, commercial success. Great expectations followed her every action, and ultimately they did her in. No one was a match for hopes that high.

The evidence clearly indicates, however, that if more than one person is hired at about the same time, the expectations of management lessen dramatically. Spread over two prime movers, the hopes become remarkably more reasonable. Each takes the blistering spotlight off the other, thereby helping both to flourish. In Cynthia's case, had a new merchandiser, let's say, been hired at about the same time she was, the firm's top officials would have been less likely to become disappointed so quickly. In short, sometimes in business the best flowers blossom only in the shade.

At small to medium-sized companies, especially those still caught in the throes of their initial entrepreneurial fervor, that condition may be hard to come by. In fact, it is common at these firms for people to be hired and fired with great regularity. The revolving-door personnel policy is mainly a result of their founders being in a phenomenal hurry to turn the tiny firm into a giant one overnight. These somewhat crazed executives therefore unwittingly surround each prospective employee with an aura of the miraculous, an imagined superhuman ability to get things done. The wooing of such prized prospects is done with consummate charm and great skill.

What happens once the prized employees accept the offer and join the firm is another matter entirely. After a brief period, during which the aura continues to linger, it is abruptly removed. Each incident at any given firm varies, and there are many differences from one firm to the next. However, analyzing a large number of cases reveals a sequence that is common to almost all of them. Prospective employees who are being courted are wonderful until they have joined the firm and settled in; after that they become inadequate, a monumental letdown. The basic reason for the shift in attitude is simple: the boss inevitably begins to project his or her massive inferiority feelings onto the no-longer-new arrivals.

Like an ardent lover who has become severely disenchanted, the boss rejects them and goes hunting passionately for other alleged supermen or superwomen to replace those now on the staff, who clearly can't fly. In this case, when the honeymoon ends, so does the marriage. The sudden emotional or actual dismissal may be a devastating blow, particularly for people who enjoy playing the White Knight's role and thought they were fulfilling its demands rather well until then.

Finding out beforehand the number of people who have come and gone in the same slot, as well as the length of time each one lasted, is a worthwhile preventative. Also, it is useful to determine the firm's general rate of turnover in positions comparable to this one. These few bits of information may be hard to come by, but we always found them worth the effort; they provided a good indication of what employment there would be like for a particular member of our sample, once the honeymoon was over.

Picking the Best Boss

If the fourth item on the job-change checklist is the number of people who are simultaneously being hired at that level, question number five is: How much clout does one's prospective boss have in the firm? Not all bosses are alike in the degree of influence they exert in their companies, even if all the companies are the same size and each boss occupies the same relative position in the firm. For a variety of reasons, some are more influential than others. To people who are thinking of working for the person, that is no minor matter; the amount of power the boss wields directly affects the quantity that subordinates, at best, will have. It is very illuminating to study two bosses in two firms, comparable in almost every important way—except that one is more powerful than the other. We usually measure that by finding out (1) how much respect their co-workers have for them, both personally and professionally, and (2) how willing their co-workers are to get into disagreements and disputes with them, as opposed to a variety of other figures in the firm.

After examining a large number of such pairs, it became clear to us that the vast majority of people are more clever than they care to admit. They know whom to start trouble with, if they're so inclined, and whom to sidestep. Like animals in the jungle, they know where danger lurks, and they are usually quite adept at avoiding it.

It isn't the power of bosses per se that this study is concerned with, but the power of the individuals who work for them. Although they are rarely aware of it, how people are treated by co-workers and especially other superiors depends on two distinct sets of factors: their own personality and position, on the one hand, and their boss's authority, on the other. The people we studied tended to notice the former but not the latter at work, and therefore they held themselves personally responsible for any contemptuous or indifferent treatment they received at the hands of colleagues. Be that as it may, their everyday lives at the firm were made easier or more difficult, depending upon how well their bosses were regarded. More important than ordinary, everyday situations, however, were the extraordinary ones connected with the question of who was to be fired when a squeeze was on.

Selecting the right boss can make a major difference in what happens to a given employee during troubled times for the economy in general or the firm in particular. Financial pressures filter down but are always felt unequally. To run through the entire sequence: the country as a whole may be experiencing economic difficulties, yet certain industries are doing well while others are suffering. Even in an industry that is hurting, a handful of companies are faring better than the rest. Within any given company, some divisions and product lines are prospering at the same time that others are fading. Finally, certain executives at a firm have stronger positions there than others, even though the two appear at first glance to be on approximately the same plane. It is no easy matter to gauge precisely how powerful a particular executive is, since a person's fortunes may change over the years. Also, one executive's star may rise or fall depending upon the degree of influence exerted by other officials who subsequently join or leave the firm. Nevertheless, the issue is too important to ignore.

Business plays favorites; it has no choice but to do so. There is only a finite amount of assets and manpower to go around, and rarely does each member of the senior staff get exactly the same proportion as the others. In fact, carefully counting the quantities parceled out in a wide variety of firms makes it plain that democracy is almost never the guiding principle of distribution. Only a few directions can be pursued by each firm at any one time, thanks to the limited resources it has at its disposal. So the people who are a continuing source of direction, either because of the force of their personalities or the strength of their ideas, are of necessity valued more highly than others. All other things being equal, these are the best executives to work for: prime movers and/or well-embedded managers, people who aren't likely to be dismissed lightly, if at all.

It is worth noting that the people who voluntarily state during an interview that they are the real power at the firm are usually lying. If they merely fooled themselves with such fibs, that would be fine. But prospective employees who thereby become convinced that they will be working directly for a dynamo, someone who behind the scenes is nearly running the company, may soon find themselves not only disappointed, but also looking for yet another job.

Why? Because the desk-thumpers and blowhards, people who insist on bragging about how much weight they have at the firm to throw around, are simply too abrasive. Accomplishing something worthwhile takes the coordinated efforts of many individuals, each with an ego. Laying claim to too much authority, and therefore seeking a disproportionate share of the credit, offends the people whose cooperation is needed most. Executives who sit there tooting their own horns during an interview are a danger to themselves, and to anyone who believes them. They may boast about how secure their position is, yet paradoxically, once the boast is heard by others on the staff—and eventually it will be—the person's position instantly becomes more fragile. Particularly where power in the business world is concerned, those who have it rarely flaunt it. (This topic is so important, we will look at it from a different angle—namely, theirs—in Chapter Fourteen.) In short, ferreting out the quiet but well-entrenched figures at the firm proved very worthwhile over the years for those members of our sample who did so.

There is one limitation that every boss has to labor under. It has to do with the size of the company. Generally speaking, the larger the firm, the less power any person in it, chosen at random, will have. In a smaller firm, less fragmentation occurs. Wide areas of operation may be in the hands of just a few people, who both plan and carry out the company's affairs in this sphere.

Why is the size of the firm relevant to people who are attempting to assess a particular executive for whom they propose to work? Because this is one issue that leads to a substantial amount of frustration and distress among highly motivated men and women. They may want very much to convince the boss that a proposal they made is sound and should be acted upon, and the boss may even agree. Yet nothing is done. Whose fault is it? The majority of people we surveyed who have found themselves stuck in this situation unhesitatingly blame their bosses. "He doesn't really listen to anything I say," one remarked. A second commented, "She just nods her head, then I don't hear about it again." These two both reached the same angry conclusion. "Why did I bother telling him (or her) in the first place?"

The complaints overlook a crucial fact: in large companies power is atomized. The boss may think the proposal is first-rate yet not have enough muscle in the firm to implement it. Under the circumstances, sneering at him or her only makes matters worse. In many of the instances we monitored, the boss felt more frustrated about the defeat than the employee who'd proposed the idea to begin with. "It makes me realize how little my word really means around here," said a dejected VP.

Will the boss tell them about such troubles? We found that to be highly unlikely, for three reasons: first, it is an embarrassing admission to have to make, particuarly to a subordinate. Second, once subordinates come to think of the boss as weak and ineffectual, in most cases they stop trying as hard as they had previously to do their work well. Third, the idea may yet find its way into the firm's policies or products (as it eventually did in the case of the temporarily dejected but persistent VP), so an admission of failure would merely be premature.

In short, those who got the best, most powerful boss they could were better able to exploit the ideas that came to mind and opportunities that came their way. Nevertheless, it was essential for them to be prepared for a number of limitations that both they and their boss would have to live with, thanks to the size of the firm.

People Who Painted Themselves into Corners

The sixth and final item on the checklist is one that less than 2 percent of the people we surveyed thought seriously about before changing jobs: namely, what to do in case things don't go well. Number six on the list therefore is, What's my fallback position?

There is much to be said for the innocence and enthusiasm with which the workers we studied threw themselves into their new jobs. They were eager to do well, and they enjoyed learning about and becoming part of a different enterprise. We'd not want that to change. What does need to be modified, though, is the step prior to the plunge. "Look before you leap" may sound like a trite cliché, yet once the sentence is given teeth, as a result of specifying what to look for, it is an extremely useful guide. So after people have checked off the first five items, it is important for them to think about what they will do if the position they are considering turns out to be unsuitable for them or is erased—and to do it *before* they become too enamored of the firm to see it clearly anymore.

The thoughts will be more productive if they are made concrete. In the first place, work has an important geographical dimension. Reporters have a beat; salespeople, a territory; and most workers, an office. They are probably going to be located somewhere once they take the job. Key question: who else is around? That is, what other firms offering comparable kinds of employment are there in the vicinity? When the answer is none, the risk associated with working there rises. People who have gone to the sole employer of that type in the community, particularly if that is the kind of work they wanted most to do, have often unwittingly painted themselves into corners. Although it is potentially a quite self-destructive step, it is apparently a rather easy mistake to make. Roger subsequently told us that he hadn't given so much as a moment's thought to the question of other employers in the area offering similar types of work. As we saw, in his case there weren't any.

One of the chief differences between the work worlds of the nineteenth and twentieth centuries is the virtual disappearance of "the company town." This was a large employer, typically in textiles, steel, coal, or shipbuilding, that had a near monopoly, not so much on any particular kind of work, but on work in general. If people wanted to be paid for their efforts, as opposed to eating the fruits of their labors on the farm, they had no choice but to seek employment there. It is essential to realize that people who take a position now at the only employer in the area who offers work of the type they like have in some ways turned the clock back at least a hundred years.

The price to be paid for doing so may be high if things don't turn out as well as they had hoped. Interestingly, we found that they are likely, under the circumstances, to do the same thing people 130 years ago did: become more cautious and restrained, concerned about making waves. The difference is that people a century ago were aware that they'd have to act in a somewhat more orderly manner or not be able to land the job to begin with. Even today, the need to keep the job one has already landed, since there is none other nearby, usually has a parallel dampening effect.

Unfortunately, a policy among employees of nervously knuckling under, adopting a low profile, turned out to be correlated with an inability by both the firm *and* the people adopting that policy to remain competitive in the field. Neither the firm nor the individuals in it did well in the long run. This casts a revealing light on the growth of clusters of businesses around the United States, all in the same field; take, for instance, Silicon Valley near Palo Alto in California; the ring of high-tech companies on Route 128 around Boston; the concentration of communications and advertising companies in New York; and the large number of commodities firms in Chicago. At first glance one is tempted to suggest that having so many similar companies near one another merely makes all of them miserable. Also, it requires each to spend considerably more of its time trying to hold on to key employees. When people can simply go across the street and get an equally good job, perhaps for higher pay, they often will. Annual turnover rates in the 20 to 40 percent range become common.

Nevertheless, it is now clear that one of the crucial reasons for the success of these clusters is that they subtly encourage the *employees* working in them to take risks every bit as much as the *firms* in the area must in order to remain competitive. The boost to employee morale is evidenced not only in the more upbeat approach they take to their work (confident that a neighboring company will have them if their present one won't any longer), but also in the larger proportion who become entrepreneurs—adding yet another company in the same or an allied field to the cluster. The setting can clearly lead to an excess of self-confidence, yet the reverse is a more dangerous excess in what is rapidly becoming a global economy. The conclusion our study produced is that *employee timidity leads to mediocrity and the eventual stagnation of the firm.*

Ready for Trouble

Let us summarize the major points covered in this chapter, and see how Roger and Cynthia could have anticipated and overcome the troubles that seemed to emerge so suddenly. Our study turned up six items, which we call the job-change checklist, that significantly improve the chances that any given switch will be successful:

Number 1. An assessment of the economic and financial health of the *industry.*

Number 2. The same question about the *company.*

Number 3. The same question about the *division* that is of interest.

Number 4. The number of other people in comparable positions being hired at or about that time.

Number 5. The power and indispensability of one's immediate superior.

Number 6. The fallback positions that are available at nearby firms.

Roger knew that government expenditures on defense, as well as purchases by foreign nations, were increasing at the time. Yet he ignored the fact that at the company he'd selected, they were decreasing. He had failed to notice that this was a troubled firm, one which was not holding its own as a defense supplier. Number six, as well as number two, therefore, were the main sources of the difficulties that eventually beset him. What could he have done to prevent them? He himself gave the answer three months after taking his new job. "If I knew then what I know now, I'd have come here to begin with."

Cynthia had been indifferent above all to number three, and that caused her to accept an offer to join what even the firm's top officials later admitted was the most vulnerable division of the company. Plans had already been discussed to phase it out, unless someone came along who could breathe new life into it overnight. Number four was also a crucial oversight: a number of people had come and gone in the position Cynthia took, none being allowed to last long enough to prove his or her merit. (The range was four to 15 months for the four previous holders of the position.)

On the other hand, Cynthia paid careful attention to number five. Her immediate boss, the vice-president in charge of marketing (sales, actually, in this case), not only recruited her for the position, but also tried hard to make the project work. She correctly guessed that his position at the firm was secure and his word respected.

However, the rapidly eroding profit picture ultimately caused all other considerations to be swept aside. As Cynthia put it, five months after starting at another firm, "Sure, he knew the business cold and was well-respected. So what? When the place is going under, what difference does that make?" The moral here is clear: Items one through three on the checklist are more important than number five—a strong boss in a dying division may not be able to do much for talented subordinates at the firm.

CHAPTER
8

A Mass of Expertise— Plugged into Nothing

IN THE WESTERN world it is common for people to feel that they have absorbed a certain portion of their surroundings. "This is mine," they say offhandedly, "and so is this." Both at home and at work they can identify a long list of things that are theirs solely, jointly, or, like the desk in their office, theirs to use exclusively.

However, our study slowly but surely revealed that the reverse is even more the case. People are absorbed by their surroundings, particularly in the eyes of their customers. The first time the realization occurred to us was when we saw a restaurant owner whose face looked very familiar but, whom we couldn't identify, without the context of the restaurant in which we were used to seeing it. We began to wonder whether the members of our sample do the same thing with most of the people with whom they do business. If so, does that affect their sense of closeness to—and willingness to continue doing business with—the person after he or she moves to another location?

We didn't have to wait long to find out the answer.

"I'm More Than Just a Salesman"

Harry Carlson is a salesman, a good one. The line of electrical supplies that he was representing ("repping," as he always called it) was big. "We have something for everyone—well, almost everyone," he said, his smile disappearing. "Almost" wasn't good enough for Harry. He wanted a line broad enough to meet a wider variety of customer needs. "That's where the *real* money is," he said, suddenly coming to life. "Once you're in the door—that's the hard part, you know—you might as well sell 'em *everything*."

After 12 years with one firm, he moved to another that had a much more extensive product line. Not only was the company larger, it was more profitable as well. As Harry commented after being hired, "I got a free car, more T & E [travel and entertainment money], and a better office and secretary. Not bad, huh?"

So much for the good news. A hint that the new position would be anything but a bed of roses appeared during the second week. When Harry changed jobs, he did so under the assumption that the associations he had built up over 12 years of serving the same customers would remain intact. "Hell, I know some of those purchasing agents as well as I know my own family," he said, in a matter-of-fact tone, two months before leaving. It was an offhand remark, yet it was far more important than he realized at the time.

The network of business relationships he had developed over the years supported his picture of himself as a professional. "They all know me by now," he said proudly, and he was right. His dealings with customers were lubricated by the familiarity that sprang from an endless number of meetings and conversations, both in person and on the phone.

That, above all, had given him the confidence to move on, to feel that he had outgrown his current firm and needed to transfer to a new one. Although he was unaware of it, the web of friendly feelings between him and his customers was the ground upon which he stood.

Overnight, it vanished.

"What in God's name is going on?" Harry asked in utter disbelief when Rick, one of his longtime customers whom he considered a good friend, wouldn't give him an initial order at the new firm. "Why not?" Harry persisted. "This line is as good and *better* than the one you've been buying from me for years."

"I'm not denying that," Rick replied, trying to do his best to keep things calm. "It's just that we're not ready to make any drastic changes right now." Had the conversation with Rick been the only one of its kind, Harry would have let the matter pass. But much to his chagrin, the same thing happened with the vast majority of his other customers. "I don't understand it," Harry said in an anxious and depressed tone during the middle of the third week at the new firm. "I expected better treatment than this from these people. I've always given them 100 percent, done my best to service each and every account."

It was clear that he was taking it personally—and that's the whole point. Harry thought the relationships that had sprung up between himself and his customers over the years went beyond mere business. He frequently referred to himself proudly as being a sales rep, yet there was no doubt in his mind that his customers valued him as more than just a purveyor of a line of goods. "They *like* me," he commented repeatedly. "I can tell: they light up, they smile, when they see me."

Not anymore. Slowly but surely it began to dawn on him that he had been laboring for years under a dangerous illusion. His accounts did indeed like dealing with him, but it was now obvious that his firm and its product line, not Harry himself, had been what was primary, had been the glue that held the relationship between salesman and customer together. He'd been secondary all along. His income now suffered, and so did his ego. "I was embarrassed," he remarked a few years later. "Nothing like that had ever happened to me before."

"Where Is My Following?"

Harry may have felt excruciatingly alone during the transition period, but he wasn't. Other people elsewhere and in other professions were having remarkably similar experiences.

Sharon Daniels is a successful stockbroker in New York, employed by one of the nation's largest brokerage firms. Unlike Harry, who basically sells switches, panels, transformers, and other electrical products, Sharon handles people's money. The savings they've worked hard and long to accumulate are, in many instances, turned over to her to invest at her discretion in stocks and bonds for a hoped for profit. In most cases Sharon's customers retain possession of their money and stock certificates but look to her to advise them about what to buy or sell, and when.

She inevitably comes to know more about the personal finances of her clients than Harry does. And that is so even though Harry spends much of his time in face-to-face contact with customers, while Sharon spends most of her time on the phone. At times she finds that amusing. "You know, don't you, that I've never even *met* some of my best customers. We've only talked on the telephone. Others I've seen for a few minutes—once—when they stopped in to drop off or pick up a check."

The greater degree of closeness Sharon has to her customers' personal, financial lives is reflected in the conversations she has with them. Although she tries to keep the topic on stocks and bonds because, as she puts it, "I don't make any money talking about their kids," she knows the names of many of her customers' children. "When the kid gets into college," she said with a feigned air of resignation, "I get to hear about it. Sometimes they drone on and on about little Timmy getting into Yale." On the whole she doesn't mind it, though. "It's hand-holding," she commented, "and you have to do it no matter what line of work you're in."

After eight years with the same brokerage firm, Sharon decided to try another. "A friend of mine went there a year ago," she said, visibly excited about the prospect of a change. "His boss asked me to drop in for an interview a few weeks ago, and I did. He offered me a higher percentage on [the commisions from] my trades. It's an offer I can't refuse."

"Will you miss anything about this place?" we asked. "Not really," she replied, smiling. "The other firm advertises on TV too, so they're just as well known. But their commercials aren't as funny."

Once she made the switch, she discovered something else that wasn't funny: her customers refused to transfer their accounts. Sharon was shocked. One of the conditions her new firm agreed to before she would take the job was that she would receive extra secretarial assistance to notify all her old clients of her new affiliation. "They kept their part of the bargain," she said. "They were happy to; they wanted the customers to switch as much as I did."

Sharon called every last one of them; she even went so far as to send each person unsolicited an account-transfer or new-account form with their names filled in. Few signed it. At that point she began to sound like Harry, only angrier. "Lousy bastards, after all I've done for them, you wouldn't think they'd act this way." She began to mimic the responses they had given her. "No, Sharon, I like your old firm just fine. Maybe after you've been at the new firm for a while, we can talk." Then, in a different voice, that of an older woman who was a longtime account, "Well, I don't know, dear. I've gotten kind of used to [your previous office]."

The damage done to her pride was buried under the anger she generated during the first few months. Although the animosity that was her constant companion during the period helped in some ways, it couldn't mask the fact that her earnings had plummeted. "I felt *cornered*," she said, nearly a year later when the situation began to return to normal. "I had to start cold-calling [telephoning potential customers from local mailing lists and the phone book], as though I were a green kid who'd just broken into the business. I hated it."

When all is said and done, Sharon was even more hurt than Harry had been. Why? Harry at least was able to take refuge behind the differences between the two product lines he had sold. "I can't say I really blame them for sticking with the old [line]," he commented philosophically four months after making the switch. "It was pretty good stuff. I can't take that away from them."

Sharon, on the other hand, had no similarly convenient excuse. She kept referring to the mass defection of her following as an act of monumental disloyalty. "They betrayed me," she said bitterly, "right when I needed them most." There was no product line for her to hide behind, from which she could draw solace. "*I* was what they were buying," she said irritably, five months after the switch, "and they simply stopped buying, that's all."

Complaints That Sound Like Advice

Many people who witnessed one or another of these two instances concluded erroneously that there was a simple explanation for all the turmoil that surfaced: the old firms were preferred by customers to the new firms. In that sense, the switch was merely a mistake. "Why move to a different place," said one observer, "that won't stand the test when your customers compare them?"

The explanation that Harry and Sharon had switched to inferior firms sounds plausible enough, but if we examine one more example, we'll see the real explanation emerge.

Jack Sanders worked for 11 years for a major computer manufacturer, first as a service representative, then as a troubleshooter who handled a variety of customer complaints. His knowledge of the company's equipment had grown to the point that he could iron out even complex difficulties without effort.

Although much of the public thinks of computers as miracle machines, most of Jack's customers thought of them as a pain in the neck. "Every week there's something else wrong," said Mike, the owner of a mid-sized paper-and-printing-supplies firm. "If it's not one thing, it's another." Mike was a regular user of Jack's services, and he usually awaited his arrival impatiently. "When the computer is on the fritz, we don't function well around here. Inventory, billing, payroll, bookkeeping—it's all in this blinking box."

Mike and the majority of other accounts that Jack serviced started encouraging him to quit. They liked Jack but resented his firm. "Why don't you go out on your own," Mike repeatedly said to him. "That way you can keep whatever you collect [instead of having to split it with your company]." Another account told Jack, "You don't need them [your firm] anymore. They're just holding you back."

Jack was flattered by the steady stream of compliments and disturbed by the equally steady flow of criticism being aimed at his employer. He knew the company inside and out, and he was aware of the many mistakes that ordinarily were made. "We do a lot of things wrong," he said, disturbed at the thought. "It's a lucky thing the customers only know the half of it."

The half they did know was enough to make them persist, and Jack eventually took their advice and resigned. "I didn't want my boss to know that I was going into competition with him," Jack said squeamishly soon after quitting, "so I told him I was going to do some traveling and then develop some interesting new software."

He did neither. After spending two weeks setting up his own shop, getting a telephone, stationery, business cards, answering service, forms, and tools, he was ready. There was only one minor problem: his customers weren't.

Jack simply couldn't believe it. "You were one of the people who *told* me to do this," he protested to Mike. "You said you'd give me your business."

"No, I didn't," Mike said defensively. "I never promised you anything. I thought it was a good idea for you—not for me—and still do."

What puzzled Jack was that, as he put it, "I'm in a position to provide my customers with exactly the same service they got before." There was even a bonus now. "And it'll be cheaper too, half the price." Nevertheless, his customers weren't budging.

For the next three months Jack devoted himself diligently to seeking new business, but when he wasn't trying so hard to work up the enthusiasm needed to entice some accounts, the underlying depression showed. He was more demoralized than we have ever seen him, either before or since. "I felt deceived," he told us seven months later. Unlike Harry and Sharon, who wanted to quit and did so happily at the earliest good opportunity, Jack had resigned reluctantly. He was motivated to make the move by his customers, not greed.

Why, then, had his customers left him in the lurch? A common excuse was because he no longer had an organization behind him. Most, though, gave reasons that sounded quite similar to those offered by Harry's and Sharon's old customers. It is time to see what these three instances, as well as hundreds of others we could cite, have in common.

First, the job change by each of the three resulted in both an emotional and financial setback. Harry classified himself as one of the "walking wounded" for months after the switch, and looked it. Sharon's and Jack's marriages plainly suffered (Harry was single at the time). Sharon claimed that she largely lost interest in sex during the subsequent two-and-a-half months. "I went numb," she said at the end of that time. "Nothing he did turned me on." Jack became inaccessible at home to his wife—"Sullen," she called him—who attributed it to the fact that "he has to be nice now to those people all day [if he's going to get them to sign service contracts]. Before, he didn't have to be; he could just do his work."

One statistic impressively reveals the extent of the financial damage in each case. Harry lost 44 of 81—54 percent—of his active accounts. Sharon lost 47 of 76—62 percent—of hers. And Jack lost 48 of 55—

87 percent—of his best customers. It was a totally unexpected blow. Prior to the move, each had estimated that, as Jack put it, "Losses will be minimal, 5 to 10 percent at most." Sharon agreed, and Harry went so far as to state, "They'll *all* stick with me."

What's Out There, Columbus?

Our survey of the 212 customers (81 of Harry's, 76 of Sharon's, and 55 of Jack's) revealed some fascinating results. The principal reason most hadn't continued doing business with the three when they changed jobs had nothing to do with the relative merits of the old versus the new firms. Something more basic was responsible: inertia. "I guess it's like the song from 'My Fair Lady,'" one of Sharon's largest former accounts commented. "'I've grown accustomed to....'" Another said, "Here the paperwork is already in place, and everything runs smoothly." A third commented, "I like [the old firm]; I know them and they know me."

The second reason for maintaining the status quo has to do with fear. Apparently, when people change jobs, they become aliens to many of their prior business associates.

Torn from the setting in which they had come to be known, they seem different, perhaps even unrecognizable, to people who may have worked with them for years. The majority of the 212 customers questioned used one phrase more frequently than any other to describe what was happening to Harry, Sharon, and Jack: each of the three was embarking on an *adventure*. Jack felt a little of that, since he was going into business for himself, but the other two thought they were doing something more pedestrian in merely changing jobs. Nevertheless, the three had separated themselves from an important part of what their customers had long used to identify and mentally position them: their firms. Traditionally, men and women in small towns entered adult society, the only kind there was, only after marriage. Middle-aged bachelors and spinsters were anomalies, and were socially invisible. Things have changed on the surface and yet have remained the same. There are so many unmarried men and women now, so many who intend to stay that way, that another social hangtag was needed, and has been found. The firm for which one works provides an essential part of one's public definition. People who have no such affiliation, or have just adopted a new, unfamiliar one, become the modern version of the small-town unmarried of days gone by. They may think that in transferring from one firm to another, they have merely switched business labels. Actually, they have done something far more drastic. In the local world of the people with whom they previously did business, they give the appearance of having fallen off the edge of the world. They have become vagabonds; adventurers setting out on solo journeys to uncertain places.

The sudden transformation made Harry, Sharon, and Jack strange but intriguing to their old customers. Without wanting to become caught up in the voyage and its dangers, old business acquaintances were very interested in seeing where the three would end up, without having to end up there themselves. As one put it about Sharon, "It's her gamble, not mine. I've got a business to run." Said another about Jack, "Let's see where he lands, and if he lands on his feet. Then I'll decide what, if anything, I want to do."

In short, when people change jobs, their old customers may sincerely wish them well yet subconsciously come to fear them. To friends, they may still look the same after the switch; their customers know that something is missing and seek to protect themselves against the new uncertainty by imposing some distance. Not too much, however. As a pair of executives told Jack, "Now that you've set off on this journey, there's no telling what your ultimate destination might be, Columbus." The two were trying to remain aloof but still friendly. They didn't want to miss out on any treasures Jack might stumble upon.

No One Is Immune

The mass abandonment by customers at job-change time may seem a hazard that afflicts primarily people in sales. That at least is the tentative conclusion we had reached after examining the first few dozen cases. Further investigation proved that we were mistaken. It affects almost everyone who works.

One of the delightful things about doing long-term research is that a pattern which emerges in one area may suddenly be seen to be applicable to another, though at first glance they seem wholly different. We had spent almost four years monitoring the surprisingly severe setbacks sustained by many people in sales-related positions as a result of job changes before we realized that the same thing might apply to other occupations. As we are about to see, the distressing experiences of a hardworking physician made us aware that the public's lethargic and phobic reactions affect, in varying degrees, all professionals who move.

Francine Parker is a pediatrician. "I was pretty sure that's what I wanted to be even before I graduated from college," she recently remarked. By the time she began clinical courses in the third year of medical school, any doubts she still had about this specialty had vanished. Her grades were excellent. "Maybe it's easier for me to remember the material," she commented modestly at the time, "because I can envision myself actually *using* it."

Once she had finished a three-year pediatric residency at a major metropolitan hospital, Fran joined forces with an older pediatrician with a well-established practice. "I'm 56," he told her during the initial interview, "and I better start thinking about someone to replace me when I retire."

She liked the fact that she was kept busy straight through the day. "There's never a dull moment around here," she said with a weary grin, two months after she began. "Any complaints?" we asked her. "Only one," she replied. "The cases I see now are almost never as serious as the ones I saw night and day in the hospital. They're not as demanding [medically], and I worry about getting a little rusty."

By the fourth month on the job, she had something else to worry about as well. Conditions between Fran and her boss were rapidly beginning to deteriorate. "He puts me down a lot lately," she said, her patience becoming frayed. The 24-year difference between their ages was showing up in an increasing number of disputes betwen them about what to do first. "My education is more modern," she stated firmly. "I'm more up-to-date." A personality clash, in addition to procedural arguments, soon made the situation untenable, and Fran quit. "I can't—I won't—work for anyone else," she said.

She opened her own office a few months later, and within three years she had a decent-sized practice. Other doctors began referring patients to her, and "satisfied patients also send their friends," she added. By the sixth year she had all the business she could handle, and then some. These were, by Fran's own estimation at the time, the happiest years of her life. She married and had a family of her own: two boys.

For two more years she remained at the same location, then decided to move. "We need more space [for living], and it'd be nice to have the office be nearer the house." She got her wish. The office wound up being attached to their new residence, which was on the other side of town. "It's exactly what I hoped for," she said cheerfully.

She must have been hoping for a catastrophe then because, much to her surprise, that's what the move produced. Most of her patients abruptly stopped coming. Her business dropped to a fraction of what it had been only a month previously. "It's not fair," she said, holding back her tears. "It's just not right. I didn't move to another city, you know." It was 11:00 A.M. and her office was empty. "It's never been like this," she said, staring off into space.

No companies were involved here. Fran was self-employed before the move and was still self-employed after it. She hadn't changed jobs, merely locations, but the reaction of her patients was similar in most respects to that which Harry, Sharon, and Jack got from their old customers. "Seeing her isn't convenient for me anymore," said one, mildly annoyed that the move had taken place at all. Commented a second, "I'm not going to lug my kids to the middle of nowhere." As far as they were concerned, Fran might as well have fallen off the edge of the planet.

As we examined case after case, it became quite clear that what happens to people in sales who change jobs can happen just as easily to self-employed professionals who change locations.

No one makes such a move expecting it to result in a *decrease* in business. Yet it usually does, and each person thinks that he or she alone has suffered a humiliating setback for doing the very thing that helped other people prosper. The key question that needs to be answered at this point is: Who gets hit hardest, and who is the least affected, by changes in job, affiliation, or location?

Do You Know Where Your Lawyer Is?

There is a tie for first place. Two types of professionals usually are little affected by a location or job change: accountants and attorneys. When we speak of the "retention rate," we mean the proportion of old customers who continue to deal with the person at his or her new place of business as though nothing had happened. Lawyers and accountants have the highest retention rates of any professions in the United States.

Typical comments were, "Yes, I'm aware that my lawyer moved [to a different part of town]. So what? Does that mean he's a less good lawyer now?" And, "Of course I'll stay with the same accountant [even though he has moved]. I don't think the change of address makes any difference."

The reason the clients of these professionals are generally unconcerned about moves is very interesting. Unlike physicians, let's say, who dispense remedies and suggestions directly to their patients, accountants and lawyers only find out details from their clients. Then, armed with that information, they proceed to render the real service for which they were hired. Namely, they act as intermediaries between the person and the IRS (in the case of accountants) or between the client and another person or firm (in the case of attorneys).

In fact, the most important actions an accountant or lawyer undertakes on a client's behalf occur *after* any meetings with the client. The meeting is merely a prelude to the serious business to follow, when the client isn't present.

That is very different from what happens with doctors. The mothers who take their children to see Fran get all the medicine (or prescriptions for it) and advice they need, right then and there. The main interchange occurs between doctor and patient. On the other hand, lawyers and accountants interact—on their client's behalf, primarily with someone else.

Obviously, then, where they are located isn't all that important, especially if there is a good reason why they are not centrally located. As one client put it, "Fancy midtown offices only add to the bill and are more for [my lawyer's] convenience than mine." Usually they are representing a client's interests against those of a bureaucratic legal or financial entity somewhere; for instance, in a courthouse near city hall or by mail with an income tax agency in the state capital. As long as they handle the written and verbal parts of their jobs well, they could be located anywhere as far as their clients are concerned, even near city hall or the state capital. It should therefore come as no surprise that retention rates of over 90 percent are common when a move is made by a self-employed attorney or accountant, or one working for a small firm. Few other professionals are so lucky.

Odd as it may sound, architects and interior decorators are two more of the lucky groups. Preliminary conversations with the client are necessary before they can get on to the real task at hand: working on the apartment, house or office. Like lawyers and accountants, they are one's representatives against, in this case, an inanimate adversary (wood, walls, paint, and furniture).

The group's retention rates, which are only slightly less lofty than those of accountants and attorneys, therefore make sense. In fact, there is an amusing twist here: nearly 17 percent of the more than 300 clients we surveyed couldn't tell us where their decorator had his or her office. "All I have is a phone number," a wealthy woman told us with a giddy laugh. "When I call it—he's never there—I leave a message and he calls me back." In that case, a change of location couldn't possibly have cost the decorator any business. By way of contrast, every client we surveyed of the lawyers and accountants in our sample knew approximately where the professional's office was located.

Location or job changes by psychotherapists produced unexpectedly high retention rates, much higher for instance than those experienced by pediatricians. Since psychotherapists at first glance would appear to have more in common with physicians than with architects, that was a surprise even in light of the more personal nature of the relationship. The reason turned out to be a straightforward one. "I don't *want* my shrink to be my next-door neighbor," was a typical comment. "It would make me uncomfortable to run into him [or her] in the supermarket." So in many instances psychotherapists were deliberately chosen from a conveniently distant part of town in the first place.

"How far is far enough?" we asked more than 1,000 patients. The consensus view was that three-fourths of a mile in an urban setting was sufficient. In suburban settings, two miles was deemed the minimal comfortable distance. (Many people in rural settings thus didn't go to psychotherapists, although they wanted to. The therapist would have had to be in the next small town to be acceptable—and either there wasn't one there or else it was too far away to be convenient for regular two- or three-times-a-week trips.)

Changes in job, affiliation, or location by psychologists or psychiatrists are therefore likely to have only a modest impact on their patient load. As it turns out, they were chosen in part because they were "out there, somewhere" to begin with; being out there, somewhere else normally causes little disruption.

Portable Accounts

Let us summarize what we've discovered thus far, together with the data gathered from a number of other professions.

Table 2: Retention Rates

	Percent
Lawyers and Accountants	91
Architects and Interior Decorators	87
Psychologists and Psychiatrists	80
Doctors and Dentists (range: cardiologists, 81, to pediatricians, 49)	69
Salespeople (range: apparel and textile, 90, to auto, 3)	48
Consultants (range: medical, 57, to computer, 12)	37
Hairdressers	11
Book Editors	4
Advertising	4
Bakers	2
Dry Cleaners	1
Pharmacists	0

Many of the numbers may seem sufficiently high for people in that particular field not to have to worry about a move, but they do. An abrupt loss of 30 to 40 percent is still a sizable blow. And often the percentage is much higher: Harry, Sharon, Jack, and Fran lost an average of nearly 60 percent of their customers overnight.

The one-two punch to the professional's emotions and finances can be devastating. Rena Stevens was a tall, blond hairdresser whose customers adored her. "She's terrific," commented one regular. "She does exactly what I want her to do, though I never know exactly what I want her to do." The following she developed over a seven-year period grew to the point where a move, as she put it, "to a less dingy and tacky place" appeared appropriate. Quietly, she let all her regulars know that she would soon switch, and they in turn assured her that they'd be right behind her.

The strong reassurance they gave her played a major role in the negotiation with the salon to which she intended to transfer. "I've got plenty of business," she told the owner. However, once she quit and made the switch, the business quickly evaporated. Although she was now only 12 blocks (five-eighths of a mile) from her former location, a mere 6 percent, three of approximately 50, showed up in the next three months.

The owner of the salon began badgering and even mocking her. "I thought you had *many* loyal fans." And, "You certainly know how to exaggerate, don't you?" On a spring day that seemed no different than any other to her co-workers, four and a half months after starting at the new place, Rena, at 47, went home early, complaining about a headache, and took her own life. She left a note addressed to no one in particular that simply said, "I'm sorry."

Bruce Shaw, an ad agency executive, had reason to believe that his expectations about "portable accounts," as he labeled them, were every bit as realistic as Rena's. Yet of 23 accounts he had handled, nine of whom he claimed to be on intimate terms with, not one moved with him when he switched to another, considerably smaller, firm. It took a while for Bruce to realize how distorted his thinking had been. "I must have been *crazy* to believe they would," he said six months later. "I'm such a horse's ass. I'm lucky to still have my job. I shot my mouth off when I arrived."

We surveyed officials responsible for ad agency selection at all 23 firms, without in any way referring to Bruce. More than half stated bluntly that size was a major factor in their initial choice of and decision to stay with Bruce's old firm. The conclusion to be drawn from this and a wide variety of other examples we examined is that people at a large firm who expect to take accounts with them to a smaller outfit, one with "a more personal and homey atmosphere," as Bruce described it, should think again. That is much less likely to occur than most imagine.

The vice-president in charge of advertising at the firm Bruce was most confident of snaring of the 23 told us, "We have to be *independent* of employee defections [at ad agencies]. In a small shop, a key figure leaves and the place falls apart. We can't allow that. With a large place, it's much less of a problem. There is always a warm, breathing body on staff to fill in [for the person who quit]."

What Bruce failed to realize was that many companies deliberately *choose* to do business with the bigger legal and accounting firms or advertising agencies. Besides access to a broader range of specialized skills, such a choice gives them a degree of protection small firms can't provide. The "friendly and cozy atmosphere" may be nice, but it isn't sufficient to offset the higher degree of risk it exposes clients to, as the VP quoted above put it, if key employees defect or die. Bruce, it had become clear, never stood a chance of landing any of the accounts.

Lawyers leaving large law firms typically find themselves in the same situation as Bruce: they go, the clients stay. To think otherwise is perilous. Most major corporations prefer not to have their legal affairs handled by a one- or two-man firm. Some critics claim that this is because "it looks better on their annual reports to have big names." Perhaps, but our study indicates that protection as well as prestige is on the clients' minds. Either way the result is the same: although lawyers and accountants generally have high retention rates, factors connected with the size of the firm can drastically reduce the rates of those who quit.

For instance, when Vic Braden decided to resign from one of the nation's largest law firms and open his own office, he thought he could take two corporate clients with him. "That would have been enough to carry me," he said. On the surface at least, the two accounts had sound reasons for transferring their business to Vic at his new firm. And he was very optimistic about their doing just that. In his words, "I was the one who personally managed their work [at the old firm]. No one besides me knew very much about their day-to-day requirements." Nevertheless, they stayed.

Retention rate for this lawyer during this job change: zero. The result: a period of panic. Five hard years later, Vic needed larger quarters for his expanding staff (6) and rapidly growing number of clients (31). He moved to an entirely different part of town, four miles from his then-present site, basically for aesthetic reasons ("I like the area"). Retention rate: 100 percent.

The first move, when he went into business for himself, caused him many weeks of sleeplessness, tension, and depression. "I won't ever forget how awful it was," he recently commented. "I honestly thought I'd starve. I didn't know *where* on earth I'd scrape up some business." The second move, even though it was much more time-consuming and complicated physically, produced nothing but smiles. "I don't mean to keep on grinning," Vic said in the midst of it. "I'm just very happy."

In the Grip of a Developing Squeeze

People who are thinking seriously about quitting their present positions and taking jobs at smaller companies should keep foremost in mind their clients' preferences about the size of the firms with which they like to deal. The preferences can play a crucial role in one's subsequent success or failure. Needless to say, size isn't merely a one-way street; there is traffic in the other direction as well. Bruce and Vic were temporarily trampled by accounts running toward large advertising and law firms. But there are many clients who find the fees charged by the bigger legal and accounting firms well beyond their reach. "We do it cheaper," said Vic proudly, and his booming business signifies that many customers agree.

Money isn't the only thing that motivates people to seek a smaller firm to handle their business. In at least one profession, publishing, the writers we surveyed told us that they were "deathly afraid of getting lost in the shuffle at the larger houses." Yet writers want what they've written to be read—and large firms usually have better marketing and distribution than smaller ones. The interplay of these opposing forces has a major impact on the business life of both editors and authors.

To see why, we need to look at a few statistics about book editors which help bring the picture into sharper focus. The first thing to note is that this is a field with turnover rates that are much higher than most people imagine. Of 162 editors whose movements we monitored during the seven-year period from 1977 to 1984, only 44—27 percent—were still at the same firm as the one they were at when the period began. We intentionally chose editors whose minimum age in 1977 was 30 or more, anticipating that they'd be over the jumping-around period that is usually part of initial positioning by junior members of any profession. However, job changes actually increased in frequency (by 16 percent) in the over–30 group, and they increased again (by 11 percent) in those over 42.

Turnover rates that high are usually associated with fields undergoing very rapid growth; for instance, high-technology firms, or else minimum-wage establishments such as the fast-food outfits Burger King and McDonald's. Yet the period under review was one of relatively slow growth for the publishing industry. Retention rates for book editors—by which we mean the proportion of authors the editor was able to take with him or her when transferring—were a surprisingly low 4 percent. (Since authors were under contract for their current book to the house, not the editor, they had to stay when the editor left. So we are referring here to the author's next book.)[1]

What effect does that have on the business life of an editor? Just this: editors who don't have the authors they need have to find them, and that means a disproportionate amount of time spent on the acquisition trail, reading manuscripts submitted by authors they don't know, rather than editing manuscripts by authors with whom they are already familiar and who are under contract. Where is the crisis, then, for editors? It's a nearly constant one. "Everybody in this business is running scared," the chief of a major publishing house told us in confidence. Sure enough, four months after making the comment, he was fired. "Everyone's track record here is poor," he had said.

As with so many other professions, all the underlying pressures rise to the surface when an editor changes jobs. That is usually not immediately evident, since there is a honeymoon period that typically lasts a few months. "They told me to take it slow and easy at first, and get to know the place," Alan Tanner, a 41-year-old senior editor, commented a few days after switching to a different house. Far from seeing himself as in the grip of a developing squeeze, Alan was thrilled at the opportunity the job change gave him, as he put it, "to leave my mistakes behind me." He was referring to the fact that most of the manuscripts he had acquired in the past had failed to earn back even the advance that was paid for them. That bothered Alan more than he cared to admit and, for the moment, made him glad that his retention rate was close to zero.

The initial sense of relief was soon replaced by feelings that were less pleasurable. "It's back to the same old grind," he said four months after starting. "I thought it would be different here, if you know what I mean, but it really isn't." Alan was alarmed to discover that his expectations of substantial improvement at the new place wouldn't—indeed, couldn't—be fulfilled. The pivotal and inescapable fact of his life as an editor was once again reasserting itself. "Good, commercial unknowns are *very* hard to find; I have to wade through hundreds of manuscripts and proposals to come up with even one that's just so-so," he said glumly. And on the other hand, "Authors who are good

---

[1] See L.A. Coser et al., *Books: The Culture and Commerce of Publishing* (New York: Basic Books, 1982) and W.W. Powell, *Getting into Print: The Decision Making Process in Scholarly Publishing* (Chicago: University of Chicago Press, 1982).

and well-known are *very* expensive; I don't get them because I can't afford them."

He had accurately sensed what was coming, for during the next three years only two of the 28 properties he had acquired made money. "And not that much, either," he added. "Maybe I should be looking for another job—before they ask me to." Bouncing back and forth between anxious hopes and jarring disappointments, Alan was clearly holding himself responsible for a situation that wasn't of his own making. Instead it was a chronic condition that afflicted the entire industry during a prolonged slow-growth period.

In short, the predictable crisis connected with job changes in publishing may be slower to emerge than in other fields. However, the low retention rate nearly guarantees that it will eventually appear, not too long (average time: two and a half years) after each move.

A Floating Mass of Expertise

To summarize the most important points covered in this chapter; the years one spends on the job produce a growing web of working relationships, as well as expanded knowledge of the field. While it may be exciting to suddenly appreciate the fact that one knows 300 to 800 people in the field and exchanges hellos with dozens of them daily, the relationships are fruitful in a business sense primarily because each person represents a particular firm or area of professional skill. A job change ruptures established working relationships. Leaving one firm and going to another is more of a disruption than has previously been recognized. Done repeatedly, there is a danger that the person will become a mass of expertise that is plugged into nothing substantial, a friendly but basically unproductive fop in his field.

We like to think of ourselves as sophisticated inhabitants of a global village now—Spaceship Earth, "every day the world grows a little smaller," and all that. Yet the fact remains that the world we actually live in, and know from daily experience, is limited and local. An enormous amount happens elsewhere that we don't, and won't, ever hear about. Primitive psychological mechanisms still operate to make people who leave our local world appear to have become more unpredictable, and that means predictable crises may be taking shape on their horizons.

The basis for this particular crisis is always the same: people come to feel that they have absorbed a part of their business surroundings. As their job-related skills increase, so does their sense of ownership. Quietly they lay claim not just to the greater knowledge in their own brains, but also to the firm's assets. If that led them merely to pocket a few office supplies as they were leaving, a common occurrence and usually done self-righteously, the damage would be minimal. Unfortunately, they also feel entitled to some and perhaps most of the firm's customers.

Trouble arises quickly as a consequence of the expectations those who are leaving build up in their own minds and, even worse, in the minds of their prospective employers. Since many are quitting to start their own firms, they deceive themselves drastically about how large an already existing customer base they will have initially. The entrepreneur's life is hard enough, and the failure rate high enough (more than four out of five new ventures by members of our sample failed in their first four years); the additional emotional burden connected with images of customers following a charismatic Pied Piper can result in depression, psychosomatic illness, and suicide. The rejection may have been wholly imaginary, due instead primarily to customer laziness, but it is taken personally nonetheless.

Many of the nation's great fortunes have been amassed by people who left a large firm with the expertise they had developed and started a fledgling outfit of their own. These firms, and the contributions they have made to the nation's economic health and international competitiveness, deserve to be encouraged. Nothing we have stated here should be taken as critical of that effort. However, *one needs to be grimly realistic about one's ability to walk off with the firm's customers, even if one had a major hand in bringing them to the firm in the first place. And the larger the firm, the more essential the realism.* It was revealing to see that those members of our sample who founded firms during recessions were significantly more likely to have them succeed than those who started them when the economy was near or at the top of the business cycle. The rampant optimism produced by the rapidly expanding economy left those who started firms during the boom poorly prepared psychologically to handle any setbacks. Inevitably, there were some.

CHAPTER
9

Easing the Transition

DURING A SUSTAINED period of rapid growth in the economy, it is common for people to expand their financial goals. The pot of gold at the end of the rainbow seems more attainable, and many find it only natural to reach for it.

During slow- or no-growth periods for the economy as a whole or a specific industry, a profound transformation typically takes place. People become significantly more preoccupied with holding on to what they've already achieved. Expansion if possible, but conservation as well, start to guide their plans. As we've seen in the previous chapter, job changes disrupt established working relationships and often make it difficult for workers to keep what they have. However, there is another factor operating here: in many cases people lose what they had because others grab it.

Defending One's Good Name

When we asked Harry, the electrical-products salesman we met in the last chapter, why his business base dropped by 56 percent after his job change, he had a ready reply. "The guys at [my old firm] have been bad-mouthing me to my accounts something fierce. They must be. Why else would my customers turn on me like this?" Sharon was even more certain that she knew the explanation for "the despicable behavior, the monumental disloyalty," as she put it of her accounts, 62 percent of whom abruptly stopped doing business with her when she switched stockbrokerage firms. "You've got to be kidding, if you think I don't know why they stopped. I got knifed, that's why. Rumors, innuendo—it was easy [for them] to destroy the good reputation I had."

Jack had a similar certainty about what had caused him to lose 87 percent of his customers, who suddenly no longer needed his help with their computer problems. "I walked out on my old firm," he said slowly and thoughtfully. "The bigwigs there aren't going to say anything good about me. Why should they? It only makes them look bad." Jack's words are closest to what the majority of people we monitored who've been harmed by job changes give as an explanation. Condensing the replies of workers in a wide variety of fields, the typical response consists of two parts.

First, "I would have retained all or most of those accounts had someone not interfered and prevented it. The clients liked me, of that much I'm sure."

Second, "The someone who interfered was my old boss and maybe others from my old firm who had an ax to grind. There were a few unsettled scores, bad feelings, in the air there. My customers loved me, but my co-workers—well, that's another matter. Some of them are very jealous people."

We have gone to great lengths to check on the accuracy of the explanations offered by Harry, Sharon, and Jack, as well as many others who have experienced similar setbacks. In a way it would have been comforting to find that they had been the target of slanderous, character assassination campaigns soon after changing jobs. Had that been the case, a strategy aimed at neutralizing the critical comments made behind their backs could have been constructed. The enemy would have been plainly visible, and his maliciousness reason enough to do something about him. A counterattack, to clear one's name if nothing else, might have been deemed to be well worth the trouble.

Unfortunately the facts rarely fit this picture of good-versus-bad guys, in which banishing the baddies isn't the goal of the good guys so much as defending their own good name is. We did encounter a number of instances in which employees who had left became the subjects of steady streams of abusive comments by those who stayed. And there were indeed cases in which the person's immediate superior both initiated and orchestrated the hostile remarks. Nevertheless, it is easy to lose perspective on this matter unless a few things are kept in mind about derogatory words uttered behind someone's back. To begin with, they take place while the person is still there, not only after he or she has left to go to another firm. In fact, many more disparaging statements are voiced *during* the time the person is employed at the firm than afterwards. Rivalries often spring up between co-workers, and the closer (either in location or function) the two are, the more bitter the rivalry. Personality clashes are also common; certain pairs of workers fit together about as well as gasoline and a match.

Distance therefore might be expected to cool the conflict, especially if it is a permanent separation as a result of a resignation or dismissal. To make certain that that is what usually happens, we catalogued the comments made by co-workers both before and after Harry, Sharon, and Jack left their old jobs. Not everyone who worked with them loved them, as they well knew. But we succeeded in each case in finding the person or persons who disliked each one the most. We were curious to know what those who had a distinctly negative, as well as those with a more neutral, opinion of the three would later say.

As it turns out, once the three left, the attitudes of co-workers quickly changed. Not only was the decrease in hostility larger than we anticipated, it occurred in a very uneven manner: the neutral remained neutral, the mildly hostile became moderately less so, while the very hostile became much less so. In short, the more a co-worker of yours detests you, the more likely it is that the person will forget about you and erase the animosity shortly after you have left. For instance, six weeks after Jack quit, we bluntly asked Gary, the co-worker who disliked Jack the most, "How come you aren't still making [vicious] jokes about Jack?" He paused a moment and said, "I don't know. I hadn't realized I'd stopped. I guess it's because he might as well have vanished into thin air."

Finding Gary in the first place wasn't hard. When he and Jack were still working together, he made no secret of his enmity. Gary openly resented the star status that Jack had attained at the firm, and he tried repeatedly to make others equally resentful. The goading worked. Gary often acted as cheerleader in a "humorous," as he always insisted, tirade when Jack wasn't around. Within a month of Jack's departure, the issue of which of the two was the best in the department, Gary or Jack, stopped mattering. Gary had won, by default. The attacks completely ceased. Out of sight, out of mind.

That happened in virtually every other case we examined. It was apparent that the explanations offered by Harry, Sharon, Jack and others in their position were soothingly self-serving but wrong. What, then, accounted for the undeniably sudden drop in business each had sustained?

Out of Sight, Out of Mind

When people change jobs, the world they leave behind them doesn't bleed endlessly. It closes its wound, either by finding a makeshift stand-in on the staff to take their place or by hiring someone new to fill the now vacant slot. For example, unknown to Sharon, the very day after she left, someone else was sending a letter to all her accounts. Far from attacking her, it was nothing if not polite. Actually the letter was fairly standard and merely served to introduce Brenda, an older woman at the firm whom Sharon liked. "I'll be your new account executive," it said, "and can be of assistance in many ways." The letter went on to list the wide variety of services the firm currently offered: everything from buying and selling stocks, bonds, options, and futures, to real estate, stamps, coins, precious metals, credit cards, tax shelters, and mutual and money-market funds.

When Sharon was shown the letter six months later, she was livid. "It looks like bragging to me," she commented angrily. She felt that it was hinting that many of the services had become available to the firm's customers only after Sharon's departure. "I could have supplied every one of those services [while I was still there], but not everyone needs them, you know."

The reader may be wondering why it is worthwhile for us to discuss what a previous employer does once someone leaves. At first glance, the matter might seem irrelevant. However, there is a pressing reason to study the subject carefully, since the actions taken by the old firm can have a drastic impact on what happens to the person who is now at the new one. And the effect is exerted in a much more indirect manner than has previously been thought.

The letters Brenda sent out were followed a few weeks later by phone calls. The combination of customer inertia, their familiarity and comfort with the old firm, and Brenda's intelligent and pleasant manner were making her efforts more fruitful than she had assumed they would be. Nevertheless, she was taking nothing for granted, and she was using a very clever approach.

Scanning the type of activity in each account, she made certain to mention to each customer a new product or service that stood a good chance of being of interest. "I want to offer them something enticing," she said. To a 31-year-old production manager whose record of transactions clearly indicated that he liked playing "high fliers," volatile issues primarily in the electronics field, she suggested a new name in their first phone conversation. "I think this stock is beginning to come alive," she said enthusiastically. "It has a very good track record."

"Oh, yeah?" he replied, obviously warming to the subject. "Send me more information on it, if you have any." She did, putting it in the mail that day. Less than three weeks later he bought over 1,000 shares. Her quietly aggressive style was paying off in two ways. Not only did she prevent the bulk of Sharon's old customers from switching to the new firm, but approximately one-third of the accounts eventually did more business with her than they had done with Sharon. Brenda made an offhand remark about the matter that was insightful. "She softened them up for me. I'd be a fool not to take advantage of it. They're not going to just sit there [and make no transactions]."

The pattern seen here was encountered in case after case. What happened to Sharon happened to others as well. One person left a firm, another moved in to take his or her place. Then the real problem began. The result in nearly every instance was a measurable decrease in the amount of business done with prior customers by the person who departed. As we've seen, that was often experienced as a defeat, right in the middle of the victory of landing and starting at a new job. An explanation was needed for the setback by the person who was transferring, and it was found. "I've been stabbed in the back."

Perhaps, but highly unlikely. We don't wish to make light in any way of the anger, upset, and depression these people experienced precisely at a time when, on the surface anyway, they had good reason to be elated. Nevertheless, the fact remains that they hadn't been rejected or abandoned by the loyal. They'd merely been forgotten. Even the co-workers who despised them had a totally different outlook. Where hatred once prevailed, indifference now reigned, and the more intense the animosity, the more abruptly it disappeared. In some cases enemies even became friends, once the two were no longer accidentally pitted against one another at the same firm.

As it turns out, the basic three-part reason for the business, and hence emotional, misfortune people may well suffer as a result of a job change is this:

(1) Their old customers are lazy.

(2) Their old firm is familiar.

(3) Their old firm is not lazy. It wants—it needs—the business that once was a joint possession of the firm and the people who have left. Employees often state that the association between themselves and their employer is a collaboration of equals. If anything, in their view the customers they have are more theirs than the firm's, so they are the primary partner in the relationship. However, whether we like it or not, we live in a business society, one in which companies have the right to do anything that is legal to maintain their existence. Since they are the source of jobs this country sorely needs, they, not the individual employee, are usually considered the dominant partner in any tug-of-war that develops and ends up in court.

Without even thinking about it, people still at the firm will therefore move to lay claim to what they see as theirs, not the property of someone who has left. The person may take it personally, perhaps deeply so, but it isn't meant that way. In the vast majority of instances, the executives there bear that person no ill will now, even if they once did. In fact, they aren't at all likely to be thinking about the departed employee, positively or negatively, when making their plans. Their goal is a simple one. They want those accounts, and although they probably couldn't spell out the reasons why they feel so justified in doing so, they will pursue them with determination.

"Without Me, They're Nothing"

When business conditions aren't good, the situation worsens. That is, when the nation's economy or a particular industry is displaying little or no growth, the pressures involved here magnify. A firm that lets an increasing number of accounts wander off, carried away by a succession of employees that leave, will soon be teetering on the brink even in the best of times. On the other hand, when the economy is less than robust, the firm is compelled to take a more enterprising stance right from the start if it is to survive.

Keep in mind that it doesn't want just any old account of an employee who is no longer there. Instead, the ones with which the person had done the most business are the ones it wants most to retain. There is trouble brewing, in that case. The economic and psychological forces at work here are about to collide in a particularly painful way because the clients with whom the ex-employee did the most business are usually the ones of whom he or she is fondest. They are the accounts whose sudden indifference is likely to be experienced as a shocking rejection.

It is irrelevant whether the harmony between, for instance, Sharon's personality and her high-volume accounts came first—that that was what led to a greater-than-expected quantity of business—or whether the quantity of business she was doing with them was large and *that* made her feel closer to them. All that matters is that she did indeed become emotionally attached to those accounts. Her sense of herself as a competent professional rested at the time on their willingness to do business with her. Unfortunately, what her old firm wanted most was the very group of customers to whom she had come to feel closest.

It is hardly surprising that so many workers who have quit one job and gone on to another, only to lose the accounts that made the work satisfying to begin with, suffer emotionally as well as financially. They accurately state that something precious, and not merely monetary, has been torn from them. Be that as it may, their old firms can almost certainly be counted upon to try seizing old customers, oblivious to the attachments, the feelings of ex-employees. It does so because it really is oblivious to those feelings. Brenda isn't cruel. She wasn't attempting to crush Sharon's psychological world. "I'm just trying to make a living," she said plainly, "and not doing all that well, either." But Sharon was crushed anyway. She wasn't the only one: the outcome was the same in a distressingly large proportion of the cases we examined.

What can we learn from this predictable crisis? Two things, one of which gives rise to the problem in the first place, the other of which allows us to prevent it from occurring. First, our illusions are at times a menace to our future well-being. For instance, we flatter ourselves greatly to think that when we die, the world will be stunned. Of course, we don't actually believe that; perhaps it would be more accurate to say that we'd merely like it to happen, like to have everyone grieve for us when we go.

The business version of that belief isn't quite so harmless. In fact, it is capable of doing substantial damage. For us to be secretly of the opinion that when we leave our firm, it will completely fall apart is understandable. We want to matter, if we're going to participate. And once we're participating actively, we want our contribution to be important. In a flash, we conclude that we matter tremendously. Naturally, then, our departure will create havoc. But there is really only one way to make that happen: found our own firms, and keep them small, so small that they can't function without us. Then our permanent (maybe even temporary) absence will indeed cause upheaval and the collapse of the firm.

However, once a company attains a certain size, it begins to have a life of its own. There are certainly key figures within it, managing its everyday operations and planning its tomorrows. Although they are indispensable, they are not irreplaceable—that is, they have to be there, but if they aren't, others will be found to take their place. (The distinction may be clearer if one thinks about the police in one's town.) Those who are in a supervisory capacity can most readily be forgiven for thinking that the company would founder without them.

Be that as it may, the people employed at the firm have a vested interest in keeping it running. They need money to live. If they aren't going to steal or be given it, they will have to earn it. Also, they are acquainted with the firm's style of operations and, while they no doubt have their share of complaints, they know and like the company well enough to have stayed. A key employee who quits and expects the firm to distintegrate as a result is usually in for a big surprise.

It is an extraordinary sight to see firm after firm be severely rattled by—but survive—the death, dismissal, or resignation of top executives. The healing, the regeneration power of companies in an environment that encourages their existence (though not their unlimited profitability) is remarkable.

The economic successes scored by Japan in the 1960s and 1970s, particularly in automobiles, consumer electronics, and semiconductors, produced a flood of books and articles in the nine-year period from 1975 through 1984 seeking the reasons for the success. One thing Americans learned at the time was that college-educated workers in Japan tended to stay at one company for their entire career *and* received steadily increasing wages each year. The former aspect didn't appeal to workers in the United States nearly as much as the latter did. In fact, the members of our sample preferred by an almost six-to-one ratio to be able to change jobs whenever they chose yet still have steadily rising incomes.

Since it is what they dearly wished for, it is not surprising that they assumed their peers were currently achieving this prized combination. For instance, 82 percent (2,173 out of 2,652) of the members of our sample who were asked the question thought that, generally speaking, a pay raise was likely to accompany a job change. Similarly, 46 percent (1,221 out of 2,652) were of the opinion that the person was likely to be moving to a physically more attractive firm as well (that is, there were environmental, nonfinancial benefits as part of the deal). Finally, 39 percent (1,035 out of 2,652) were convinced that the person in addition had been promoted (that is, had improved upon the title he or she previously held). In sum, thanks to the better pay, position, and working conditions people were usually thought to obtain for themselves as part of a job change, the conclusion of our panel was that the people in question did all right for themselves.

This general perception of job-change bliss contributed substantially to making people who did not achieve it, through their own job changes, miserable. After all, they were doing poorly in a situation where everyone else typically does well. What they did not know is that this is one of the great myths about business life in America. To be specific, nearly 36 percent (953 out of 2,652) of the job changes we monitored during the period 1975–1983 (one per person) resulted in a pay *decrease*. Far from being recent entrants to the work force, the people undergoing these setbacks were well established in their careers; the majority had family responsibilities and were in their thirties and forties. To add insult to injury, in more than two out of five of these cases (417 out of 953) the move also brought with it less attractive working conditions (smaller office, no secretary, more noise, no window, no carpeting) or an outright demotion.

Ever since they were old enough to talk, the message they had been hearing was "onward and upward." Their activities in the business world decades later, it was implied, would merely be a continuation, an automatic fulfillment, of that slogan. Yet here they were in their prime years with what they couldn't help but feel was a dirty little secret. What is worse is that they were condemning themselves for their failures to advance at the very time that they needed, for public relations purposes, to put on the best possible face—if they were at least to limit the damage done to them by the actions of competitors and the inaction of old customers.

A Gift for Customers

The members of our sample who proved most adept at handling the turbulence that job changes create were those who somehow sensed that customers, as well as peers, believed a step up rather than sideways or down had occurred. Since an improvement had allegedly taken place, this preconceived opinion of customers was exploited, whether or not it was accurate.

To choose the best example of adroitness in this area that we have encountered; as soon as the switch was completed, David Coleman immediately began bragging about how much better his present company was than the prior one. People who were superficially acquainted with both firms could see little difference between them; perhaps precisely for that reason they were tempted to accept Dave's comments at face value. After all, he had now had a chance to see both firms as only an insider could.

Dave was an articulate and very convincing fellow. But it was generally true that people who changed jobs with a maximum of success were significantly more likely to *entice* their customers into coming with them—rather than use bullying or self-pitying tactics, complaining about disloyalty to achieve the same goal. The main reason gentle persuasion and commercial seduction worked, whereas badgering was resented, goes back to the public's bias in favor of believing that someone who has changed jobs has taken a step up in the world.

In that case, without putting it into so many selfish-sounding words, they want to know how they too can benefit from the person's increased wealth or position of power. Dave made it seem as though he was ready to share it with them gladly, at least if they were willing to do business with him at the new firm. This subtle, almost smug approach ("What I've got now is so good, I don't have to use a hard sell to get people interested") proved markedly effective, especially in contrast to Harry's, Sharon's, and Jack's visible annoyance and shock.

The defeatist approach all three unwittingly used ("Oh my God, I've been abandoned and there is nothing I can do about it") confirmed customer impressions that each of the three had taken a step down. People go where good things are to be had, and the gloom and doom radiated by these three made it clear that even *they* didn't think they had anything good to offer, much less something better than what they had been offering before.

There is another aspect of the situation that needs to be discussed here. Our studies indicate that the earlier people tell their best customers that they are thinking of switching firms, the better. Not only is it an honor to be the recipient of such inside information, but more than three out of four members of our sample assume that if someone who had been happy at a firm suddenly is no longer there, the person probably got fired.

That interpretation becomes increasingly likely the higher up people *or* their customers are in the business world. For instance, it made perfect sense to workers with lower and entry-level positions that someone simply decided on a moment's notice to quit. "Yeah, I feel like doing it on plenty of days," said an assistant shipping clerk, "and one of these days I will, too. I'll show 'em who's boss." An assembly-line worker expressed similar sentiments. "Sure, I could see it [someone abruptly quitting]. I'm not tied here. Nothing's keeping me here. If I want to go [one day], I'm gone, in nothing flat." On the other hand, that attitude made no sense whatever to upper-income, upper-echelon employees. "Why would anyone throw away what it took so long to build?" replied the vice-president of a forest-products concern. The advertising director of a cosmetics company responded, "No, I can't see myself 'chucking it.' Oh, I think about it occasionally, don't get me wrong. But I'm not about to do it."

"Showing 'em who's boss" wasn't the overriding issue in their business lives. People in their position had gotten over the seething rebelliousness that was encountered with much greater frequency among holders of lower-level jobs. In addition, workers occupying higher-level slots had spent years getting there, and they had a major vested interest in staying there. Many spoke about it in terms of fatigue. As a 41-year-old middle manager put it, "I don't want to have to do it again—I'm too old to."

In fact, continuity was the underlying theme of most of the comments they made, when they were asked to project themselves into the situation of someone who is suddenly no longer with a given firm. They knew that each step up the ladder meant that more authority and responsibility would be theirs. In order to get it, and keep it, they were aware that they would have to appear stable, not given to jerky movements and thoughtless gestures, once they had been handed the reins. In short, with career continuity a central value, and adolescent rebelliousness a distant one, their interpretation of a hasty departure was that the person had in all likelihood been fired.

These factors must be taken into account when considering a job change. People have developed biases, interpretive inclinations, that make them leap to a verdict on the basis of what is usually meager knowledge of a situation. Once someone abruptly terminates a relationship with an employer, it is too late for public explanations. The business audience will already have jumped to a conclusion and the explanation will strike them merely as face-saving. It is important then to start early and say the right thing.

What "the right thing" is depends on the position of the listener in the corporate hierarchy. Those on a lower-level usually assume the person quit anyway or that, if he was fired, he deliberately provoked the episode. So, in essence, it was his decision all along. People voicing a criticism in order to lay the groundwork for a job change with this group of listeners should be aware that comments such as, "My boss is a real jerk," are far preferable to, "I don't like the direction my company is taking."

The majority of workers in middle-level positions want to move higher and fully expect to do so one day. The attitudes they adopt tend to have much in common with that of those at the top, the people whose jobs they want. They sense that the correct outlook, on the one hand, and candidacy for an executive position, on the other, go hand in hand. Where the topic under discussion is concerned, these two all-important groups, the middle- and upper-echelon occupants, are therefore appropriately treated as though they were one. The most effective comment to make to this combined group may seem bland at first glance, but it works very well. It is, "I don't feel that I really fit at my firm, don't really belong there."

The remark strikes a responsive chord in these listeners because they too want more than just money from their work, they seek a measure of personal fulfillment as well. Whatever else it is, their occupation is supposed to provide an opportunity for self-development and self-expression. That can't happen if the match between person and firm isn't a good one. Even a healthy seed can't blossom in poor soil. Employee and employer have to be right for one another. For a person, let's say Dave, to state publicly that the match isn't quite what he thought it would be—in fact, is downright disappointing—gently detaches him from the firm in his listeners' eyes. Equally important, it is his listeners, not he himself, doing the detaching; they almost automatically end up urging him to find a more satisfactory position elsewhere, while at the same time encouraging him to retain his current position until one more to his liking has been located.

With this audience, criticizing the boss is a real mistake in helping lay the groundwork for a job change, though it is a common occurrence. To call the boss a jerk to this group is meaningless. So is theirs, at least in their view. But they are working around him or her, making slow headway year in and year out in spite of their boss's obvious inadequacies. They are likely to consider someone defective who evidences an inability to do the same.

One benefit of leaving complaints vague and sticking to a simple story of mismatch is that a substantial proportion of listeners will conclude that the person is too good for the firm, and that that is what is causing the difficulties to begin with. The first few times we saw this reaction, we were puzzled. As a growing number of examples were encountered, we discovered that there are two important factors in operation here. The first is that not gunning down the firm or a supervisor is elegant behavior that stands out because of its rarity. In the listener's view, the diplomacy is admirable—and upbeat, clearly not the action of someone who has been defeated. Some people can destroy an opponent with sarcastic remarks delivered sweetly. At times that is fun to watch, especially in the theater; but it goes over quite poorly with an upscale business audience where job changes are concerned. The caustic comments may make them laugh for the moment but will leave many with the feeling that the person issuing them is merely an intolerant buffoon, one who will soon be in equally hot water at the new firm as a result.

The second reason vagueness works well with this audience is that it allows them to project themselves more fully into the speaker's shoes. Once they have, they are far more likely to see the situation in a light that is complimentary to him. After all, they aren't about to insult themselves. If they can empathize with him, they will inevitably take his side against the firm's.

To briefly review the key points covered in this chapter, the outcome of a job change can be improved significantly by keeping two points in mind: first, prepare customers for the coming event, and the sooner the better. In most cases it is best for people to avoid using the most common route, which is to condemn or openly ridicule their employer, who may fire them if word gets back. Dropping a number of non-specific hints about a profound mismatch between themselves and their firms has repeatedly produced superior results—and still leaves the door open in case one chooses to stay or is summoned to the boss's office to explain the remarks one made in public.

Second, it is essential for customers to feel that the move involves an increase in prestige for the person undertaking it (something they are strongly inclined to believe in any event), because the new firm is of higher quality in some way than the old one. That holds out the enticing hope that they too might be bettered in some way. Laudatory comments about the dedicated and knowledgeable approach of one's new co-workers—statements such as "They're in a class by themselves"—have proven very effective.

IV

THE FORTIES

ANXIETY ABOUT
BECOMING
OBSOLETE

CHAPTER
10

Becoming Indispensable to the Firm

WATCHING A WIDE variety of workers enter their forties is exhilarating. By this time, they appear able to handle almost any business problem. While they have plenty of gripes, one is left with the net impression that these are people in their best years, and they know it. Their diverse experiences, together with the time they have spent polishing their particular crafts, make them feel that they have reasonably secure futures, barring an economic collapse. In a word, they seem to have sizable amounts of momentum.

First impressions have rarely been as deceptive as they are in this instance. Our research makes it clear that, contrary to the most widely held view and our own initial one as well, the forties is the most dangerous decade for people in business. There cannot be any question that many go on to achieve great things and make major contributions to the world around them during the decade. Yet the day-to-day behavior of this group graphically conveys that most feel they are treading on thin ice instead of a rock-solid foundation that has been two decades in the making. The problem is the very thing that seemed such a blessing a few moments ago: momentum. It is wonderful if people have it, but what happens when they lose it?

Keep in mind throughout the next three chapters that it becomes much harder for workers in their forties to continue to think of themselves as shooting stars, up-and-comers, young geniuses about to experience a rapid rise in pay, position, and renown. The rate of advancement normally slows. The mileposts pass by nearly unnoticed.

Few have yet arrived at the top-management stage. Attempts at labels—such as the two most frequently used tags, middle manager and junior executive—seem awkward and somewhat self-demeaning ways for 45-year-old men or women to describe themselves. If workers in their twenties are often stuck between school and the work world, those in their forties are straddling, for the last time, the gap between promise and fulfillment. The period when they could get by on the basis of potential alone has come to a close, yet only a small proportion have had a chance to show what they can really do. No one has handed them the reins of a firm. Many start to doubt that it will ever happen.

Waiting for Permission

"I have a lot invested here," said Gary Walker at 41. "I've got to be careful not to do anything stupid. I have been with this outfit for eight years, and I understand this place. Getting used to a whole new office routine somewhere else would be a pain." Gary had moved up rapidly during the period and was now a divisional merchandise manager at one of the nation's largest department store chains. He was happily married and had two children, but other than his family, little distracted Gary from his work. "No, I'm not big on hobbies, or vacations, or parties," he commented at 36. "My wife and I are kind of homebodies. We keep each other company."

Gary was a large man, 6'1", about 200 pounds, and he was easily recognizable even from a distance because of his energetic, loping stride. It would have been hard to imagine him walking slowly. In conversation, the same excess energy often made him bounce from topic to topic, not letting any of them drop. It was a verbal juggling act that kept many of his listeners mystified and an equal number amused. He clearly knew what he was talking about, yet he was usually of the impression that most of the people around him didn't.

In spite of Gary's reluctance to consider moving to another firm, he wasn't nestled happily in the current one either. Something was wrong. Over the years, Gary had maintained a positive approach to the world, even in the face of a few sizable setbacks at work—including being summarily fired one Friday a decade before in a major but belated corporate reorganization (the firm subsequently went bankrupt). His focus was usually his work, not its immediate financial rewards or trying to beat out co-workers. "I'm happy to let my accomplishments speak for themselves," he had said at 35. However, six years later, he'd become restless and uneasy, qualities that hadn't been there before. "I'm not always sure what I'm doing here," he acknowledged the following month. "Most of my time is my own—you know, no one watching me—I can do what I want." Gary had long been averse to hoodwinking his bosses into believing that he was busy when he really wasn't. "I don't like the idea of faking it," he told us at 27 during our initial interview. Fourteen years later, his attitude on that score was even stronger. Still, the excess time he had on his hands was bothering him more than he cared to admit.

As an undergraduate, Gary was a pre-law student and had completed a major in political science. "My father is an attorney," he said with a smile during our first meeting, "and it seemed kind of like an exciting field." By the time he was a college senior, though, he decided to go to a graduate school of business instead. His reason: "I wanted to [be equipped to] handle all the firm's problems, not just the legal ones." There were offers from some of the nation's largest companies as he was receiving his MBA, but Gary decided to stay with medium-sized firms. "The trip to the top isn't as long," he commented. The price to be paid for the choice was that some of the companies weren't sound enough financially and, as we've mentioned, one went bankrupt two years after he joined it. "That was a damned shame," he said at 32, a few weeks after the firm failed. "If they hadn't made such a *secret* of their difficulties, a lot could have been done to save them."

That was typical of Gary's hands-on, problem-solving approach. This was no "armchair theorist." More than once he remarked, "Plans, good plans, are necessary, but it's how you put them into effect that matters." What was conspicuous about Gary between the ages of 27 and 41 was the endless series of good suggestions that flowed from him as a result of his intense involvement in his work. Since he had concentrated on finance during his graduate studies, he was among the first to realize that the building supplies manufacturing firm he was working for had gotten itself into a severe cash squeeze by being lax about collecting its receivables—that is, the money it was due for merchandise it had sold. As Gary put it at the time, "It's really nuts; the more we sell, the closer we're coming to bankruptcy." We asked him, "Why is that?" He replied sarcastically, "Because we're laying out a small fortune to buy raw materials and not getting paid for what we ship. Management is operating this place as though it were a charity."

As Gary moved up the ladder, trouble developed because, once he had entered his forties, there were fewer people each year to whom he could tell his good ideas. What was happening to him was quite the reverse of the stunted adolescent antagonists we met in Part Two, who sought to make their mark by always opposing someone else's proposals. What motivated Gary instead was a desire to contribute to the overall effort any way he could. At 41, he was suddenly finding that, although good listeners among his contemporaries at work had previously been plentiful, they had now become quite scarce.

What accounted for the change? In his twenties and thirties it was appropriate for Gary to bring his proposals to his supervisors. He was their assistant, and the innovative comments he frequently made were appreciated. "He's a real self-starter," one of his bosses said, when Gary was 33. "You don't have to tell him what to do. Most times, he knows. And does it." While Gary was no less enthusiastic eight years later about being productive, he had fewer superiors to whom he could hand over his worthwhile suggestions, secure in the knowledge that they would be acted upon. Now *he* was expected to run with the ball himself. Although Gary was unaware of it, his world had shifted radically in the past few years from vertical to horizontal. On his way up the ladder, he had focused mainly on the ladder. Suddenly his own rung mattered more than he realized. Given his upper-middle position in the hierarchy (he would have been an assistant vice-president if his firm had used such titles), his continued focus on the highest rungs was a recipe for frustration.

The majority of people in Gary's position are under the unfortunate impression that power emanates from the peak. Therefore, if they hope to implement what they consider a good idea, they first have to get the ear of, and then a go-ahead from, the person at the top. That may be how it looks to a casual observer, but a careful, long-term analysis of the situation indicates that middle managers possess much actual power themselves.

Gary was too close to the process to see it. On occasion he did notice that one of his own suggestions was coming back at him, as though his boss had discovered it to begin with. Wisely, Gary let it go rather than insist that the idea had originally been his. Having spent nearly two decades doing it, he was still looking up, hoping for a green light. In fact, he was continually waiting for a reaction or permission. What he didn't understand is that he had already been given it. It came with the position he now held.

Disappearing Clones

"Gary is no fool," someone who knew him well might object. "If he couldn't see all the latitude he had, maybe he didn't really have it?" If we look at one other typical example and see what the two cases have in common, it will be more apparent why so many people in their forties unwittingly bring their own career progress to a screeching halt.

Alice Miller is one of the most down-to-earth people in our sample. "I thought about becoming a nurse in high school," she said, at 26, during the initial interview; but she majored instead in psychology. Her interest was more practical than abstract, and psychometrics (the measurement, for instance, of intelligence and personality) appealed to her most. So did marketing. She took all four courses that were offered on the subject at her college. A year of graduate school followed. "That was enough of the classroom for me," she said.

Alice had the usual share of problems making the transition from school to the work world. Her principal complaint during the second year on the job was, "Too much of what I have to do each day is dull. I wish more of it were exciting." However, she stuck with it, anticipating better things ahead. As she slowly rose in the financial-services firm to which she transferred after three years at her first position, the work became substantially more interesting to her. "I'm getting involved in some of the juicier projects now," she said enthusiastically, referring to the development, packaging, and test-marketing of new financial products being offered to customers. The fact that the public was expressing interest in a variety of different services—mutual funds, credit cards, and pension plans—intrigued her.

Alice was tall and slender, 5'7", though she seemed taller than that thanks to her slimness. When she was working and thought no one was watching, or when she talked on the phone, her right hand would automatically reach up and unravel a lock of her long brown hair and twirl it. If the conversation grew tense, the lock was twisted tighter and twirled faster. During other, more relaxed, conversations the lock became a mustache, held in place by a curled upper lip. A voice-stress analyzer could never have shown what two minutes spent watching Alice play with her hair would have.

Like Gary, by the time Alice was in her late twenties she was largely free of the confusion between independence and insubordination. If she heard one of her bosses or co-workers suggest a worthwhile idea, she felt no compulsion to contradict it publicly as a way of making her presence felt. "There are some very good people here," she said at 28, and meant it. In any event, she had plenty of good ideas of her own. The combination of her intelligence and involvement nearly guaranteed that that would happen. However, by the time she was in her early forties, Alice found herself in the same kind of limbo that was disturbing Gary so much. Pay raises and promotions during the past 18 years had brought her to a level comparable to his, but the time factor weighed more heavily on her hands. "It's strange," she commented two months before her 41st birthday. "On some days I have almost nothing to do, and could sit here and read *War and Peace*. Other times, for weeks on end, I can't even get a moment to breathe."

The on-again, off-again nature of her work wasn't the problem, since that is characteristic of every job, except assembly-line manual labor. The real difficulty was that Alice had lost her traditional bearings. Her way of guiding herself during the prior two decades had been so successful, she continued using it long past the stage at which it was still appropriate.

What, specifically, were the points of reference that had served her and Gary well in the previous two decades and now posed a threat to further progress? For one thing, they were used to discussing their ideas with co-workers. Now, almost overnight, there seemed to be no one around who was suitable. "I'd like to have a sounding board," Alice said at 41, "but everybody is busy, or wouldn't really know what I was talking about. They've got their own areas to worry about."

Gary and Alice had overlooked a crucial pyramid factor that typically makes itself felt most strongly once people enter their forties. While both were in school, they had had an abundance of friends. They and their peers were taking the same classes with the same teachers, and hence they had plenty to talk about. Whatever the subject, there was usually a ready listener, particularly since the conversation was likely to be based on common materials and experiences. When school ended, this important feature of their lives remained nearly unchanged. During their first decade in the work world, it was typical for others like themselves to be doing the same kind of work at the firm. "I'm surprised that he can keep our names straight," Alice quipped at 27 about her boss. "There are five of us [all of comparable age], and we even look a little alike." Make no mistake about it: in their twenties, Gary and Alice resented the presence of the others. "I'm not sure he'd notice it if I took a three-hour lunch," Alice said sarcastically at 29. "He'd see one of the other four and think I was still there."

In their thirties, the number of workers like them at the firm— clones, Gary called them—steadily diminished. In fact, the higher up in the corporate hierarchy, the fewer assistants of the same type as themselves were to be seen. That was one of the key, unseen reasons Gary and Alice felt more special in their thirties than in their twenties. The feeling of uniqueness was to some extent a consequence of the decrease in the number of occupational carbon copies of themselves they saw each day at work. Nevertheless, neither Gary nor Alice noticed the disappearing clones; what they were aware of instead was the emergence of their own individuality at the firm.

Now, in their forties, the clones had just about vanished. That should have called for a celebration, yet Gary and Alice were becoming visibly uneasy and disoriented instead. Ironically, they missed the very group of professional peers whose local presence they'd so resented in their twenties. What made the matter much worse is that they didn't realize what was ailing them at work and therefore continually misdiagnosed the source of their troubles. "The responsibility they give me," Gary said at 43, "but not the authority." Alice used different words at 42 to say essentially the same thing. "I have no real power of my own; I can only *suggest*." As they saw it, the reason for their frustration was simple: they'd been given a job to do but hadn't really been given the go-ahead by top management to do it. The excuse may have made them momentarily feel better but, as we'll soon see, not only did it not work, it backfired. The rationalizations they were dredging up for their discomfort were so wide of the mark, it was almost inevitable that their situation would deteriorate further.

What actually went wrong? A basic fact was not recognized: As people move up and develop their craft, they eventually become the sole specialist of that kind in the company. Only their intense competitiveness blinds them to their increasingly unique position, making them react defensively when anyone else in the company even sets foot on their terrain.

Unappreciated and Disoriented

The firm usually doesn't want or need two of the same kind. We live increasingly in a world that depends not just on specialists, but subspecialists. Duplication is acceptable only at the lower levels of the corporate pyramid for three reasons: there is a great deal of basically nonspecialized work to do; the workers employed at these levels are relatively inexpensive; and last but by no means least, it is a good way to round up a handful of candidates to undergo in-house assessment to see which ones will be promoted. With a rise in status, workers gain in certain ways and lose in others. An important loss over an extended period is in feedback and compliments from peers. They fall away slowly as the years pass and the pyramid narrows, so slowly in fact that people are unlikely to be aware of their growing absence. Besides, most are viewed as rivals, not allies. Gary at 42 didn't remember how pleased he'd been eleven years before, when a co-worker his age told him, "Gary, that's a super idea."

The unnoticed changes on the horizontal level produced visible changes on the vertical one. What Gary and Alice couldn't get from peers, they tried hard to get from superiors—precisely at a time when such behavior was likely to be viewed as infantile and no longer appropriate. Nonetheless, as Alice insisted at 41, "I need guidance from somewhere." Unable to get it from her associates ("They're always too busy with their own things"), she was thrown back on what had worked so well in her twenties and thirties. Gary and Alice therefore kept gazing up the ladder, waiting for the go-ahead they had already received. What confused them, and made them think they were doing less well now than they had done only five years previously was this: not only did compliments from co-workers decrease as the clones were asked one by one to leave, so did compliments from top executives who considered it normal to give fewer of them to 42- than to 27-year-olds.

Gary and Alice knew only that they felt less plugged into the firm now than at any time since their first year in the work world. That distressed them because they had consciously, as well as unknowingly, shaped much of their thinking and behavior to mesh better with their respective firms. They genuinely wanted to do well, not only for themselves, but also for their employers. To end up feeling unappreciated and disoriented after so many years of sustained effort seemed a bitter reward.

We can summarize briefly the reaction of these two and others who find themselves in this situation. They launched intense lobbying efforts to prove that they were needed. They certainly didn't feel it. At a time in their lives when one might have anticipated a high (perhaps the highest) degree of confidence coupled with competence, they instead began to continually seek reassurance.

"I'll bet nobody else could've come up with that," Gary said to his boss, after being told that his proposal was a good one and would probably be adopted. The remark was a desperate and self-defeating bit of arm-twisting, and somewhere within, Gary sensed it. "Maybe I shouldn't have said it," he later volunteered. Alice was doing her share of the same. She began to air her thoughts seriously with people who, in the past, heard only casual comments from her, mostly of a social sort. She had long had a well-developed sense of who was interested in something she was working on and who was not. Now that inner guide seemed to be missing. It was bizarre to see her ask people their opinion of a subject that they knew little about and didn't wish to know more. There is some justification for a politician to repeatedly ask, "How'm I doing?" He got the job because a majority of the electorate put him there and, with one vote per person, each person counts. But Alice wasn't running for office. She merely wanted support, apparently from everyone.

"Have you heard anything about me?" she asked one of the most indifferent workers at the firm. "I mean, did they say anything about me at the meeting?" Even had he heard, he would probably not have remembered. ("This place puts me to sleep," he told us more than once. And on another occasion, "I come here to rest [during the day] so I'll be in shape to party [at night].") However, he recognized that she was concerned about her current status at the firm, and he replied as he walked away, "Don't worry, they didn't say anything bad about you." The remark didn't soothe her.

Alice had a very flattering view of what she was doing at the time. In her words, "I'm a senior person here now, and can help [the others] in many different ways." No doubt that was true. Yet no sooner did the conversation start with each person than it turned into a discussion of her and her work. In one form or another, she was continually asking her co-workers, in some cases ones she barely knew, to review her performance positively and boost her sagging self-esteem.

Of all the people she approached at the firm, one was more effective than the rest combined at doing just that. Nicky was 31, exactly ten years and six days younger than Alice. "He's just another loudmouthed salesman," she had said when he was 28. It's not that his personality changed during the next three years; Alice's needs did. The confident and outgoing, even brash, manner that struck her as obnoxious when she was 38 appealed to her much more at 41. "He means well," she now said, smiling indulgently, "underneath the bravado."

They slept together four times in the subsequent three-week period. Then it was over. Whatever she had hoped would be there—and was initially—had disappeared. "It was nice physically," she later said, "but it didn't do much for my head." It was the first extramarital fling in the eleven years of her marriage. A month after their last sexual encounter, the magic gone, she found herself calmly asking, "Why him?"

A glass of white wine took Nicky's place. On the kitchen counter each evening while she was preparing dinner, her glass was filled two, three, sometimes four times. It seemed unobtrusive—"I don't want to hide anything, if I don't have to"—and appeared to work. "It steadies my nerves," she said. Nevertheless, she continued to cast her net wide at the office, trying to pick up any scrap of encouragement she could find, though no more bedmates.

Like Alice, Gary began aiming his requests for reassurance in every direction. The brunt fell on his wife and two old friends, neither of whom worked for his firm. The attempts were verbal not sexual in Gary's case, but they proved equally empty. "I think they're considering me for something big," Gary told one of the two friends. "I get the feeling something good is about to happen." It wasn't so. Gary wasn't usually given to making up tales out of whole cloth, yet the growing hunger for reaffirmation of his worth was getting to him. Unfortunately, whatever good the initial uplift from friends did, it soon turned into the opposite. For the people he told about his allegedly pending promotion kept raising the topic long after Gary could milk anything further from it. "I don't think they're being malicious," he said two months later. "*I* was the one who told them about it. I just wish they wouldn't ask me about it anymore."

Gary seemed obsessed with the idea that everything he'd worked for years to build now seemed on the verge of collapse. "It's pretty fragile, you know," he said, referring to his and every other firm. "It doesn't take all that much—a few bad seasons—to bring [this place] to its knees." The company was in good shape financially. Gary was really talking about what he himself had constructed. As he put it, laughing uncomfortably to relieve his tension, "If I broke my leg or something and were out for a while, I wonder who'd be here [in my chair] when I got back?" Six months later he "jokingly" asked us, "Do you think I'd still have any friends if I got fired?"

The Need for Reassurance

Without realizing it, Gary and Alice had launched a relentless campaign to prove one thing above all: that they were important, not so much personally as occupationally, to their firms. By the time they were in their forties, they had been working for sufficiently long periods of time in their respective fields to want to be praised as veteran professionals and be deemed essential by the firm. In spite of the intense lobbying effort, they were having little luck. "I'm *sure* they like me," Alice said at 42. "That's not enough. I want them to be unable to do *without* me." The need to be needed was well on its way to causing very real crises.

Instead of feeling on top of the world, ready to handle increasingly major challenges, they felt isolated—more so than ever before—and were continually questioning their own competence. Their feelings made them turn to friends and co-workers and subtly ask for help. It didn't produce the intended results. Gary's old classmate and Alice's new bedmate couldn't even put a dent in the problem. Moreover, the situation was beginning to feed on itself, since their attempt to convince themselves that they mattered was coming at the expense of their work. Paradoxically, the harder they tried to prove that they were needed, the less needed they saw themselves as being.

Gary was the first to state that he was doing something self-destructive. "I'm having difficulty concentrating lately," he said at 42, "and that's because I'm not concentrating on the right thing." Alice also was aware that she was misusing her time and energy on a grand scale. "I've lost my grip on the pieces," she said at 41. And at 42, she added, "There's always a hint of trouble in the air. I guess it was there in the past too. I'm not handling it as well as I used to."

Gary and Alice may not have been able to get their bosses or coworkers to give them what they wanted, but they had moved far enough up the ladder by this time to have plenty of people beneath them. Both now began to display an alarming ambivalence toward their assistants. In fact, it is fair to say that all the internal pressures the two were experiencing during the period poured out and engulfed those who occupied lower rungs.

* * *

Although Gary was eight years older than Tom Lambert, the two worked well together throughout Gary's 38th to 41st years. Gary had a clear idea of where he was going at the time, and Tom didn't seem to mind in the least following Gary's lead. "He's one bright guy," Tom said in a tone of admiration. "Seems to know everything that goes on around here."

When Gary's anxieties began to afflict him in his early forties, and his bosses and peers offered no effective aid, Tom was a natural person to turn to. Now, after Gary finished describing something to Tom, he would explicitly ask, "What do you think?" Tom was pleased by the question and realized it hadn't been included before. He took it as a sign of maturity. "I must be ready for bigger shoes," he said proudly.

Gary's new approach could not have been intended to elicit a fuller response, since Tom was usually happy to state his opinion anyway. From the start, he had been polite but candid about his reactions to any plans Gary revealed to him. It wasn't business that Gary wanted reviewed this time; it was himself. By repeatedly asking, "What do you think?" Gary was hoping that Tom would go beyond the specific topic under discussion and offer some supportive comments. As far as Tom could see, two things had changed: he was being strongly encouraged to play a larger role in the decision-making process with Gary. Second, Gary seemed more vulnerable and open. "He's not as aloof," Tom said, still surprised at the recent development. "I think he really wants to know what my thinking [on the subject] is."

It therefore hit Tom like a ton of bricks when he brought a pet proposal of his own to Gary and was met with a critical and hostile response. The first time that happened, Tom was hurt but inclined to dismiss it. "I must've got him at a bad moment," he said, trying to forget the incident. Gary, however, wasn't about to forget it. "You give some people an inch," he said, a few days after the episode, "and they want the whole mile." Nevertheless, Gary's need for reassurance was growing, and Tom still represented a likely source. The fact that Gary continued to seek him out, use him as a sounding board, and then explicitly ask for a reaction fooled Tom into believing his analytic abilities were being tapped. They weren't. All Gary wanted was applause.

Alice's behavior with her subordinates was rife with the same type of ambivalence as Gary's. She wanted reaffirmation of her occupational worth, and hence she opened herself up to those on lower rungs. "She's become nicer [lately]," said Rachel, age 29. "She didn't stop and talk to us this much [before]." Interestingly, Nicky had said the same, and it was one of the principal reasons he had become involved with her. "In the past, I didn't think she cared whether I lived or died."

The greater accessibility that Rachel and Nicky were convinced they were seeing made them seek Alice's assistance in promoting projects of their own. That was a major mistake. "The nerve of that twerp," Alice said angrily about Nicky, a few weeks after their fourth and last sexual encounter. "He's still wet behind the ears and wants me to go to bat for him with [the executive VP] and get him more accounts. What does he take me for, a fool?" Alice went on to state that it was out of the question in any event, because she supposedly had ideas of her own that she wanted to press for during upcoming meetings with the firm's top management.

To Rachel she was even more harsh. Rachel came up with a plan that would have allowed the regional branches of the firm more autonomy, and for a good reason. "I think we're getting out of touch with them [with our centralized approach]," she said, clearly excited about the changes she was about to propose. "The branches could be more useful to us if we gave them more rope." She did as much work on the idea as possible without going over anyone's head or stepping on someone else's corporate territory. Since Alice seemed receptive of late to contact with younger members of the firm, Rachel expected a cordial response to her well thought out plan.

Less than five minutes into the meeting in which she presented it, Alice interrupted her with, "When I *want* your opinion, I'll *ask* for your opinion." Rachel was stunned. As she later put it, "I couldn't believe my ears, so I went on [hoping to get her to listen]." The more Rachel tried to hurry, "to get to the good part," as she called the core of the argument, the more tension there was in the air. A few minutes later Alice asked her to leave, saying, "I've got more important things to worry about."

Rachel cried when describing the incident the following day, but they were tears of anger. "They ought to fire that menopausal maniac," she said sarcastically. However, her resentment didn't last long, because the day after that, Alice was once again as friendly as she had recently become. "I can't figure her out," said Rachel, and she let the matter of decentralizing the firm's operations drop.

Losing One's Bearings

In Chapter Four we examined the difference between independence and insubordination. We saw that it is common for workers in their twenties and thirties to think they are being remarkably original when they are merely being hostile. Not only do they mistake their own animosity for ambition, they also attempt to make their presence felt by instantly opposing the plans or procedures of their peers and bosses, people on the same or higher planes. The attacks they launch as a way of publicly proclaiming their individuality are usually aimed horizontally and upward.

Odd as it may sound at first, Gary and Alice were doing something quite similar now, only they mistook their anger for executive decisiveness—and aimed their attack downward. Neither of these two hardworking and decent people had gone through a self-destructively rebellious period at work during their twenties and thirties. They had wanted to make contributions but hadn't resorted to the simplistic approach used by stunted adolescents: take an idea of someone whose status is equal to or higher than theirs, stand it on its head, and claim to have come up with a brilliant new idea. This mechanical approach may make people who employ it feel very creative, yet it is a shabby substitute for truly independent thinking of the kind Gary and Alice had been doing all along. Content to let the merits of their proposals speak for themselves, they looked at each situation anew—not at all horrified that they might arrive at the same conclusions as others— and often came up with genuine insights as a result. As a bonus, they were viewed as pleasant and easy to work with.

Not anymore. Now they automatically opposed any suggestion made by a subordinate. They were well equipped to beat back even undeniably worthwhile thoughts. If the idea was good, the assistant who proposed it was labeled swellheaded and impudent. On the other hand, the idea itself could be defeated by reversing it, reducing the situation to "either/or," claiming that both had been considered and the better one already implemented.

Why were they behaving this way? What made them be pleasant one moment and act like cornered rats the next? Nothing set them off so quickly as seeing a subordinate with a sense of direction. What made that such an overwhelming threat was that they had lost their own.

Gary and Alice stood out during the previous decade thanks to the fact that, unlike many of their peers, they allowed their dedication to their work to serve as their rudders. They considered each potential job change carefully, not wanting to wind up accidentally taking a dead-end detour. There was a "rightness" to the steps they took along the way, and they could sense it. Nothing was to be permitted to interfere with what they viewed as their natural and, for the most part, pleasurable involvement with their work.

Yet in the end, everything seemed to have gone wrong. They had taken a detour without noticing it. Alice asked, "Is there a flaw in me—something I was born with—that's only now starting to emerge?" As Gary put it, "Maybe I'm just trying to prove that I really am the meanest son-of-a-bitch in this outfit." In the next chapter we'll see what was actually causing their distress.

CHAPTER
11

Pressure from Above and Below

OBSOLESCENCE WOULD APPEAR to be every bit as relevant to workers in their twenties and thirties as those who are over forty. People of every age in the work world worry about whether or not they are falling behind, yet the evidence we've accumulated indicates that those in their forties worry more about it than any other age group, and not always consciously.

Keeping Anxiety Within Limits

Gary loved having his assistants follow in his footsteps, as long as he had a sense of direction. When he slowed down a little in the past, he became concerned about their bunching up behind him. Usually, that condition didn't last long. A new idea would strike him before long and away he would go, carrying them along happily in his wake. By the time he was in his early forties, though, he often slowed to a dead halt. Then, having alert young workers such as Tom trailing along only a small step in back of him became a hazard instead of a joy. "Why are you on my heels every time I turn around?" Gary, at age 42, asked Tom irritably.

Alice was plagued by the same uncomfortable feeling of being shadowed. When eager subordinates tried to be helpful, she frequently found herself demanding that they stop. That puzzled and annoyed them, since they thought they were merely doing what was expected of them. "I give the marching orders around here," she said, at 42, to Rachel. But as Rachel later astutely observed, "That's the whole trouble. She's not *giving* any marching orders. She apparently just wants us to stand around, doing nothing."

To understand what happened to Gary and Alice during the remainder of the decade, we need a clearer picture of occupational obsolescence. There are two separate parts to the picture. The first is a given person versus a body of knowledge. The second is the person versus the other individuals who possess that knowledge. Most people would rather think about keeping up in terms of the first version. If staying up to date means digesting a mass of new information, they may feel anxious about it, but the anxiety usually remains within bounds because the outcome is up to them. The matter is in *their* hands. All they have to do to overcome the problem is set aside the time needed to master the material. "I'm going to get around to it soon," they frequently say. "I know what I have to do, and I'll do it before long, you'll see." In brief, there are two elements in this picture, one animate, the other, inanimate. There is a person, and there is also a stack of books or papers that have to be read.

Although people may feel tense and uncertain when facing such a task, it is much less anxiety-provoking than when they are pitted against another person. The situation suddenly becomes much more complex, and unpredictable. A stack of books has no choice but to sit there and wait. Another person, however, may decide not to be so obliging. Instead of waiting, he or she may be dedicated to absorbing and trying out the new material, doing it and loving it, and by now that person may be miles ahead.

In short, it may be more comforting for us to imagine that obsolescence pressures force us to confront our ignorance. What they really do, though, is force us to confront one another. It is an unending race, an intense competition, in which those who can remain in the lead for any length of time are richly rewarded by the work world, while those who fall behind are increasingly ignored and face a heightened chance of being fired.

When Gary and Alice lost their sense of direction in their early forties, they had good reason to start worrying. They may not have been keeping up any longer but, as they were well aware, the people immediately behind them were. There was nothing vague or abstract about the fear. As the decade progressed, they became more and more concerned about the people occupying the next lower rung on the ladder.

To repeat, Gary and Alice weren't really frightened about their ability to master new bodies of information. They were bright, had been good students, and knew they could somehow handle the task. The bodies they were actually worried about were their own. They had sound justification for suspecting that they were on the verge of being painfully trampled. When all is said and done, *obsolescence anxiety is the conscious evidence of a subconscious fear of being thrust aside or run over by those who are better informed.*

That is not how Gary and Alice either thought about or discussed it, for that would have made the matter too personal and threatening, a nose-to-nose battle between themselves and their subordinates. To keep their anxiety limited, Gary and Alice came up with an explanation for it and a plan to combat it. "I'm going to start taking some courses," said Gary at 43. When she was 43 and again at 44, Alice commented, "I need some refresher classes in [multivariate] statistics and maybe math too." Both decided that learning more about computer programming as well would make them more modern and thus less fretful about becoming out of date.

Key question: did it help? The surprising answer: not at all. To begin with, they didn't do very much, although they talked frequently about the subject. Gary had taken a course in computer languages in college, and Alice had taken two statistics courses as part of her psychology major. Twenty years later, when they became scared about the prospect of becoming obsolete, there was great security to be found in turning to something familiar as the solutions for what was upsetting them. "Yeah, a couple of [night] courses would fix me up in a jiffy," said Gary at 44, trying to make himself feel calm and in control. Alice had the same view of what ailed her and was attempting the same cure. As she put it, "When you get to be as *busy* as I am now, you need a little help keeping current. There's a seminar at [a nearby university] that meets for two hours a week. I really should sign up for it. I'm sure [my firm] would be happy to pay for it."

As we said, there was much more talk than action here. Yet we know from a large number of comparable cases that, even had these two spent half of each day in school, boning up on the latest developments in their respective fields, they would still not have found the peace they were seeking. What complicated the problem enormously was that they were running at top speed down the wrong road. School may have been a familiar route for remedying a lack of knowledge, but it was a useless cure for what ailed them.

They had lost their sense of direction; as a result they had become frightened that they would be crushed by the stampeding junior staff members right behind them. Although obsolescence is often a disturbing prospect for men and women in their twenties and thirties, these people are still amorphous and energetic enough to confront the fear and turn it to their advantage. For the young, keeping up may be a terrible strain, but it is also an awesome opportunity. In a way that few other things ever will, it holds out the promise of allowing them to upstage their elders.

Since Gary and Alice were typical in not wanting to view obsolescence in such brutal, person-versus-person terms, they spent the entire decade of their forties worried most about one thing. On many a night, they woke up in a cold sweat. And the subject of their recurring nightmare? Computers.

Getting People off One's Back

Once automation became labeled as the alleged cause of all their woes, Gary and Alice took some predictable steps. Since they themselves were focusing more on the subject now, reading about it, even taking a technical course or two, they expected others to do the same.

Who? Their bosses, for one. In a number of meetings with his superiors, Gary raised the issue. "There's a whole new generation of computers coming out that might interest us," he said on one occasion. On another, "We ought to look into some of these minis and micros." Alice was making similar suggestions at the time. "They can solve problems much faster than we can," she told her supervisor.

For two to three years, Gary and Alice were able to use the subject of automation to derive a sense of self-direction, one that they could even discuss with key executives. However, it wasn't really suitable, because each firm already had someone in-house who was a highly trained and experienced expert in the field. "The guys in [the] data processing [department] know more about this than I do," Gary found himself saying in the middle of an important meeting devoted to the topic. Alice too realized how much of a novice she was in the area, though she had been making use of a variety of hardware and software combinations for years. Much to our surprise, she came close to stating outright that she wasn't doing herself much good by hopping aboard this subject. As she put it, after being asked a number of questions by her bosses that she was unable to answer, "It's tough to wage a war with borrowed horses."

Although Gary and Alice couldn't make much headway with top management on this score, their own subordinates felt its sting. Gary began to criticize what his assistants were doing as "stale" and "out of date." Alice too started using that as the unkindest cut she could deliberately deliver. After being shown a proposed format to be utilized in a new marketing campaign, she sneered, "It looks *old* to me."

Instead of being devastated by the criticism, Gary and Alice's subordinates were galvanized into action by it. They clearly enjoyed the challenge of being required to come up with the most modern version of the technique, style, or apparatus in question. Gary and Alice were in their forties, but with few exceptions the subordinates with whom they had daily contact were in their twenties and thirties. "Asking me to find out what's new," said a recently hired 27-year-old assistant of Gary's, "is like asking a bird to fly. Say the word, and I'm on the wing."

The thrill that these younger workers experienced at having to dig up the newest and latest—something they were inclined to do on their own anyway—helped deepen the hole that Gary and Alice were unwittingly digging for themselves at work. They had originally started slamming their subordinates and criticizing suggestions as "old" as a way of getting the crowd to back off. And it worked, temporarily. Then, these youngsters came roaring back, making even bigger pests of themselves than they had been before.

Instead of taking the initial rejection personally, they took it as a command that they not bother their bosses, Gary and Alice, until they came up with something sufficiently new to warrant attention. However, once they had done so, once they found what they considered innovative or improved ways of doing things, they weren't so easily put off again. "This really *is* the best method for doing it," Gary's new assistant said, nearly shouting, "but that lunkhead won't listen." Then came the crushing blow. "And *he* is the one who asked me to find it in the first place."

In brief, if Gary and Alice wanted to get the people behind them "off my heels," as Gary had put it, they could not have chosen a worse way in which to do it. Now they had their subordinates on their backs instead. Worried about being labeled "old" themselves, they repeatedly labeled the work of their assistants "old" and set off a forest fire with themselves in its midst.

Armed with the newest and the latest—which they accurately insisted they had been told to find—the assistants not only became annoyed, they had proof at last that their bosses weren't paying attention to whatever was most up to date. The assistants were in the lovely position of being able to rightly claim that anyone who was ignoring them, after all the spade work they had done, had to be falling behind. Before leaving the firm to take a better job elsewhere, one went to both of Alice's immediate superiors and unloaded. "I spilled the beans about what a *nothing* she is," said Ronnie, now at the new firm. "All she does is block progress, not create any, and they finally know it."

The incident could not have occurred at a worse time for Alice, who had turned 45 two weeks earlier. In addition to the chronic uneasiness about her career that she had been feeling for years, there was egg all over her face now, and it wasn't about to disappear. "That's the first time we've heard anything like that about you," Alice's boss said to her, and then asked, "Is it true?" Alice felt her heart begin to race. She defended herself as best she could, knowing that her spotless record had become a thing of the past. Nevertheless, from the serious way in which the question was put to her, as she commented, "It was obvious I couldn't exonerate myself. Anyhow, I was so nervous, I'm sure they think Ronnie was right."

Dealing with Subordinates

Gary had a few close calls of a similar nature—fed-up or departing workers who thought about venting their spleen to top management—but apparently none did. To make certain that it didn't happen in Gary's case or happen again in Alice's, both decided subconsciously in their mid-forties to stop acting as impediments to progress and become its proponents.

Alice was the first to put the new policy into effect. Now when an assistant of hers came up with a worthwhile proposal, she would relay it at the earliest opportunity to her superiors, giving credit to the person who had come up with it. "You know Rachel, don't you?" she asked her boss in the hallway. "Well, she made an interesting suggestion...." Gary actually spelled out the reasons why he thought the new plan was necessary. "You can't get in the way of a good idea whose time has come," he said philosophically. "So why not pass it along?" The new policy seemed to be, "If you can't beat 'em, join 'em."

However there was less altruism here than it seems. In fact, the policy contained a very clever escape clause. If the idea that Gary or Alice passed along turned out to be one that management liked, the originator of the idea wasn't the only person to be commended. Gary or Alice also were since it was assumed that they had hired, encouraged, and helped the person, and then selected and communicated the particular suggestion. Everyone shared in the glory.

The built-in escape route could best be seen whenever Gary or Alice passed along an idea and it was vetoed. Gary had barely finished describing a new management-training program that an assistant of his had put together when he heard, "That's one for the circular file. It stinks." Gary didn't waste a minute making absolutely certain he emerged from the interchange unharmed. "I *thought* you'd say that," he said casually to his boss. "I had doubts about it myself. But I figured I'd check it out with you anyway."

Neither Gary nor Alice were aware that they had adopted a new policy for dealing with their subordinates' upward thrusts. That made it easy for the two to rationalize the fancy footwork they had to do instantly when a suggestion was hissed instead of applauded by the firm's top management. "If I'd told you I [also] didn't like it," Alice said to her boss, "it wouldn't have gotten a fair hearing. This way [by pretending I liked it], you could be the judge."

What she really meant was that no one could accuse her of being a boulder in the path of progress anymore. If anything, she appeared to be making a diligent effort to be the reverse. Rather than thwarting her assistants' best ideas, she acted as their promoter—even to the point of saying she liked many of the suggestions that she actually didn't. She was proud of her new stance. The tactic also succeeded in removing her and Gary as targets for the wrath of bright underlings. "I went to bat for you, kid," Gary said to one. "Did the best I could. But the big brass said no, and that's the end of the line. Next time [with a different idea], maybe it'll be different. Hang in there."

Gary and Alice felt expansive when describing any episode now in which they played the intermediary. They considered their behavior appropriate to the more senior image they were trying hard to project. Not once did they acknowledge that they resorted to acting as conduits only after disaster seemed to be looming on the horizon or, in Alice's case, had already occurred. The new policy's superb defensive benefits were also skillfully downplayed. Nevertheless, both were well aware that their subordinates could be brash and outspoken at times on behalf of a good idea, and that something had to be done to contain the potential damage such dedication could cause. The youngsters weren't fond of suffering silently.

The plan they were using certainly seemed at first glance to be working. Alice at 47 even came right out and said to one of her assistants, "Don't blame me [that nothing is going to be done about it]. I'm on *your* side." It appeared to be very effective. There were no further protests for the moment. Be that as it may, they had unwittingly adopted a high-risk strategy. In spite of the greater confidence and at times cockiness they felt, they weren't nearly as well protected as they thought. Their greatly enhanced ability to duck bullets from below, all the while collecting plaudits from above, turned out to be an illusion.

That became painfully apparent to Gary a month before his 47th birthday. In what was by now a practiced manner, he mentioned an assistant's brainstorm to his own boss and got the reply, "Have him write it up. I want to see the details." The boss's tone had been hurried, almost indifferent, so Gary gave the matter little thought. "Put it in writing," he brusquely told his assistant, "and make sure you do a good job. We don't want him to think we're a bunch of amateurs, do we?" Four days later, Gary got the report, glanced at it briefly and gave it to his boss's secretary to give to him. "I knew everything that was in it," Gary subsequently said, "so I gave it the once-over and that was that."

There was no reaction for over a week. Then Gary got a call. "I'd like to see you," his boss told him, sounding serious but friendly. When the two got together that afternoon, Gary's boss said excitedly, "This is a first-rate piece of work." Gary had heard praise before from his superiors about the work of his subordinates, and he expected this to be another instance of the same. "I thought he'd say, 'You're doing well—all of you—keep it up,' or something like that," Gary later told us.

Instead, he was amazed to hear his boss add, "Whoever wrote this knows more, much more, than is on these pages. I'd like very much to meet him. Have him here at 2:30 tomorrow." This time Gary didn't have a snappy rejoinder. On virgin turf now, he'd not had a chance to perfect a few casual comebacks. As he later put it, "When I asked, 'Do you want me there too?' and he said, 'No,' I knew my goose was cooked." It was the first time he had ever been deliberately excluded from such a metting.

What Gary feared and his boss hoped for came true the following afternoon. The session lasted from 2:30 until 5:00, not the 30 minutes for which it had been scheduled. "How did it go?" Gary asked as nonchalantly as possible when his assistant finally emerged. "What did you talk about?" The short reply upset Gary more than he had anticipated and prevented him from pursuing the matter further at the moment: "Oh, everything. We touched a lot of bases." That was on Thursday. What Gary did not know but eventually discovered was that on Friday the boss got permission to grant the youngster a promotion. The next Monday, Gary's boss told him to do just that. "You're the one who should tell him," his boss said cheerfully. "He's two notches below you. From here on, he'll be only one."

Gary dragged his feet a while before doing what he'd been asked, and he developed severe abdominal pains prior to delivering the message, unusual for someone who often bragged about having a cast-iron stomach. As he put it, "I was about to say to [the boss], 'Hey aren't you moving kind of fast? Shouldn't you find out more about the guy first?' But I could see that he had already made up his mind." Then, with one hand on his abdomen, he asked rhetorically, "Can you believe this? I'm going to witness my own hanging. Put the noose on my own neck."

"I Get Away with a Lot Here"

Events at Alice's firm unfolded in a different manner during the period. Herb Evans, the vice-president in charge of marketing, a key figure at this particular company, had been with the firm only three years. Before that, he had been at a major competitor. From the day he came aboard, Alice was wary of him. "I better keep my eye on him," she said at 44. "Herb's got big plans for this place, I can tell. He's trouble." Her prediction ultimately proved accurate but took so long to be fulfilled, she had forgotten about it. A pleasant working relationship had sprung up between them in the interim.

"I'm not happy with the way many things are done around here," he suddenly told Alice at a meeting with six other people present. "I haven't been since I arrived." Herb had apparently been holding his tongue, carefully scrutinizing the division's procedures and personnel, and now he was ready to make a few changes. "We're no match for our competition," he told the group. "We need better people—sharper, more with it. We're *antique* by comparison with what others [in this industry] are doing."

The sentences made Alice squirm. Herb appeared to be talking to everyone there, and he looked around the room frequently as he spoke, yet Alice felt that she was the main target of his comments. For one thing, she was next in line in the corporate hierarchy and responsible for most of the day-to-day operations in her area. As she put it, "If something is wrong [in this area], it can't be anyone else's fault. It has to be mine."

The second thing disturbing her was that he used very much the same phrases she would have used, had she been in his position. In the last half-dozen years, she had become increasingly strident about things being "state of the art" and "brand, spanking new, created only yesterday." A co-worker even joked about Alice's single-minded focus on the subject by singing, "Everything's up to date in Kansas City." Herb, however, had not only stolen her thunder but, as far as she was concerned, was also aiming lightning bolts at her with devastating effect. Nervously, she asked, "How do you think I felt in front of [the others present], with him making me eat my own words?"

Whatever chagrin Alice felt at hearing her own words coming back at her didn't begin to match the discomfort that resulted from the next suggestion. Herb hadn't called the meeting merely to criticize. He wanted changes made in the staff. "You've got to get rid of a few of the people you now have—we don't have the budget for more—and replace them," he said firmly. "We need people who have market smarts, really savvy types. No more sleeping on our feet."

The remarks sent Alice reeling. She had spent most of the decade worrying about being run over from the rear by her bright young assistants. After trying a variety of approaches, she had finally found one that allowed her to experience a modest measure of security: she played "the good guy" and let her bosses be "the bad guys" when they rejected proposals made by her subordinates.

Now, all of a sudden, she was being ordered to make her own life miserable. Alice had stumbled upon the tactic she was using only after a great deal of subconscious trial and error. For her boss to tell her to dismantle that defense—the only effective one she had—made her bounce back and forth between rage and despair. "I can't tell him I won't do it," she later said, as fidgety as we had ever seen her. "He'll fire me. I mean, I can't just say no. And if I hire people who are no better that the ones I've got, he'll know it. He's got everyone's number."

The pressure from both sides, from above and from below, had been there throughout her forties. Now it seemed to be intensifying to the point where she might no longer be able to handle it. In fact, it was difficult to tell whether she was more concerned about being adjudged inadequate by her superiors or by her subordinates. "He couldn't think very much of me," she said tensely, referring to Herb. What brought her to that conclusion? Because, she went on to explain, he would not have told her—he'd not have *had* to tell her—to get a better quality staff if she had been capable all along of doing her job. "He says, 'Get rid of the deadwood,' but who does he *really* have in mind? Maybe it's me. I don't know."

On the other hand, the prospect of hiring some "dynamos," as she kept calling them, terrified her as much if not more. "They're big on winners here—it's a kind of star system—and I'm not much of a star [by their standards]." There was little question in her mind that, once top management realized that they had someone new on staff who was definitely going places, in her words, "the person will leapfrog me, pass me by like I'm standing still." Like Gary, she was being asked to have a hand in her own execution.

Gary and Alice spent the next four years in an agitated state. They did their jobs as best they could—which is quite a statement, given the internal tension they generated almost daily and, lest we forget, nightly as well. Nevertheless, the massive worries they carried with them into their early fifties were the same ones that had assaulted them subconsciously in their early forties and emerged into their conscious perceptions only in the mid-to-late forties.

Alice did as she was told, although she managed to let almost eight months go by before hiring the first one. ("Good people are *very* hard to find," she repeatedly said to Herb.) Another year passed before she hired a second. Gary too learned how to drag his feet in a way that immobilized the enemies above and below. For instance, he often made it seem that he couldn't possibly begin a new project he was being assigned until he completed one he had previously been given. "You know me," he would say convincingly. "I can't stand doing a half-assed job. And I don't want to tell the 'geniuses' I have working for me to rush. They get so damned flustered."

For the most part, it worked. As Gary candidly admitted at 50, "I get away with a lot here. Nobody knows for sure what's going on in my department but me, thank goodness." It was a comment that would have been totally out of character fourteen years before, when hoodwinking his firm in any way would have made Gary extremely uncomfortable. But much had happened along the way. More than a solid decade of desperately defending themselves had made these two cynical and devious to a degree that they would previously have found odious.

One thing was certain: their ambitions remained largely intact at 50, and they still scrambled madly to get whatever attention and acclaim for themselves they could. If anything, they were more viciously competitive at 50, where their peers were concerned, than they had been at 35. In spite of the intense and continuing battle they had waged up, down, and sideways, they had remarkably little to show for it. They had made almost no real progress during the decade and a half in terms of pay and promotions.

The reasons why weren't hard to find. When Alice was 50, Herb got an offer to become president of the firm he had left six years before. He jumped at it. Once he was there, we held a series of interviews with him and asked, "Is there anything you'd do differently if you could do it over?" High on the list was one item he had already mentioned to the other senior executives before leaving: "I should have fired Alice. She doesn't deserve to have that position." The lack of progress in Gary's case was summarized by his immediate supervisor when talking to a friend. "Gary?" the supervisor replied to the friend's inquiry. "He's a hack. A scared rabbit. The guy is dead in the water."

Heading for Trouble

The earlier that people realize difficulties are developing, the better. The evidence indicates overwhelmingly that finding out that one is on the wrong road in terms of one's everyday business behavior is something that must be done as soon as possible. It is easy to take the detour too far and then be unable to come back and start over before one runs out of time. A career is only so long.

It may have been possible in the past to get away with not keeping up, since the business world wasn't nearly as competitive as it is now. Today, merely remaining in business for an extended period, just surviving as a going concern, has become an achievement for each firm. Moving on to the next step, attaining a decent-sized market share and doing it profitably, is more than thousands of companies can currently hope to attain. With corporate bankruptcy rates at the highest levels since the Depression, and foreign firms taking huge bites out of the American economic landscape, the pressure is on.

Try as they might, Gary and Alice were unable to hide the fact that they had fallen victim to the single most common—and predictable— affliction of people in their forties who are in the business world: a loss of momentum. Instead of recognizing the problem for what it was and doing something about it, they compounded the error by becoming irritable and defensive. Since they were attacking the symptoms, not the cause, the matter only worsened.

In the next chapter we'll see how the whole problem could have been prevented in the first place.

CHAPTER
12

Staying in the Mainstream

GARY AND ALICE had known about computers ever since their teen years. They had grown up during an era in which the industry was also growing. Soon the machines peppered the corporate landscape and became an everyday part of the operations of thousands of businesses.

Yet is wasn't until Gary and Alice were in their forties that the machines suddenly seemed to them a menace. In their twenties and thirties, forward-looking people that they were, they considered computers interesting but weren't particularly fearful of them. Something had changed drastically. It could not have been the mere fact that they had grown older. There were many people their age in our sample who entered their forties and experienced none of the apprehension that plagued Gary and Alice throughout the decade.

Who's Afraid of a Big, Bad Computer?

Before we see what accounts for the variation from one person to the next, even though the two seem comparable in every important respect, it is worthwhile to take a closer look at the following question: How worried is any given person about being replaced at work by a computer? How much does he or she feel threatened by automation?

The reason the question is crucial is this: The more threatened people doing white-collar office work feel, the more likely it is that they are losing their sense of direction.

In their twenties and thirties, Gary's and Alice's business lives were overflowing with purpose. They knew what they enjoyed doing, where they wanted to go, and what they would do once they got there. However, by the time they were in their early forties, they'd lost their bearings. It was then—and only then—that they were subject for the first time to acute attacks of obsolescence anxiety. We now know that to be an unmistakable sign that serious problems lay ahead.

Others who were comparable to them, but who managed to maintain a strong sense of direction during the decade, escaped the affliction entirely. They were too busy pursuing their professional interests to worry much about the topic. Their deep involvement in what they were doing, its pleasures as well as pains, made them view the whole idea of being replaced by a computer (when we raised the question) as absurd.

A typical comment, which came from a portfolio manager who is six weeks older than Gary, was, "Look, I'm going to wrestle with these [stock and bond] markets until I'm too old to see the telequote machine. When—and if—someone invents a computer that does this better for the clients than I can, I'll quit. But not before then." He then went on to remind us that institutional investors (banks, insurance companies, pension and mutual funds) had plenty of computers to go along with their piles of cash, and thus far they had managed to use these allegedly brilliant machines primarily to help them take thumping losses whenever the market declined.

Like this fellow, the vast majority of those who were happily grappling with the substance of their field—instead of fighting an endless war on three fronts, up, down, and sideways, with superiors, subordinates, and peers—never even thought about the matter. If automation was going to overtake them, it would have to take them unaware.

If that attitude seems cavalier, perhaps even naive, consider one monumentally important fact: over the last two decades, computers have actually become less menacing, not more. The reason behind the shift could hardly be simpler. Companies that manufacture these machines want to sell them—to every firm, large and small, and to individuals now as well. At one time, computers were thought of as esoteric, high-tech, and even exotic. So were the people who had anything to do with them. The typical customers for computers therefore were very large firms, universities, or the government. The size and complexity of such institutions made their data-processing needs obvious. They could also afford the high price of the machines and, equally important, they were willing to staff the requisite specialized department devoted solely to working with such equipment and the data it was designed to handle.

Where was the department? Usually hidden away. (Water cooling systems that had to be used in addition to air conditioners to meet rigid operating-temperature requirements often made that necessary.) Only a tiny proportion of the people employed at the firm even knew where the EDP (Electronic Data Processing) department was. As for the people working there—well, as we said, they were considered a little strange. As one viewed them, "The people [in it] remind me of the yucky math club kids in my high school."

Computer manufacturers realized early that they would soon be in trouble if they sold only to huge firms. Eventually they would saturate the market, and then what? So during the 1960s and even more so during the 1970s, they tried hard to broaden the customer base. When they failed to do so, or didn't move rapidly enough into the area, new manufacturers sprung up or expanded—for instance, Digital Equipment and Data General—that took the small-computer market seriously.

The upshot: the machines ceased to be housed only in the bowels of the nation's largest corporations and ultimately came to be seen everywhere. The manufacturers succeeded in broadening the market immensely, while at the same time, the machines came out of hiding and lost their mystique. Mass-market acceptance required nothing less.

Not everyone was happy about that. There are computer scientists and electrical engineers in our sample who liked the idea of scaring people into believing that, "You'll soon be replaced by a computer." Call it the Revenge of the Math Club. As one put it in 1959, "It's a power trip for me, I guess. I dream of coming up with machines that will throw millions of people out of work." Said a second in 1960, "I wouldn't mind having people tremble when they see me coming and realize that maybe their jobs are in jeopardy."

The companies that manufacture the machines had other goals in mind. They were less interested in power than profits. Instead of taking people's work away, they wanted everyone to believe that the machines would help make their work easier and go faster. "You'll be more productive," was a common sales pitch. A common retort was, "No, I won't. Not if I have to spend all my time learning how to program these boxes, and even more time debugging each program."

The last two decades can therefore be summed up in a simple phrase. There has been a massive effort on the part of computer manufacturers to make the machines more "user-friendly." That's just a nice way of saying "less intimidating and easier to use." So now everyone can buy one; small firms, individuals, and, of course, teenagers. The companies don't even want potential customers to ask whether or not they really need the machines. That might prevent each of them from getting one. The only question they want people to ask is, as the salesman in the local computer store put it, "What *level* of computing power do you need?"

In short, if worrying about being replaced by a computer is a groundless fear, why is a larger proportion of the work force concerned about it now than was the case twenty years ago? There are indeed employees who have good reason to worry: manual laborers and assembly-line workers. But these people have been undergoing displacement by mechanical inventions for centuries. The fact that electromechanical (robot) devices will do the same in the future merely continues the labor-saving trend.

However, the people we have focused upon in our studies aren't manual laborers. The vast majority are white-collar office workers. Their fears about automation may seem very real to them, and we certainly don't mean to make light of their concern. But, as anyone who has watched the computer industry develop over the years and knows even a little about new product plans can confirm, the anxiety is unwarranted.

Once again, then, we ask: If there is little cause for alarm, why are so many people worried? To see the answer, we need to spend a few minutes talking about a subject that at first glance seems worlds apart from this one: the sexual anxieties of youngsters a century ago.

Getting Back on the Right Road

If children are repeatedly told that everything connected with sex is filthy and forbidden, they'll eventually believe it. Instead of seeing it as merely a normal part of life, they may try to scrub their minds of any allegedly dirty thoughts associated with the subject.

Once puberty hits, though, the severe repression often leads to trouble. Nature wants them to think about the topic, whereas they, in order to please their parents, would rather not. The internal civil war that starts during adolescence and continues into adulthood can be severe. They may find themselves extremely anxious and not know why, when in fact the underlying cause is that they are at least mildly aroused. If they have been taught to believe in the Devil, they may feel they have fallen into his hands. "Get thee behind me, Satan," is a phrase that is not nearly as popular now as it was in the nineteenth century, but in one form or another it is still heard.

It is very revealing to talk to people who believe in the Devil and who are convinced that erotic thoughts, not to mention acts, are the result of his work. They interpret their anxiety when they are sexually aroused to be proof that the Devil exists. As one put it, "I can feel his evil presence in my loins." The point here is that their anxiety tells us little about the Devil, since we can't physically prove or disprove that he exists. But it does tell us in many instances that they are aroused, something we can measure.

"What in the world," the reader may be asking, "does any of this have to do with computers and the success of a business career?" An enormous amount.

Not many people believe in the Devil anymore. Even those who believe in God (more than 65 percent of our sample) don't give much credence to the idea (well below 1 percent). Nevertheless, bizarre as it may sound, the Devil plays more of a role in their thoughts about their business activities than they might imagine. What confuses them is that the figure is no longer dressed in black, with a cape. Instead, he has been superseded by a machine—a computer—with whirring tapes and blinking lights.

People who are deathly afraid of sex, because they think it is obscene and disgusting, use an image of Satan as a *reminder* to stay on the right track and away from the subject. And people who deeply believe that they should be working hard, but who have in fact temporarily lost interest in doing so, also need a way of prodding themselves into behaving properly day after day.

The Devil served the purpose well in the past, when suppressing sexual thoughts was one of polite society's highest goals and people were praised for succeeding at the task. Now, in the post-contraception era, we are more comfortable with sex; so the internal reminder that the Devil used to provide in this area is no longer necessary. But it is still necessary in another area, and for good reason. College-educated adults in particular hold work in very high regard. To them, it isn't just a job, a mere source of income. They have infused it with a higher value and now want it to give them many of the deepest satisfactions they will have in their lives. In not doing their work, or in having a mere job, they feel they are cheating themselves.

But no Devil appears in their minds to tell them they are doing something they shouldn't. Nor does their boss, because in most offices no one stands over their shoulder every minute of the day to make certain they they don't goof off. The impetus to work must come from within—and hence so must the reminder. Fear of the Devil doesn't provide it any longer, but fear of the computer does.

In short, people who suffer acute attacks of obsolescence anxiety are reminding themselves that they have wandered off the right track. They are not working and they know it, even if no one else does. Since they are violating one of their highest values—that work should be personally rewarding and meaningful—they seek to nudge themselves back onto the correct path. If they don't do it to themselves, for themselves, who will? Who else can, before it is too late?

That is why the question about how worried people are about being replaced by a computer is crucial. Long before they have wandered so far off the right road that a career crisis is unavoidable, it will let them know that serious trouble awaits them in the not-too-distant future.

The Effort to Keep Up

Even when a belief in the Devil was widespread, people didn't always invoke his specific image to keep themselves in check. Old diaries and letters indicate that a more abstract image was used far more frequently: Temptation, always spelled with a capital *T*. In fact, one of Satan's other names that was very popular at the time was the Tempter. The word was equally useful since it pulsated with the same kind of anxious reminders to stay away from forbidden thoughts and activities.

Office workers today can't always count on the image of a powerful computer springing to mind to get them back on the track, lest the machine take away their jobs. Besides, some people are well aware that a computer, no matter how advanced, could probably not do their work as well as they can. It is therefore very common for the needed prod to assume a more abstract form: obsolescence anxiety. People agonize about the fact that they aren't keeping up, that they are falling behind, losing touch, and becoming out of date.

Misguided critics have labeled this as evidence of the fickle and faddish concerns of outer-directed Americans, an effort by each to remain part of the all-important crowd. To some extent that is so. But this greatly overemphasizes the group-oriented aspects. To a much larger extent the concern is an attempt by an energetic, hardworking, and ambitious people to keep themselves motivated—on their own. In Europe, before emigrating to these shores, people typically had been embedded in tightly knit social fabrics that carried each individual along quietly. However, in this country, people were (and are) free to rattle around in wide open spaces in which, if they chose, no one could monitor their everyday behavior. As a result, they found it necessary to do it themselves.

Internal coercion systems were created to take the place of external coercion systems that now were missing. The consequences were major. People who are controlling their own behavior successfully don't need, and usually resent, having an outside agency tell them how to act. There is little reason for them to pattern themselves after a model of their "social superiors," a concept Americans scoffed at in the past, and still do. Most already have all the self-restraint they need. In the nineteenth century, traveling evangelical preachers howled at them about Lucifer and his fiery Hell, providing people with a powerful inner reminder to carry with them on their unwatched wanderings. The twentieth century has given them IBM as a substitute for the Devil, and Obsolescence Anxiety in place of Temptation.

That means that the subtle reminders they send themselves that they are deviating from the best course—the one most likely to help them get ahead—are very important. However, the reminders won't always be embodied in the image of a flashing, whirring, clicking electronic box coming after them. It would be convenient to have something that vivid available to help keep one on track, yet what most dedicated workers experience instead is the vague, gnawing fear that they are becoming outmoded and irrelevant. That may be less visual an indication but it is every bit as valuable as an unmistakable early warning sign.

Once Gary and Alice ignored those signs, the series of troubles that eventually bested them occurred in predictable steps. First, they tried to mask the fact that they had lost their sense of direction. Nevertheless, they still had to handle the consequences of the loss: the fear of being found obsolete and dispensable. There were younger workers around who were more dedicated to keeping up to date, and that made it easy for top management to make some potentially embarrassing comparisons. Being at a smaller firm would not have helped these two, since our studies indicate that they would have been subject to the same high degree of internal and external scrutiny elsewhere. The business world was becoming increasingly competitive. As Gary put it, "There's no place to hide anymore." Each smoke screen tactic that he and Alice used therefore merely required yet another. Nothing seemed to work, except briefly.

Soon they lost sight of the fact that they had ever even had a sense of direction. It amazed them that they had gotten as far as they did. From what they could now see, there was no justification for their rise, much less for them to keep the jobs they currently held. But they had no place else to go. Although they had lost their old senses of direction, they had not acquired new ones. So, in spite of feeling dated and old, they were determined to hold on to what they had somehow attained. What consumed them now was the outcome of each day's skirmishes, since there was nothing to make them look beyond the squabbles and hence render each more bearable. There was no forest, not even trees; they only watched nervously for pitfalls. All they could feel were the brambles along the way.

Looking for Praise

How did they get into the mess in the first place, and what is most likely to cause others to find themselves in same situation? The most basic answer has to do with praise. Our studies turned up the fact that people in business get less of it between the ages of 37 and 53 than when they are on either side of that age range.

When people are younger, their elders will compliment them, if for no other reason than to inspire them. That isn't to imply that their words are false. They usually mean what they are saying, but with children and young adults it is considered acceptable, even mandatory at times, to exaggerate. Their need for approval is openly recognized, even if it is rarely fulfilled completely. If the job they hold in their twenties and early thirties is even moderately well matched to their abilities, they will obtain a certain amount of applause, though in most instances it will be less than they ideally would have liked.

Once workers are in their middle-to-late fifties and early sixties, they will also receive a certain amount of recognition. (The problem here is that it is difficult to distinguish the genuine from the counterfeit article, as we'll see in Part Five.) Younger workers frequently make a special point of displaying respect for senior figures in the firm. Here too, as with the young, in many instances it is less than the amount desired by the older recipient.

However, people in their forties are in a barren zone. *Statistically speaking, the group making the transition through its forties receives the fewest work-related compliments by far; in fact, in the majority of instances, they receive none. Inner satisfaction is therefore of crucial importance.* The pleasure that comes from doing their craft well, and from deepening their ability at it, must carry them during the period. They received a number of compliments in the prior decade and will get them again in the next one, assuming they can somehow survive the decade-long drought. But for the moment, they can consider themselves extremely fortunate if they have even one person each who serves as a source of legitimate and heartfelt praise.

Does it matter? Enormously. Is is supposed to matter? No. People in this age range for some reason are assumed to be free of the need. Not only is that a myth, it is a very destructive one. People who run scared at this level are in a position to wreck a company. Once they turn from furthering the firm's goals to boosting their own egos in a direct and personal manner, they become a dangerous and disruptive force. In a large number of cases that we've documented, they have brought healthy firms to a state of disarray and subsequent collapse. Nonetheless, these men and women yearned for what they weren't getting, and pay and promotions simply weren't enough to keep them plugging away peacefully on the firm's behalf. The policy they instead adopted was, "Praise for me is more important than prosperity for this company."

If only it were that simple. The distinction may be neat when people are in their twenties, but if they've been serious about their work all along, it becomes much harder to make once they are in their forties. A loss of momentum doesn't change one of the central values that guided their lives for decades. Namely, that work is supposed to be, and once was, personally meaningful. A temporary halt in career progress may bring them into conflict with that value but certainly doesn't erase it. Wishing it were gone won't make it disappear, particularly with nothing of equal weight to take its place.

In brief, by the time the people we studied were in their forties, they had spent many years adhering to an approach to life that makes dedication to one's work satisfying. Trying to do an about-face in order to reduce the inner conflict that results from a loss of direction at work only triggered an internal alarm, repeatedly. The result was acute and recurring bouts of obsolescence anxiety, signals they ignored at their own peril.

Regaining a Sense of Direction

What, then, is one supposed to do when the alarm sounds? First, stop looking for praise. Telling people in their forties not to expect much applause at work may seem like a meager bit of advice at best. However, our experiments with volunteers who were told in their late thirties that they were entering a period during which they would receive little or no praise indicate that this information is remarkably helpful. People who aren't anticipating a compliment are much less disappointed when it doesn't come. And it was the disappointment, not the lack of approval, that hurt adults most. In this arena, to be forewarned is indeed to be forearmed. Those who were alerted suffered significantly less letdown.

It is also worthwhile to note that synthetic compliments from manipulative managers just above them did nothing for the workers we studied. Ironically, the most common reaction was an increase in cynicism and irritation. Typical comments, "I hate being treated like a pawn," and "What do they think I am, an eight-year-old?" Approval dished out in so mechanical and cosmetic a fashion, whether it was issued almost daily or on a monthly basis, struck them as empty theatrics, mere foolishness.

Second, and most important, it is imperative during this decade to become a self-starter. What is odd is that it is primarily workers in their twenties who are repeatedly encouraged to be self-motivated. Being a get-up-and-go type is widely and officially admired at that stage.

What makes it odd is that no employer really wants people to be self-starters when they are in their twenties. Quite the contrary, the firm certainly wants them to be willing to work energetically but wants to be able to tell them where, when, and how. Having one's own special style and approach, assuming they are well-defined at that age, is usually a nuisance. The firm wants young employees, especially those who show promise, to adopt *its* style and make their contributions within that framework, rather than sweep away the old approach and introduce something radically new.

It is when people are in their forties that being a self-starter can make or break their career. To be specific, when Gary started getting almost no positive feedback from peers and superiors in his early forties, he lost his bearings. Their warm words had been a key part of what he had been using to orient himself all along.

He took the lack of explicit approval to mean that his superiors now disapproved of what he was doing. They didn't, but they were no longer willing to praise him daily as a way of inducing him to do his work. They expected him to become significantly more autonomous, without putting the message into so many words. Had he been prepared for that, in all likelihood he would have been much less rattled by the deafening silence it is typical for good workers to experience during this decade. Then, he could have gone on to step two and used his own sense of direction to see him through.

Sharpening one's sense of direction, and therefore keeping one's self on track, is easier once it is realized that specialized skills are the ones needed most by modern firms. We all have a diversity of interests, and it certainly would be fun to be able to do something different each day, depending upon what caught us up at the moment. Entertaining as that might be, it would soon pose a threat to our ability to make a living. Hopping whimsically from one area to the next, milking each for any kicks or applause it yielded, would stop us from developing enough depth and expertise in any one field to find a secure place for ourselves occupationally.

Odd as it may sound, it would also prevent us from enjoying ourselves. The people we studied who were indeed able to do whatever they pleased each day throughout their forties—because they had enough money and decided not to work—rather rapidly became bored. That surprised us. We believed it when workers told us that their dream come true was to do, as one put it, "everything, anything, or nothing on any given day." Yet once they had the opportunity to do just that, month after month, they eventually grew restless and irritable, not overjoyed and content.

Particularly when people are in their forties, it is clearly quite important for their daily activities to have a strong sense of purpose. When all is said and done, they need a work-related activity they enjoy sufficiently to do for years on end—without wanting to switch. It has to catch them up, absorb them hour after hour, so that the time passes without their being impatiently aware of every tick of the clock. Not only will the activity keep them absorbed, as a critical bonus it will also keep the people around them organized.

In fact, the best way for them to cause chaos in their office is to do nothing. That is what Gary and Alice unwittingly did, and it threw the people around them into a tizzy. Especially because both were such movers and shakers in their thirties, always busy, constantly trying to find different or better ways to get things done, they had gathered behind them some equally innovative assistants and associates. Coming to nearly a complete halt caused Gary and Alice to be bumped into regularly and hard.

One can avoid the most serious, predictable crisis of the decade. If necessary, one may have to force oneself to be a self-starter after 40 by finding a series of projects that are interesting, significant, and co-ordinated—not random—and that help the people behind one to fall into formation. Even then, one shouldn't expect to look over one's shoulder and see an orderly line of baby ducks in one's wake. If one is really propelling oneself forward successfully, the co-workers and sub-ordinates who are involved will have things with which to busy themselves that, at least in one's own view, are constructive and worthwhile. The pattern may not be as visible as with birds on the wing but, if all is going well, one will have become the leading point of a flying wedge.

It is important to mention that people who lose their sense of momentum aren't always attacked by feelings of obsolescence. Even those who have lost their sense of direction entirely may not think about sophisticated computers coming after them or state-of-the-art electronic hardware replacing them. Instead of experiencing the problem psychologically, in terms of obsolescence anxiety, they experience it in social terms, as being "out of the mainstream."

There is a very real demographic dimension to their concern: the huge postwar baby-boom generation, the largest in American history, has come of age. Between 1946 and 1964, 76 million children were born in the United States, and now, with many of them already in their thirties, they are an economic force to be reckoned with in the work world. Since this group constitutes nearly a third of the nation's population, it is small wonder that so many executives in their forties and fifties are asking themselves, "Are my concerns those of the up-coming generation?"

Regardless of how the anxiety is experienced, whether it be psychologically or socially, the underlying problem that gives rise to it is the same, and so is the solution. Overcoming the uneasiness requires people to regain their momentum. Workers in their forties with a clear sense of direction have no reason to fear the upcoming generation. A strong sense of direction is what these young adults repeatedly tell us impresses them most about those just ahead of them.

In short, only a dedication to deepening one's abilities, perfecting one's craft, will carry one through the barren zone of the forties with a minimum of inner turmoil and a maximum of productivity and fulfillment. The compliments people got in their twenties and thirties may have helped them sustain their feeling of purpose at the time, but in their forties they will be lucky to receive any honest compliments at all. Although young workers in their first years on a job often complain about being merely "a cog on a wheel," it is when they are between 37 and 53 that they will truly be expected to lick their wounds privately and function day after day as if they are brilliant and tireless robots.

If they hunger during their forties for approval, the situation will go from bad to worse. And as they slow down, they will be attacked by a variety of fears, all interconnected: "Have I fallen behind?" "Maybe I'm outmoded." "Perhaps I don't belong here any more." "I wonder if I'm still pulling my own weight." It is imperative for them to heed the warnings they are giving themselves and get moving again.

They can count on the fact that it will frequently be lonely, and there are many occasions when they will have to consciously compel themselves to be self-starters. However, the rewards in time will arrive, though perhaps not in the form in which they were anticipated. In the interim, personal satisfaction will have to carry them. Throwing themselves into projects that absorb them and sharpen their skills is the most effective way to find peace and advancement while avoiding substantial, and what often turns out to be permanent, harm to their career.

V

THE FIFTIES

THE PROBLEM OF
NO HEIRS

CHAPTER
13

Manipulating the Boss

WHEN WE FIRST began our study during the 1950s, the stages of the life cycle was a widely discussed topic. Erik Erikson, in particular, called attention to the subject in 1950.[1] In spite of all the interest that was generated, unfortunately neither the theory itself was ever fully developed for adults (since Erikson's main focus was on childhood and adolescence) nor was the existing theory measured against the real-life experiences of contemporary business people. From the start, we felt that this was a worthwhile and even essential goal.

Erikson's view was that the excessive attention paid to how much young children need their parents had blinded us to how much the older generation is dependent upon the younger. The desire to be needed is a strong one, Erikson felt, especially in one's more mature years. The observation was hardly new, but Erikson's contribution was (1) presenting the desire in a structured setting as a specific stage in the life cycle, and (2) in doing so, making it the most important psychological need for all human beings during the seventh of the eight stages into which he felt their lives are naturally divided, or should be.

Erikson used the word "generativity" to describe the desire, and he defined it as a concern with establishing (by which he meant giving birth to) and then guiding the next generation. Since people in business couldn't spawn the appropriate subordinates on cue, the analogous step in this case involves "adoption." A senior executive either consciously or subconsciously adopts, in an informal manner, someone who occupies a more junior position at the firm. From then on he or she serves as tutor, as well as boss, to that person.

What happens to people in the seventh Age of Man who fail to act in the manner the model suggests? The alternative to generativity,

---

[1] Erik Erikson, "Chapter 7: Eight Ages of Man," *Childhood and Society*, 2nd ed. (New York: W. W. Norton, 1950).

according to Erikson, is stagnation and self-involvement.[2] With no one else's growth to concentrate upon, no fledgling in need of their guidance and advice, they become preoccupied with themselves and end up excessively self-indulgent.

As a theory, that sounds fine, but two serious obstacles to generativity quickly become apparent when one examines the day-to-day lives of business people. The first obstacle is that by the time college graduates enter the business world, they are moderately fed up with school. In their view, it has delayed not only their income-earning years, it has also postponed their maturation. Now they actively seek opportunities to be in charge and to expand their abilities through on-the-job practice. Reverting to the student role strikes them as an unwelcome step backward. If they have to do it, because one of the firm's elders feels like being generative, they will, but they emotionally resist the arrangement more than most care to admit.

The second major obstacle to generativity concerns competition. Why this topic receives so little attention in Erikson's work we're not sure, but the subject and its effects on people's behavior simply cannot be overlooked in the business world. In the 1950s, it is fair to say that seniority—that is, a hierarchy based on length of service with the firm—went far to restrain competition between older and younger employees. A senior executive who wanted to informally adopt a subordinate and act as mentor therefore had much less to fear from his pupil than would be the case in more recent decades.

The 1957 launch by the U.S.S.R. of Sputnik I, the first space satellite, and the election of Jack Kennedy in 1959, ushered in an altogether different mentality. We had fallen undeniably behind the Soviet Union in an area of technology that represented a clear threat to United States military and commercial interests. The nation—and the business world—suddenly elevated scientists and engineers to positions of high status. Since the federal government was spending tens of billions of dollars on the space race, and corporations large and small wanted to be eligible both for the research and development funding and suppliers of high-tech products as well, bright young graduates in these fields were eagerly hired straight out of school and given substantial salaries.

Whatever respect for seniority that had previously existed suddenly vanished. In fact, the whole system of establishing peace within a business enterprise by giving everyone a vertical ranking based on age

---

[2]In some books and articles Erikson has set generativity against stagnation, while in other writings and classroom lectures it is set in opposition to self-absorption. We have combined the two. See "Growth and Crises of the Healthy Personality," *Symposium on the Healthy Personality*, Josiah Macy Jr. Foundation (March 1950). Reprinted in *Identity and the Life Cycle*, International University Press, 1959 and W. W. Norton, 1980.

now seemed to have been stood on its head. Youth, especially technically trained youth, was prized most. Power and decision-making ability was handed to these recent graduates in many cases without their even asking for it, and more than 52% of the executives in our sample told us in 1964 that these young workers were now the appropriate source of direction for the firm. Less than 12 percent felt that way in 1958–59.

To say that the new high-tech mentality that had seized the business world posed a threat to generative feelings understates the case. Actually, the two mentalities now existed in a state of direct opposition. It is hard for senior executives to adopt and guide someone who is widely viewed as being better qualified to do their job than they. The pleasures that come from parenting, from watching and fostering the development of their progeny, can be substantial. Yet here, thanks to the nation's obligatory emphasis on science and technology, they had pupils who might leapfrog them at any moment and end up being *their* superior.

There was a solution, and we expected many executives to choose it. They didn't. The firm's senior members who wanted to express their generative inclinations could have adopted subordinates with non-technical backgrounds. The threat such pupils posed on this score would have been decidedly less. The advantage of adoption in the office, as opposed to having real children at home, is that one gets to pick and choose. However, there was no question who the prized subordinates were. The firm's officers all wanted to adopt a winner, and that meant someone with a science or engineering education. Humanities majors yearned to be included but were passed by repeatedly, left to languish in the corporate nursery. Like moths to a flame, executives in the 1960s were drawn to the very protégés they secretly feared most.

Under the circumstances, it is hardly surprising that stable, generative pairings between younger and older members of the firm decreased markedly between 1958 and 1963. Erikson's comment in 1963 that generativity involves "production and care"[3] seemed both obvious and divorced from reality. It was now clear that the theory was not only too simple to have any explanatory power, it also omitted the most important psychological realities people at this stage of their lives experienced day to day.

As the 1960s came to a close, and government spending on defense and the space race wound down, we expected to see generative pairings on the job increase. After all, by late 1969 scientists and engineers were no longer viewed by either the nation or the nation's businesses as

---

[3]*Childhood and Society*, p. 274.

saviors. We thought their removal from the pedestal would foster more mentor–protégé duos involving, not only those with technical backgrounds, but also those with degrees in the humanities. It didn't happen. The reason is that a new group of favorites emerged that forced both of these groups to the rear. MBAs quietly became (there was no Sputnik to herald their arrival) the new corporate darlings.

There were striking parallels between the way business leaders viewed MBAs in the 1970s and scientists and engineers in the 1960s. The generative impulse still beat within the breast of executives, but now they preferred that it be aimed at someone with an MBA. To put it quantitatively, approximately 43 percent of the executives in our sample told us in 1973 that young workers with a graduate degree in business administration were the appropriate source of direction for the firm. Scientists and engineers got less than 11 percent of the votes, nearly an 80 percent decrease from a decade before.

Nevertheless, the new "miracle workers" were every bit as much a threat to generativity as scientists and engineers had been in the previous decade. Once again, executives were drawn to the very people who might be adjudged more qualified to run the firm, in spite of their lack of experience, than the officers currently running it. Also, job-hopping made such pairings difficult to establish and maintain, as annual turnover rates in the 20 to 40 percent range became common for the favored group of the 1970s (just as it had for a different but similarly prized group in the 1960s). Wary, tentative vertical pairings were once again the rule.

By the early 1980s, the bloom was off this rose too. With MBAs becoming a glut on the market and their inability to work miracles for their employers a fact demonstrated and commented upon repeatedly during the stagnant 1970s and early 1980s, executives in 1983–84 became enamored of a new breed of recent college graduate: computer scientists. However, this round of infatuation differed dramatically from that seen two decades before. Whereas 52 percent of the executives in our sample told us in 1964 that engineers and scientists should provide corporations with a sense of direction, and 43 percent of a comparable executive group told us in 1973 that MBAs should, in late 1983 *less than 1 percent* of the executives we surveyed felt that computer scientists should be given this type of power or decision-making responsibility. Top corporate officers were certainly seeking computer-literate employees, but by no means were they ready this time to hand them the reins of the firm. In fact, the expertise of the group was viewed in much the same light as that possessed by plumbers and electricians. Nevertheless, with more than a quarter of a trillion dollars likely to be spent between 1984 and 1989 in the United States on computer hardware, software, services, and staff, the field possesses a degree of glamour that plumbers couldn't hope to match. Interestingly, this time it is students and young workers, not corporate officers, who are most enthralled by new computer products and the people who create them. The fragile, generative pairings of the two previous decades, first with scientists and engineers, then with MBAs, are undoubtedly helping executives to maintain their sense of perspective during the current period.

In this chapter we will look at a few representative examples of what happens when an executive unwittingly adopts a subordinate and attempts to foster his or her business and professional development. The examples are chosen from the areas of law and public relations, fields that were much less affected than most by the trends in executive infatuation discussed above.

Preaching Versus Teaching

Most people thought of Arthur Cummings as hard-boiled. "He's fair," said a longtime colleague, "but tough. When he wants something, he goes after it and doesn't quit till he gets it." Said another, "Art's one guy who stands his ground. I've seen him compromise and be easygoing, but only when he has to."

Arthur was an indifferent student. His middle-class parents worked hard to send him to college, but World War II erupted when he was a junior and, instead of going on to his senior year, he was sent to Belgium, where he was wounded in the Battle of the Bulge. When he came home, he completed college and attended graduate school on the GI bill. "I couldn't have gone any other way," he said at 39. "My father had died that year of a heart attack. I had to work nights and weekends to cover the cost." According to a friend who knew him in school, native intelligence saw Arthur through: "He was half asleep lots of times in class from working and then studying late the night before. I don't know how he did it. I couldn't have."

A one-man band in his early years after becoming a member of the bar, Arthur didn't want to be corporate counsel at a large firm. He set up his own. But, as he put it, "I like to eat, and I couldn't afford to on what I was making." So when a prestigious law firm he had soundly beaten in an important case subsequently offered that he join them, he did. Arthur may have been a middling student, but he was a conscientious lawyer. The judges and adversaries who've watched him work over the years rated him as "forceful, quick on his feet and well-prepared."

Through his own efforts, as well as those of the other partners and associates, the business expanded rapidly and is now one of the 50 largest law firms in the country. Throughout his forties, Arthur experienced many of the pressures from above and below that are typical of the period. "I hate it," he told us calmly at 43, when he saw bright, young law school graduates moving up the ladder faster than he had. "Or should I say, "I hate *them*.' It comes so easy for them."

Arthur was a junior partner in the firm at the time, "and I get paid like one," he repeatedly said, meaning that his hourly billing rate was substantially lower than that charged by the firm's senior partners. Only a strong sense of direction (he decided to specialize in his first love, securities law, during the period) saw him through the decade with less strain than average.

Even though his wife bought him a handsome leather briefcase for his fiftieth birthday, Arthur frequently jammed his papers into any available manila envelope and went to his next meeting. With his tie loosely knotted around his neck, he always had a windblown look, as though his clothes and hair rearranged themselves of their own free will.

In Arthur's 52nd year, a new element began creeping into the picture. He wanted a younger associate whom, in his words, "I can teach, once and for all, instead of always having to *tell* what to do." Arthur wasn't an easy man to work for, but one of the main reasons for that had been, in the past anyway, that he preferred to tell, not teach. "Maybe I'm just getting on in years," he said, trying to brush aside his own remark.

Maybe. Yet it emerged again at 54, 56, and 57, stronger each time than the time before. "These young know-it-alls," he said sarcastically at 54. "They really think they've got nothing to learn." At 56, "I know they've got brains—they were at the top of the class. But they're not willing to *listen*." And at 57, "The music they play [so loudly] must be making them deaf. I tell them something valuable and they don't hear it. [Later] they tell me I didn't even say it. I have a very good memory; I *know* what I said. They don't retain anything. Got minds like sieves."

It would be easy to dismiss Arthur's string of comments as those of a self-made man who was growing crabby and old. That is certainly what some of the firm's younger associates who had worked with him in recent years concluded. "He gets you in his office [lately] and wants to lecture you," said one irritably. "Who needs it?" Nevertheless, there is more to the story here than meets the eye.

Marie Roberts is Arthur's age, but her field is public relations. During our first interview with her when she was 39, she joked, "Nobody starts out *deciding* to be in PR. You fall into it backwards, after you've done something else for a while." She had originally wanted to be in television, doing documentaries. "I look good on screen," she said in her usual excited and bubbling manner. "I've been told I'm *very* convincing."

When Marie Roberts was still, there was a look of excess about her—too much makeup, too much hair, too much jewelry, colors that were too bright—but once in motion, it all played together like a well-practiced orchestra. The jewelry tinkled happily as her hands flashed through the air, eyes sparkling, while she described her latest project. The listener was swept away by her excitement, not always recognizing a true professional at work.

An English major in college, Marie was certain she would wind up lounging around the house in a bathrobe, pin curlers in her hair, writing short stories for women's magazines, and from time to time, huge sagas for the soap-opera set. "I love the gooey stuff," she said, scrunching up her face as though she had just bitten into a bitter lemon. "Romantic fiction will be around *forever*." Her first few jobs after graduation were doing office work at manufacturing firms. She didn't try to put a happy face on this one. "Being there was the last thing I wanted, but [right after college] I couldn't get anything else."

For twelve years, she worked hard at the two firms, where she was remembered as "driven," "usually ahead of schedule," and "very cooperative." As she rose, her work brought her increasingly into a full-time role in the firm's public relations department. "Some department," she scoffed, thinking about it in retrospect. "It was one person, a public information officer, who didn't even know the right time of day. A primitive operation."

The work caught her up—"There was never a dull moment, *that* I can tell you"—but to keep herself fully motivated, she turned out short stories on evenings and weekends. "I was married, had two children, and I thought I could write Erma Bombeck-type essays about septic tanks, suburbs, and spoiled kids." Things didn't go quite as she had planned. "I couldn't even give the stuff away."

Giving at the Office

Her luck changed abruptly when a grizzly accident occurred near her children's elementary school. A teenager driving too fast ran a stop sign and slammed into a small van that was serving as a local school bus. Two children on board were killed, three were injured seriously. The car's driver was decapitated. Marie first heard about the accident at the grocery store she had stopped at on the way home. "Oh my God," she said. beginning to panic. "My son may have been on that bus."

He was, but aside from a bloody nose and chipped tooth, he was uninjured. When things calmed down a few weeks later, Marie did some digging and found out that, although there were a growing number of safety standards being imposed on cars, there were almost none for buses. The article she wrote on the subject was timely and was published in the local newspaper.

"It was the first time anything I did wound up in print," she said proudly. Marie decided to stay with non-fiction, since it had broken the ice for her. Rather than having an effect on her leisure-hours hobby of writing, the event changed the way she viewed her day. Previously, she had thought of her work as being for money while her writing was for fun. The difference was easy to see when the day involved non-fiction for her firm, and the evening, writing fiction for herself and the general public. Now, suddenly, the two areas drew nearer. A major division, one she had considered it appropriate to maintain for over a decade, came to an end.

Within the year, she joined a mid-sized public relations agency. "I could do it all day now, and on nights and weekends too," she said, thrilled at the thought. For the next seven years, until she was 41, Marie remained at the same agency. Then she moved to another, much smaller firm, taking some of the best people with her. She has been there ever since, and the agency has grown steadily and prospered.

Marie gives credit for that to the nature of the business itself. "Do you realize," she said, genuinely amazed at the thought, "that this field hardly even existed before World War II? Look how big and important it has become. How did anyone ever get along without it?" However, it was the consensus of the nearly two dozen people we interviewed who had worked with her between 21 and 39 that she had the brains, energy, and dedication to succeed at anything she put her mind to. That, they felt, is what finally occurred.

Becoming a junior executive at her firm in her early forties gave Marie all the direction she needed to carry her through the choppy waters that would otherwise have upset her at the time. A natural self-starter, compelled to become even more so by the rapid expansion of her firm, she had no trouble remaining the lead point of a moving wedge during the decade. In fact, as her subordinates pointed out repeatedly to us during the period, they often had to run just to keep up with her. Collisions with Marie because she had come to a standstill seemed an amusingly remote possibility.

However, when she entered her fifties, banging heads with subordinates not only became possible but increasingly probable. And none of the parties involved found it amusing. "What's the matter with her?" an assistant asked when Marie was 53. A month before Marie's 55th birthday, another commented, "She seems fed up," and then added sarcastically, "With what, us or herself?"

Keep in mind that, as in Arthur's case, these collisions were not caused by a slowdown in Marie's work pace, much less a loss of direction. In their fifties, Arthur and Marie were even more focused and productive than they had been a decade previously, which is saying quite a bit. They knew which projects they wanted to tackle, clearly had the appetite for the job, and were successful in most instances at accomplishing what they set out to do. Nevertheless, the degree of friction between these two and their respective assistants was high and growing higher.

Marie's words began to sound much like Arthur's but had a distinct flavor of their own. "This is the laziest group I know," she said at 53. "I wish I could make myself invisible, and come here when they can't see me. [Then] I'd catch them napping. I know they're busiest [only] when I'm around." At 55, she said, "They all think they have it made. I talk to them, they 'yes' me, and nothing registers." At 57, and angry, she said, "I can't get through to them. Just can't get through. I'm trying to *help* them, and they stare at me. Dense, that's what they are." Marie's assistants were even more certain than Arthur's that their boss was becoming old and crabby. Were they right? People in pain do indeed tend to be short-tempered, and the mild infirmities associated with middle age were beginning to make themselves felt in both cases. Among the stream of physical ailments that undoubtedly affected their mood and manner during the decade were vision, lower back, teeth, and joint problems. Both had put on a little weight, ten to fifteen pounds. The major complaints, which were never voiced to subordinates and usually withheld from peers as well, were some arthritis in Marie's hands and left ankle, and, in Arthur's case, shooting pains in the area of his right hip, which he claimed were a result of a recurring but not disabling injury suffered during the war.

That these maladies contributed to their irritability on certain days seems beyond question. "I had trouble keeping my mind on what he was saying," Marie commented at 56, after an important meeting during which her ankle was sore. Arthur had his share of similar experiences. "I couldn't find a comfortable position [in which my hip didn't hurt]," he said at 55, when his day was done. "It's distracting, dammit." Both reacted to bitterly cold or inclement weather more now than they had in the past.

On the majority of days, though, all was well. Basically, these were two vigorous adults in good physical condition. Neither one jogged, played tennis, or took part in any program of regular exercise, but they did walk quite a number of miles each day, preferring it to cabs, and were almost continually in motion. Most of the time, they felt no pain or physical discomfort. The point is that even on days when they felt in the pink of health, they voiced disparaging remarks about their subordinates' willingness to listen and learn. (All the quotes about the subject in this chapter are taken from interviews on days on which they felt fine.) Physical discomfort wasn't generating the kind of complaint both began voicing frequently in their mid-fifties. Something else was at work here.

Besides, such remarks are often heard from younger workers about *their* subordinates. "He's really thick," a 33-year-old told us about a 26-year-old assistant. Said another, age 34, about one who was 29, "I might as well not tell him anything. Talking to him is like banging my head against the wall." Despite the superficial resemblance between these comments and those voiced by Arthur and Marie, there is a crucial difference. What is it? Competition.

Workers in their twenties, thirties, and forties usually make competitive remarks publicly as a way of boosting themselves while putting someone else—to whom they feel comparable—down. Instead of grandly sharing the information they possess, they want to lord it over those who don't have it, always making certain to know just a little more than their underlings. Above all, they are eager to highlight any alleged differences in ability or intelligence, while venting some stored-up frustration as well.

By the time Arthur and Marie were in their mid-fifties, if that was a factor, it was a minor one. They did not see the younger workers who were the target of their carping remarks as realistic, near-term candidates for the top positions they themselves wanted at the firm. Ten to fifteen years before, Arthur and Marie weren't so sure. Then they worried that anyone and everyone in the firm was beating them out in the race for promotions. Only a strong sense of direction in their forties prevented them from nervously looking in every direction, constantly hyper-vigilant and worried, as were Gary and Alice.

Now, for the first time in their lives, concern about being overtaken by those right behind them was beginning to vanish. As we said, their powerful sense of purpose had kept the number of times they looked anxiously over their shoulders in their forties to a minimum. Without realizing it, they had taken the next step now. They were starting to be able to look upon those immediately below them in the firm with a genuine beneficence.

Here Today, Gone Tomorrow

Educational beneficence, that is, not financial. They weren't interested in adding new names to their wills, but they did want to impart to subordinates some of the wisdom they had learned over the years. "I've picked up some pretty nifty tricks of the trade [in the last 30 years]," Arthur said gruffly, with a little grin. "And these dimwits don't even want to hear them. They don't know what they're missing." What, then, was stopping the transmission of such useful information down the ladder? Two main factors, one of which operated to inhibit the elders, the other of which hobbled the younger members of the firm. Let's take the senders first, then we'll see why the receivers typically turned a deaf ear.

There is no question that Arthur and Marie wanted to act in a tutorial as well as managerial capacity to those under them. However, one thing stuck like a bone in their throats whenever they started to quietly discuss suggestions of real merit. As Arthur put it more than once, "Why should I tell them *anything* that's valuable? They're only going to leave anyway." Marie was even more cautious with information that she thought had commercial value. "Here today, gone tomorrow," she said with a sweep of her hand. "Anything they pick up here, they'll [soon] be using against me [at another firm]. I can't tie them to this place, you know."

Job changes play a sufficiently large role in American business, and they can be undertaken with such ease, Arthur and Marie simply couldn't ignore them. "Look," Arthur said, "they're a fact of life." As Marie put it, "It's something I've got to live with. I don't have a choice." However, she and Arthur did have a choice about how much information to disclose to subordinates. Of equal, if not greater, importance was the attitude that accompanied such disclosures. In both Arthur's and Marie's cases, it was full of caution and doubts.

Until now, we have given the impression that Arthur and Marie *knew* that they wanted to be instructors as well as executives at the firm. They did not. Had it been a conscious desire, they could have said to themselves, "I'd like very much to pass on what I've learned, but the high frequency with which job changes take place here is stopping me." In that case, the bulk of their annoyance might have been aimed at an employment system that encourages such changes. As it was, they didn't realize that they wanted to teach but were prevented from doing it by their own rational reservations. At whom, therefore, did they aim their abundant annoyance? Their subordinates, the very people they wanted to have as adoring students.

That was doubly ironic, for it caused the situation to deteriorate still further. All the makings of a vicious downward spiral were present. Since Arthur and Marie didn't know what was keeping them bottled up and wary, they wound up criticizing the people they wanted most to help—which only added to the distance that existed between them to begin with.

The upshot: at times, they were downright nasty to the subordinates they had subconsciously selected for front-row seats in their invisible classroom. "You don't want to *listen*, do you?" Arthur barked at two of his favorite young associates. Yet the fact remains that he was as much responsible for the barrier as they. The barking caused them to back off, which made it even harder for them to hear the words of wisdom he was trying to communicate.

Had Arthur and Marie suddenly adopted a warm, advisorial tone, they both still would have had a great deal of remedial work to do just to bring the situation back to neutral. The animosity in the air needed to be removed before there could even be the hope of establishing an effective teacher-pupil pairing.

What is fascinating is that money and loyalty repeatedly emerged as the chief excuses that Arthur and Marie gave themselves for their reluctance. The rationalization could hardly have been simpler. In essence it was, "I'm a key part of this firm and want to see it do well. If I tell the junior staff here the secrets of how we operate and everything else I've learned over the years, they'll eventually leave with that invaluable information. I'll have acted disloyally to the firm and also have done it financial harm. Better to be very cagey about any momentous insights."

Arthur and Marie were typical, though, in not being able to hold out forever. Each had at least one talented subordinate to whom they would have liked to impart some hard-earned insights. After holding off for a while, they could no longer resist their own impulses. The atmosphere wasn't conducive to relaxed, informal instruction, but both gave it a try in any event. What happened next brought all the underlying forces to the surface.

Arthur told Brad Mitchell, an associate of his, something he considered extremely useful and Brad promptly forgot it. Arthur couldn't decide whether to be livid or stunned. "I am absolutely dumbfounded," he said, shaking his head. "Here I go and tell him something I shouldn't have in the first place, and he doesn't even remember me telling it to him." Since Arthur and Marie were operating under self-imposed prohibitions against revealing anything worthwhile too easily, they expected the recipient, when they violated the prohibition, to be appropriately grateful. It would be difficult to overemphasize the importance of this point. When the youngsters, first, didn't say "thank you," and second, forgot the advice altogether, Arthur and Marie could only brand their subordinates monumental ingrates.

How mad were they? Mad enough to swear to themselves that they would never again be disloyal to their firms *and* to themselves. As far as they were concerned, when you give someone a gift of cash, you are entitled to some gratitude. And when you give someone advice that is worth money, perhaps a small fortune, in this case too you are entitled to some gratitude. Maybe a great deal of it. If none is forthcoming, or worse, the person throws your verbal financial gift away, you know not to be so generous next time.

Such seeming stupidity on the part of the recipient has to affect the donor's judgment of the person's competence. After all, the transaction is taking place in a business setting and is related to work. The act seems flagrantly irresponsible, so why ignore it?

One of the most important changes experienced by people moving up the corporate ladder is that a growing share of the firm's assets— plant, equipment, and personnel—are turned over to them for capable management. The fact that their words are taken more seriously now, affecting decisions that involve an ever larger portion of the firm's employees, is of major importance. If a subordinate has acted idiotically after receiving a nugget of precious wisdom, how can a senior officer overlook that? To promote the person and give him or her more authority may jeopardize the jobs of everyone at the firm. As Arthur put it, both about his own situation and when counseling others, "You have to be very careful about selecting a successor. The wrong one can ruin everything."

That, in short, is how Arthur and Marie spent the remainder of their late fifties and early sixties: trying to give gifts that, it seemed to them at least, no one wanted. Not even people who clearly needed the advice. It upset them both terribly, time after time, and poisoned the atmosphere around them at a period in their lives when they might reasonably have expected more satisfaction than they found.

Confessions of a "No" Man

We said earlier that there were two parts to this story, that the recipients had their own reasons for acting as they did. What were those reasons? One matters more than all the rest combined. It has to do with how the young in America view their elders in business. Usually, when people are surveyed regarding their attitudes toward the elderly, they understand by the phrase, first, something abstract, an amalgam called "the elderly," and second, those who are 65 and over, thus likely to be retired.

But that is not the group we've been asking employees about. The people in question were their bosses and, hence, were quite specific individuals. Second, very few were over 65. The overwhelming majority were between 50 and 65. So let's call them the firm's elders, as opposed to society's elderly.

Moving from the first category to the second usually results in a definite increase in sympathy. Apparently it is easier in many instances to feel sorry for people once they have vanished into an abstraction. However, as long as the 60-year-old, say, was still active in business, a concrete individual with the power to promote or hinder the careers of others, he or she was viewed by the junior staff with suspicion at best and, in a surprising number of instances, contempt.

Getting honest answers to the question of how people in business between the ages of 20 and 50 perceived their bosses who were over the age of 50 was very important, and it occupied us throughout our study. Typically, we had to wait until one or the other left the firm in order to hear the truth. "I had my reasons for not wanting to tell you this before," said a 41-year-old, after finally admitting that he despised his boss, who had recently moved to another company. "I didn't want it to get back to him."

Two incidents capture the underlying essentials. The first involved Marie; the second, Arthur. Marie had just finished talking to a client on the phone about an extensive publicity campaign that she was doing for them. One of her assistants, Lois Moore, age 38, overheard the conversation, since the two had been having a meeting when the call came in. The discussion Lois overheard could have been of real use to her, because Marie, who was 57 at the time, was a veteran practitioner by then of the art of public relations. Regardless of her reluctance to part with any secrets, just watching her at work was an education.

That didn't interest Lois in the least. In spite of the lavish praise she heaped upon her boss to her face, Lois considered Marie unstable. "She's worse than the weather. I have no idea what's next. Will something nice or awful come out of her mouth?" Then, with obvious bitterness, Lois added, "Marie is full of surprises." Lois had been with the firm for four years but had already developed a comprehensive strategy for handling such unpredictability. "'Go with the flow,' that's my motto," Lois said proudly. "If she wants to say it's blue when it's green, I go along with her. Who cares?"

For the most part, it worked. Marie was thrilled that Lois seemed so attentive to any tips that were offered. "She is a very heads-up person," Marie said expansively. "She's going places." Somehow, Lois had picked up on the fact that just sitting there and listening was as good, if not better, a compliment than the ones she actually gave voice to. "I let her prattle on and on, whenever she wants to," Lois later said. "It makes her feel good."

"Do the conversations do you any good?" we asked.

"Yes," Lois replied. "It makes her think I admire her."

* * *

Arthur's favorite in the firm was a junior partner named Ted Yates, who was 12 years younger than he. Ted, like Lois, seemed very hard-working at first glance, always busy with one thing or another. Yet, first and foremost in his mind was to make the right impression on Arthur. "That's where it's at around here," Ted said calmly. "He needs a lot of stroking, and I give it to him. He loves to play the big cheese. Everybody else thinks he's a cantankerous old son-of-a-bitch." That left the door wide open for Ted to appear to be one of the few people— often the only person—willing to let Arthur go on at length about anything that was on his mind. Not surprisingly, Arthur came to the same conclusion about Ted that Marie had arrived at about Lois. "He's very sharp," Arthur said at 58. "Ted gets the whole story—has perspective, if you know what I mean. A really levelheaded guy."

Arthur and Marie clearly felt better as a result of all the counterfeit praise they were receiving from their subordinates, but trouble developed as soon as an independent opinion was solicited. There was none to be had. Arthur and Marie had been talking, all right, but to themselves.

"I'm not sure I handled that so well," Marie turned to Lois and said, as soon as she hung up the phone. Marie liked being flattered as much as the next person does, yet this time she was seeking some assistance. At the very least, she wanted a candid appraisal of the situation as seen through the eyes of someone else in the profession whom she trusted. What she got instead might as well have come from a record player. "You did just fine," Lois said confidently without a moment's hesitation. "There's nothing to worry about. Besides, they're jerks, those people. They don't know *what* they want. Nobody could have handled them better." Marie had been around long enough to know that that wasn't so. Nevertheless, she found the words consoling and let the matter drop. "Lois has such a relaxing effect on me," Marie said at the end of the day.

That was true, and highly unfortunate in this instance. The client sued. Unhappy about what seemed to them the cavalier way in which they had been brushed off by Marie, they decided to air their grievances in court. It took nearly two weeks for the eruption to occur and lawyers' letters to start sailing back and forth. When it did, Marie commented, "I *knew* I should have called them back and explained what I was doing. I was uneasy after that call. I don't know why I didn't." She had forgotten how easily she had been lulled into a stupor by her prize pupil.

Arthur found himself in a worse predicament as a result of the skill with which he was being manipulated. He gladly went along with the adulation, pleased at how successful and distinguished it made him feel. "I think of myself as an elder statesman [of the firm]," he boasted to us right after Ted had done a particularly good job of stroking him. "I left him walking on air," Ted later commented.

Fine. But as in Marie's case, the real damage was done when Arthur needed some legitimate feedback and couldn't get any. Needless to say, he thought he *was* getting it. He asked Ted for his considered opinion on an important matter regarding expansion possibilities for the firm. The topic was the legal work involved in corporate merger activity, and Arthur guessed (correctly, as it turns out) that the firm should make an immediate effort to obtain more of this lucrative business. Unlike Lois, Ted often made a point of openly contradicting Arthur, "with all due respect," he would always add. "Why do it?" we asked. Ted answered quickly and easily, "Because that way he doesn't think I'm a 'yes' man."

Where keeping up is concerned, alert older executives frequently obtain the views of their younger colleagues who are more in touch with mass market tastes and trends. For Arthur to do what he did was entirely appropriate. What Ted did, on the other hand, was appalling. No one expected him to have every answer, but to give the matter no thought—indeed, to brush it off as part of a continuing effort to create a slick image for himself—led to a disaster that bothers Arthur to this day.

Instead of being "just a passing fad," as Ted labeled merger and acquisition activity when roundly dismissing it with Arthur, it was responsible for making major firms out of some of Arthur's smaller competitors. Miffed, Arthur's partners later chastised him quietly but sternly for allowing a significant opportunity to pass. Nor was this a mistake that could be remedied. As Arthur explained it to us when we asked why not, "We can't get aboard now. The [legal] firms that have the *reputation* [in this area] are the ones that everyone wants. That's where they're going. I put out some feelers to our clients. It's too late to make up the lost ground."

Victims of False Praise

Lois and Ted were lucky to have close relationships with at least one of their superiors. Most of their peers did not. In fact, less than 20 percent (11 of 63) of the employees at the two companies who were between 30 and 50 felt close to anyone at their respective firms who was on a higher rung and in the 50 to 65 age range. As a 33-year-old lawyer at Arthur's firm put it, "Don't get me wrong, we're friendly [my boss and I] and work together well, but we're not friends. I definitely wouldn't say we're friends. No, he doesn't take me into his confidence." Since this was a highly motivated group, on the whole they were content with the arrangement. "I kind of prefer it this way," said a co-worker of Lois. "I'm in touch with my boss [Marie] a couple of times a week, even if one of us is out of the office. That's enough."

The remoteness of the relationship may have given junior partners and middle managers the latitude they wanted, but it made them see their bosses primarily as (1) a source of marching orders and projects to work on ("See what you can come up with for the ABC account"), and (2) a temporary impediment to further promotions ("When he retires, maybe I'll be given his job"). Instruction and encouragement were a miniscule part of the picture. Like compliments given to workers in their forties, they were deemed superfluous. "You're not a schoolgirl anymore," Marie snapped at the co-worker of Lois's quoted above. Arthur evidenced the same attitude repeatedly. As he put it to one of Ted's peers, "Do I have to watch you every minute? Should I take attendance in the morning when I come in?"

Ted, Lois, and their more ambitious peers didn't invent the system in which they found themselves. After being a part of it since their early twenties, they had absorbed its operating guidelines and tried to fit into it as best they could, obtaining the maximum benefit for themselves at each step. Since they weren't led to expect a close relationship with an older, well-established figure at the firm, they didn't miss it. And if they had been looking for one, they'd have been bitterly disappointed. For, as Ted and Lois were well aware, that is not what was available. As Ted put it, "A mentor? Don't make me laugh. He's a windbag, using me as an ear."

A great deal of drivel has been written in recent years on the subject of mentors. Yet the fact remains that achievement-oriented workers see a mentor merely as a way of speeding their progress up the ladder, someone to sponsor and clear the way for them. Receiving wisdom is secondary, if it is in the picture at all. As for the mentor, Ted's opinion may put the matter harshly, yet it accurately characterizes what most of the wide variety of such pairings we've studied have actually been: an older person spouting off almost at random to a younger one at the firm. Far from being valuable instruction, the "lecture" is typically a collection of self-pitying complaints and self-congratulatory comments by the senior partner of the duo.

Why, then, shouldn't the junior partner in any such pairing seek to ransack the relationship for all it's worth? Since it has no real internal content, its only use is as an external implement to speed one's climb. That is the view that many privately admit they feel themselves being pushed toward. As far as they are concerned, they aren't learning anything from the contact that will enable them either to accelerate their rate of self-development or obtain promotions—if not at the current firm, then at a future one. Hence "the relationship" might as well serve as a catapult to boost them rapidly to the next level.

Manipulating older executives into giving such aid has been refined into a highly polished art form in American business circles. What masks the maneuvering in the United States, while leaving it plainly visible in other countries (especially Japan), is that middle managers in America are astonishingly skilled at taking refuge in the comment, "I don't need anything from my boss. If I can't get what I want here, I'll get it elsewhere." This statement, which is the functional equivalent of the Declaration of Independence updated and proclaimed in a corporate context, is the best smoke screen imaginable. Both Ted and Lois used it frequently. In the meantime, the stroking and wheedling continued unabated.

Of necessity, they'd have argued. At each firm, power to make key decisions resides in the top managerial layer. Regardless of how many times people change jobs, some tactic must eventually be found to deal with any superior who prevents them from continuing to move up. A fact not lost on Ted and Lois, to mention two of many, is that the senior officials, particularly of mid to large-sized firms, tend to be in their fifties and early sixties.

It is here that the emotional needs of such elders come to play a prominent role, for they mesh neatly with the impatient aspirations of the junior members of the firm. The end result, sad to say, is poor in most cases, tragic in some. The handful of instances in which the pairing is truly productive for the firm as well as the pair are joys to behold, but they are rare sights indeed.

The Chairman's Dilemma

It won't do to indict "the system" and let it go at that, since there is nothing immutable about any of this. There is much room for local change. However, as things now stand, what we found is that, as people enter and pass through their fifties and early sixties, the growing desire to find a corporate heir stands a good chance of getting them into serious trouble. How? A fiercely ambitious young worker, generally with a casual manner, will catch them with their needs showing and exploit them fully. As Arthur and Marie learned, it is no way to cap a career.

Backing away, refusing to help anyone in a subordinate position at the firm, won't solve the problem and typically makes it worse. First of all, that is what most top officials do anyway. Giving commencement addresses at school graduations is the only thing acceptable to them since, a few hours later, the youngsters will disperse instead of becoming permanent educational burdens. Second, doing little or nothing on this score will cause one of the most pressing desires in this stage of their lives to remain unfulfilled.

CHAPTER
14

Choosing the Right Heir

IT IS NOW clear that, without a great deal of effort, the final decade of a business career can contain major satisfactions not available at an earlier age. Obtaining them, however, requires people to have a clearer picture of their own needs as well as those of the junior staff with whom they work. The first thing to realize is that the public's impression that entering one's fifties and then sixties merely means winding down is flatly contradicted by the facts. Some desires wane but, as it turns out, others become stronger, one of the most important of which is an interest in passing on what one has learned. It was revealing to find that the more a person in our sample had achieved, the more intense that interest was likely to be.

When executives in their fifties started to become increasingly intolerant of their subordinates' seeming inability to listen, we therefore felt it was worthwhile to consider a number of possible explanations for the behavior. Perhaps a particular subordinate was indeed incompetent, though not *all* of them could be, as some people in supervisory positions unwittingly were claiming. Second, perhaps the executive was more "old and cranky" now, as many described themselves when the heat of the moment passed. There was also a third possibility, and we found it to be accurate more often than the previous two. The intolerance was a signal that the executive wanted to offer, not just a single piece of advice, delivered angrily, but a steady stream of it, voiced in a calm and friendly manner. Institutional impediments, not psychological ones, were standing in the way and generating a sizable quantity of frustration.

As things now stand, there is an enormous gap between the top and middle layers in most firms. The gap is based on distrust, a concern that valuable information will be carted off by junior executives looking to feather their own nests at a competitor's. The high rate of job changes makes some caution inevitable and even appropriate. Nonetheless, the central point here is that the caution has been vastly overdone, so much so that both senior and junior members of the firm are now being harmed by it.

The junior staff cannot modify the situation since they aren't in charge. Key managers must take the lead, if anyone is to, and *slowly* make the necessary changes. This is one "top-down approach" that works only when the senior personnel involved understand and fully believe that they are doing it for themselves as well as their subordinates. What we want to review in this brief chapter are the most important conditions that allowed such senior-junior staff pairings to function productively or caused them to fail.

Executive Privilege

If people want their subordinates to listen to them, it is essential for them to offer something thought-provoking, useful, or entertaining to listen to. Complaints are none of the above. When executives who entered their fifties told us that henceforth they would try "to act in a less remote manner with subordinates" (we didn't ask them to do this; it just seemed like a good idea to many), they often interpreted that to mean they had been given the go-ahead to bellyache. Some did manage to keep the focus of the conversation primarily on business topics, for instance, the nature of the industry and the operations of the firm, but they still threw in a considerable quantity of griping.

It wasn't necessary to ask them why, since they usually volunteered the fact that, as far as they were concerned, they had earned it. It was part of executive privilege, one of the perks that came with the position they had finally attained at the firm. In addition, they felt they were due something merely for trying to be of assistance to a subordinate "above and beyond the call of duty." They weren't certain whether or not they had actually helped the fortunate recipient, but they acted in a manner that left little doubt as to their view. "I'm sure my advice was worth *something*," as one put it, then he proceeded to cash in the resulting IOU by venting his accumulated dissatisfactions about the firm to his captive audience. Amusingly, these utterances too were labeled by him as meaty morsels, "real business insights," and therefore they entitled him to an even greater right to complain. It was a wonderful position: the more IOUs of his listeners that he cashed in, the more were owed him. Mafia mathematics.

The fly in the ointment here is that the listeners we interviewed told us that *they* were the ones who felt owed. "That guy is the biggest blimp since the Hindenburg," was a typical comment. The listeners were disgusted and determined to get something in return. The wheels had accidentally been set in motion for an adversary relationship rather than a warm one. The implication here is clearly that the attempt to form senior-junior staff pairings badly is worse than not attempting them at all.

The most serious mistake made by executives trying to befriend a subordinate was to tell the person how *they* would have handled a situation, one they usually had just complimented the person upon. Even-tempered subordinates found this every bit as irritating as those with shorter fuses. Apparently, no one likes to be second-guessed in business, especially if the goal was achieved in the first place. Failure might call for some helpful suggestions; success rarely does. Playing Monday-morning quarterback made listeners think the boss was merely flaunting his or her rank. The interpretation offered most frequently by subordinates was that the executive is generally insecure or, in this particular case, scared because the matter was handled well without any assistance from him or her.

It is essential for well-meaning executives, particularly those who manage to avoid the accidentally egotistical behavior discussed above, to be very selective about which subordinates they start telling personal, professional, and company secrets to. Here, the differences between a schoolroom in an academic setting and what should occur educationally in an office are greatest. Since teachers don't get to select which pupils are in their class, when a student does poorly, it is relatively easy for the teacher to dissociate himself from the failure. Blame is readily aimed at parents, community, television, the youngster's friends, or prior teachers. The executives we studied were rarely able to make use of similar excuses. A teacher is with a high school or college student only a handful of hours each week. However, an employee is on staff for at least ten times that amount of time, year round, year in and year out. Ignorance of a subordinate's shortcomings is almost never accepted as an excuse by one's peers. When Arthur, as part of a last ditch self-defense, finally blurted out to eight of his partners at a meeting that, "Ted misled me. He told me the wrong thing," they were incensed rather than placated. "And you *believed* him?" one replied, openly annoyed. Asked another, "Well, whose fault is that?" As Arthur later commented, "They didn't want to hear it."

Many of the executives who established productive business pairings with a subordinate did so quite consciously. From the start, they let a junior staff member know that they enjoyed his or her company or else that person would not have been joining them, but they also told the protégé there was a larger purpose in mind. "A picture is worth a thousand words," said one executive to an assistant just before a key client arrived. Another commented, "I can't describe what I do—I'll be too busy doing it—but you might pick up something by being there."

There are times when participating proved more valuable to subordinates than watching. As one executive put it to an assistant, "The only way to learn is by doing. When we get there, you're going to do the talking." The assistant started to become visibly nervous; that hadn't been their procedure during the ten months they had worked together thus far. "Don't worry," the boss reassured him. "You know what to say. And I'll be right there in case you accidentally put your foot in your mouth." Said another to a middle manager, "Usually, I write the report for top management and you review it. This one you are going to write and I'll review it."

We mentioned earlier that such changes normally have to be made slowly, for there is a learning curve involved on both sides. To begin with, it takes people a while—in some cases, quite a while—to realize that they have truly been granted both responsibility and authority. As one subordinate, who four years later became the president of the firm, remarked, "It was given and then taken away in the middle so many times in the past, I wasn't sure this time they were really going to let me run with the ball."

Since the skills required to do so don't emerge overnight, a certain amount of time must be allotted subordinates for the next step in their development. Hurrying the process often leads to grief although, interestingly, it was usually subordinates, not superiors, who were trying to accelerate the pace. Americans are generally in an enormous rush to advance their careers, and it is easy for them to bite off more than they can chew. Not only were superiors disappointed in such instances, so were junior staff members who found themselves failing in the spotlight, with no place to hide. That was especially likely to happen to people who are very persuasive, who at times put forth compelling, even heartrending reasons why they should be given a major project to manage. Their impatience made them overlook the complexity of the operation they wanted to, and sincerely believed they could, run. Even such failures served a productive purpose in the long run, for they erased the trivialized view of the firm usually held by people who are far from the seat of power, and therefore it made them proceed more intelligently as they themselves became executives. Repeatedly, we found that only outsiders and lower-level workers consider a modern business simple and easy to run.

A Risk Worth Taking

One of the most pleasant surprises experienced by executives who had chosen the right protégé occurred during moments when the subordinate rose to the occasion. The opportunities, provided by the senior officers, resulted in the subordinates' doing more than they ever thought they could. One thing our study taught us is that there is a huge quantity of dormant ability in the business arena, and it will remain dormant unless it is fostered to a much greater extent than is currently the norm.

United States business leaders have shown themselves to be remarkably skilled on balance when it comes to placing the firm's financial assets at risk. They generally know when and where to make a worthwhile investment. Not every venture succeeds, of course, but the analysis and planning done beforehand help define the best route. And since no one has a crystal ball that works, careful vigilance is usually exercised along the way, to make corrections or limit losses.

Taking a similar approach, not only with the firm's financial assets but with its human ones as well, can pay comparably large dividends. An investment in plant and equipment, which uses money, needs to be matched by an investment in key subordinates, which primarily requires time. Patience also is needed in both areas. There are many similarities between the two types of risk, and our study convinced us that both are worth taking.

Investing in one's staff will be most productive if one has chosen the correct site for the capital one is committing—that is, one's time, knowledge, and energy. Which subordinates are the most appropriate vehicles for this type of funding? Although every individual is unique, and each case must be considered on its own merits, some important generalities emerged from our studies. The first is that the people one takes under one's wing should not be more than 20 years younger than oneself. Keep in mind that what we're discussing here is a very personal form of investing. With a few notable exceptions, an age difference of 25 or 30 years is apparently too large an abyss to bridge. For executives who are between 50 and 65, that means choosing people who are at least 30 to 45 years old.

However there is usually a big difference between subordinates in their thirties and those in their forties. As it turns out, people in the 50 to 65 age range are significantly more likely to establish a successful teacher-pupil pairing in a business context with someone from the older than the younger group. Two reasons account for the bulk of the higher success rate. First, workers in their forties are better prepared for the additional responsibilities that they'll be shouldering once one starts working more closely with them. Those in their thirties talked a good game, and they were better at convincing a superior in many instances to trust them than were those in their forties. But it was usually more of an ego trip for them, a personal victory to boast about. Those in their forties, on the other hand, mainly took it as an acknowledgement of the skills they had developed over the years. For them, it was a welcome, professional opportunity. As one executive put it after trying comparable people drawn from both age groups, "The younger want applause; the older ones, they just want to do the work."

The second reason for the higher success rate is that people in their forties were not only better prepared, they also were more grateful. We've already seen in Part Four that many capable individuals in this age range feel isolated, more so than they were before the decade began or will be once it is over. During this period, though, they need more feedback—particularly compliments, if deserved—than they now receive. There is an important natural alliance, then, between subordinates in their forties and superiors in their fifties and early sixties. Unfortunately, little is being done to put it to good use.

Both parties to the pairing could reap vastly more than they currently do. That is particularly so because nothing drastic is called for in order to obtain the many benefits. When these duos are functioning at their best, they are rather loose and flexible arrangements, built on mutual need and respect. Tying each to the other in any rigid manner breeds resentment, not productivity and satisfaction, since each has his or her personal method of accomplishing the goals they both have deemed desirable. As one chief executive officer put it, "I can see now that getting too picky—arguing about every detail—doesn't make sense. He's got his own way of doing things, and that's all right with me as long as the job gets done."

As Arthur and Marie would be among the first to attest, the fact that one has selected someone from the right age range does not in and of itself guarantee success. Additional criteria are required to distinguish the good candidates from the bad. The main reason the executives in our sample had trouble on this score is that they were unable to make a monumentally important distinction. They couldn't tell the difference between talent and tension.

Someone who was tense struck them as driven. In a business context, that was viewed as a good thing, and it might well have been—had that been what they were actually seeing. However, in the majority of cases, the tension was a result of the abundant hostility the person was carrying. To confuse the two was a drastic mistake.

Neil Shaw, for example, worked in Arthur's firm. When he was busy with a project that brought him into contact with no one else in the office, all was well. He was interested in law and could focus on legal matters hour after hour; that is, as long as he was alone *and* he didn't think about his peers. Once he so much as envisioned them, even when they weren't nearby, he reacted to them as though they were. Their image consumed him. Instead of merely thinking about them, he would dwell on them incessantly. They were his dreaded competitors, and he didn't want them to get ahead of him even by an inch.

For some people, having a few rivals provides a bit of added impetus. It is an extra incentive to work. To others, the motivation is a tidal wave. Inundated by the aggressive emotions the contest generates, they are unable to focus on the project at hand without also thinking about the other contestants. The image of their rivals' progress becomes laced through their involvement in their own work. Now, they are no longer alone, even if they don't see a soul from the office for days on end. It is a self-torturing form of imaginary company, and it spawns a maliciousness that knows few bounds.

My Buddy at the Office

Arthur couldn't see it. He noticed that Neil was tense, but he took it to signify a restless and impatient talent trying to burst free, and left it at that. Arthur did recognize Neil's enormous need for approval. In childlike fashion, Neil would run to him with a piece of work in hand and nearly plead to be told, "Yes, it is outstanding." However, that wasn't the end of it in Neil's case. When he got the approval, and even more so when he did not, he immediately swung in the other direction. "I don't need anything from him, or anyone," Neil would say angrily. "I shouldn't have been asking him [to begin with]."

Marie had two subordinates who behaved similarly in her office, and her conclusion about them was the same. The intense manner of all three struck Arthur and Marie as a sign of dedication rather than what it was: the malicious competition of people who are deathly afraid of being beaten out and prepared to do almost anything to prevent it from happening, no matter how devious or destructive.

Unfortunately, both Arthur and Marie promoted such people regularly (that was unfortunate because they tend to be very divisive in a firm, turning each person against the others, leaving only themselves as an alleged "friend of all"). Sensing an instability, though, neither Arthur nor Marie chose them as partners for an ongoing educational pairing. Needless to say, the people they did choose, Ted and Lois, were every bit as bad.

Now we can ask the central question of this chapter. "Who *are* the most appropriate subordinates for such a pairing?" The answer obviously isn't the Teds, Loises, and Neils of the business world. Instead, far and away the best candidates are the competent and, in many instances, relatively quiet people whose work one most respects. In both Arthur's and Marie's offices there was at least one such person who was overlooked, yet who would have been overjoyed at the opportunity.

Arthur and Marie acted in an altogether typical manner in neglecting these people in favor of the more chummy types they chose. What was it they liked about Ted and Lois? They claimed the two subordinates were intelligent and hardworking, but that's not the real reason the two were selected. First and foremost was the fact that they were skilled conversationalists, fun to be with—and people who knew how to flatter their bosses with false praise the instant an ego boost was needed. In short, they simply were good to pal around with.

It was profoundly disturbing throughout our study to see top executives at major as well as smaller companies repeatedly select the wrong candidates. Eventually it became clear that what they were choosing were sidekicks, not students; people to entertain and who could in turn entertain them, not learn from them. They weren't going to find that out until it was too late. The pairings usually take years to gel and, once formed, tend to stay intact, in spite of any cracks that begin to appear. As Arthur put it about himself and Ted, "You could say we've attained a certain amount of momentum." Marie's assessment of the relationship between her and Lois was even more on target, "I guess I have a lot invested in her after the years we've been together."

Long before people become so heavily invested in a subordinate that they are hesitant to sever the bond should things start to go wrong, they need to see the pairing for what it is. An amusing sidekick rarely makes a good student. And the flatterers don't give a hoot about their superiors' "teachings." They are only too happy to boast later to their peers that the boss is a pushover and a fool, not a fountain of knowledge. That hasn't prevented an enormous number of executives from following their own worst instincts and tying up with hustlers anyway, subordinates who were merely out to manipulate them. What our studies demonstrate is that executives who want entertainment would be better off going to a movie. If they need flattery, they should get it from someone who doesn't work for them full-time.

We return, almost automatically, to the issue that gave rise to management's caution in the first place: defections by key employees. One must be prepared for the possibility that some and perhaps all of one's star pupils will leave. That mustn't be allowed to interfere. The process is more important than any of the pairings, both for oneself and the world at large. Finding another heir, instead of feeling abandoned and bitter, is essential. The executives who were most successful on this front thought of it this way, "My legacy is growing, being carried to distant places by my former subordinates."

What is fascinating is how little similarity typically exists between the partners in the best senior-junior duos. In fact, the differences between the two are often large enough to cause observers to rate them as "the odd couple." Revealingly, the senior partner in such pairs rarely brags about the younger's charisma or charm. Instead of having a scintillating personality, the subordinate is usually a workhorse who thrives on the labor and is thrilled at the results.

One indicator will tell executives a great deal about whether or not they have got the right heir for their business wisdom. When the pairing was a mistake, even just moderately so, the senior partner felt it to be, in the phrases voiced most often, "a drain," "a chore," "a one-way street." That is a signal that must not be ignored, and for a very good reason. For more than 25 centuries, great teachers have always learned as much from their best students as the other way around.

VI

HIGH ACHIEVERS

CHAPTER 15

The Hidden Pitfalls
of Self-Employment

PEOPLE IN BUSINESS for themselves tell us repeatedly that they know all about the employees who work at large corporations. And those in big firms are equally convinced they know all about the kinds of people who start their own small ones. Both are certain that there are essential differences between the two groups and that, more importantly, the differences were present all along.

Nevertheless, the differences were not there in the beginning. They develop over the years, in response to the highly dissimilar working conditions that characterize the daily routine of each respective group.

Spillover

The chief distinction between the day-to-day business lives of the two groups in their formative years on the job is territoriality. When one accepts a position at a mid- to large-size firm, it is apparent right from the start that the piece of turf that will be one's own is small. It may be a very important piece and unlimited in scope, but it is quite limited in size.

Stepping on someone else's corporate terrain causes an immediate and usually negative response. Sometimes politely, at other times rudely, the owner of the space will issue a reminder that one needs explicit permission to trespass on their ground. In the vast majority of instances we monitored, newcomers learned within their first year at the firm to abide by the boundaries of each person's position. After that, the matter was accepted as one of the givens, much like the location of the elevator, and received little further thought.

The group that does give the matter additional thought is the self-employed. To an extent that amazed us when we first began to measure it, those who are in business for themselves think about and refer

231

almost continually to the pinched size of the turf occupied by members of a large firm. Sometimes it seemed they never tired of congratulating themselves on the greater latitude their business lives allowed them. There was little doubt in their minds that it was one of their primary sources of strength and success.

To some extent, they are right. But having the potential to do something and developing that potential to the point where it brings one the rewards one wants are entirely separate issues. Our sample includes a considerable number of self-employed people who certainly didn't lack intelligence and energy, yet who have accomplished little and are upset about it. Being in business for themselves didn't produce the rapid abundant flowering they (and we) had been led to expect it would from the self-laudatory comments of people on the path. Indeed, they claimed to feel sorry for any worker who had accepted what in their view amounted to "a horse's stall" in a large firm, rather than being able to roam free.

It took us a number of years to discover just how central a role self-discipline plays in the business lives of those who go on to become successfully self-employed. When we think of the term "discipline," a picture of conscious shaping of behavior springs to mind: a drill sergeant barking orders or a runner pushing himself to go a half-mile farther today. Yet, as we've seen, in a large firm people come to respect the territorial limits of others without giving the matter much thought. Nearly 40 percent never even take it to be an issue. As it turns out, this is the more important type of self-discipline for the self-employed.

It is critically important because when people are in business for themselves, there is no one in the office next door to prevent them from spilling over and doing other jobs in addition to their own. A source of strength? In some cases, yes. In many others, definitely not. In fact, it is the single greatest cause of failure for the self-employed.

Take a look at two representative instances of bright, dedicated, and resourceful people who seemed destined at one time to succeed, but much to everyone's surprise, have not and aren't likely to.

Vera Marshall is an interior designer and has an office at home. "I never thought I'd wind up doing this," she said three years after starting at 28. "I wanted to be an artist but I couldn't make a living painting." A continuing interest in architecture and a firm grasp of period furniture ("I took courses in college and at [the museum] across town"), together with the innovative use she made of available space, made her knowledgeable and in demand. "Not in the beginning," she was quick to add. "You don't break into this business overnight. It takes time for people to get to know you." For the first three years, she did work primarily for her friends, usually couples in their thirties who were moving up in the world and had just bought cooperative apartments or brownstones in the city. "They're easy to work with," she said happily. "We can always agree on a budget and a style."

Born and raised in the Midwest, Vera recoiled at the mere thought of being labeled conservative once she moved to New York. In some ways she became more of a New Yorker than the natives, buying series tickets to cultural events, seeing Broadway shows as soon as they opened, and diligently keeping up with whatever was "in" at the moment. Vera was a little above average height, at 5′ 8″, and wore her light brown hair short. She felt it showed her fine bone structure to its best advantage. Her lips, a bit on the thin side, were offset by her eyes, which were wide set and blue. Vera scorned shopping the usual department stores for clothes and preferred finding her "treasures" in small, offbeat boutiques specializing in ethnic wares from around the world. Full skirts and sandals were what she most often wore.

Her initial customers may have been "no problem," one of her favorite phrases, but the work also produced almost no income. "I need older, wealthier clients," she said. Kenny, her husband, is a graphic designer, and he makes the bulk of his income designing dust jackets for publishers and technical manuals for a large computer manufacturer. "We have enough to live on," Vera commented, "but the best-paying [design] jobs come from people with lots of space *and* money." And that meant a better established clientele than Vera, with great effort, had thus far been able to land.

Slowly, the number of calls and assignments grew, as satisfied customers mentioned her name to their friends. "I have two large assignments now," she said excitedly near the end of her ninth year in the business. When the two were completed though, they weren't followed by additional work. In fact, for over five months, she had nothing. "That's the way this crazy business is," she said, as dejected as we had ever seen her. "It's feast or famine."

Her manner and mode of dress were deliberately restrained, part of what she considered a picture of good taste. "You are judged by how you look and live," she said on a number of occasions. On the other hand, there was, as she described it, "an artistic spirit [in me] that wants to burst out." After trying for eleven years to pour that mixture into the field of interior design ("A fixed space to be filled with ideas and art," is how she often characterized her task), Vera became interested in other avenues.

Actually, she had been traveling on them all along. But now, as her 38th year was drawing to a close, she started to aim a greater portion of her ambitions in a variety of different directions. In her view, the artistic urge within was forcing her to examine alternative ways of expressing herself. One seemed especially attractive. Ever since her mid-twenties, she had been actively involved with home-furnishing fabrics. Knits and wovens for furniture and wall coverings intrigued her. "The right ones can make a room come alive," she said at 32, "and look wonderfully elegant." The attention that she had paid to the subject throughout her thirties didn't seem to her (or to us) a departure from her main line of work.

However, by her late thirties and early forties, it became one of the principal outlets through which she hoped to release her creative energies. Had Vera been employed at a large firm, she would have been aware of the magnitude of the step she was taking. Instead, in her situation, it seemed a mere extension of what she was already doing. Trying to learn about what goes on in a knitting or, more important for her purposes, weaving mill was the first bit of information she sought. It took her on trips to small, local textile producers and to a few major ones in the South as well.

Learning about the various types of machinery (*coarse* and *fine gauge*, *circular* and *flat knit*, *water-jet*, *jacquard* and *interlock* were terms that suddenly entered her vocabulary) was only the beginning. Acquiring the basics of fabric design was consuming a sizable chunk of each week. "I can *draw* the patterns I want to see," she commented at 42, "but the fabrics don't look like my drawings." Much to her distress, she soon discovered that a knowledge of yarns was needed too. It annoyed her that there were so many pieces to the puzzle, but persistence had always been one of her strong points, and she plunged ahead.

When she was 44, the owner of a small mill offered to let her try her hand at designing a group of fall fabrics. "I was ecstatic when he asked me," she said at the time, "and scared." Vera still had some interior design clients, and the amount of time they took up was substantial. Pulling a room together required her to meet with even more people than designing a fabric did. "But there is this difference," she quipped. "All I need for the room is money."

Putting a salable line of fabrics together required much more: a knowledge of fashion trends; weights and quality the market was looking for; and, last but by no means least, appropriately priced goods. In spite of extensive help from the technical people at the mill, the line was a flop. The technicians had given her exactly what she wanted, but it wasn't what the public wanted.

"No one can sell this garbage," the sales manager told her after trying repeatedly to do so. Yet she was totally unwilling to attempt it herself (or in conjunction with the sales force), in spite of her claim that she knew the right buyers to see. "I'm *above* that," she said angrily. "I won't sink to that level." Her ego sank instead as the dismal results poured in. She had accepted a royalty arrangement based on sales volume, rather than an outright fee. Vera hadn't seen a cent. "It's not my fault it didn't sell," she said to the mill owner. "No, I guess it's mine," he replied. "I got exactly what I paid for. It cost me nothing, and that's what it's worth."

To add insult to injury, trouble had long been brewing on the interior design front and now it erupted. Two of her customers resented what seemed to them to be Vera's haphazard and indifferent approach to the work they wanted done. "I can't reach you when I need to," one told her, "and it takes you forever to return my calls." A second commented sarcastically, "I didn't know you were a mail-order designer. Can this work really be done by mail?"

The complaint was based on the fact that it wasn't being done at all. Vera had been paid $7,500 to install a wall of bookcases, and had a contractor lined up who had agreed to do the job. After taking $5,500 from her (she was going to keep the other $2,000), he disappeared. Vera subsequently discovered that he had run up an enormous pile of debts, collecting all the advances he could, and now had declared bankruptcy. She had to find another contractor to do the work and paid for it herself. "I'm 46," she said in disgust, "and going nowhere."

Word among her old contacts was out that she was undependable, and her business dried up. In order to keep herself float, she began joining various women's organizations', hoping, as she put it, to "network" herself into a new circle in need of her interior design skills. While some of the new friendships did pan out, the business it brought was sporadic and most of her earnings went for club dues, clothes, and lunches. Fiercely optimistic, however, and still proud of "being on my own," she attacked each job, large or small, with equal fervor. "I have a feeling this one could really lead to something," she said, at 55, about her latest project, the house of a friend in Englewood, New Jersey. "It might make *Architectural Digest*, and then I'll be set for life."

It may seem as though we are suggesting with this example that self-employed people who don't succeed by the time they are in their forties won't. What the evidence instead indicates is that people who use the determination and energy that is present in abundance during their twenties and thirties to create their own personal style—even if it exists solely in their minds at the time—stand a significantly better chance of succeeding in the later decades of their business lives, especially if they are self-employed. Apparently it is quite important for people who go into business for themselves to spend the first decade thinking about what is unique about their approach to their chosen field.

That doesn't mean success will come their way overnight. It may take some years for the world to be ready to accept their particular style or view. Also, and this was a common outcome, they may wind up seeming to stumble into success merely because of a golden opportunity that later came their way. The irony is that, in most such cases, the project that brought them wealth and renown barely resembled the unique approach for which they had been trying so hard to win widespread approval.

Why, then, did they succeed? Because the determination they had to push one approach, *any* approach in which they truly believed, allowed them to continue to take themselves and their work seriously until other people finally felt the same way about them. Vera was the reverse; she mistook her nearly total lack of direction for what she kept calling her "wonderfully eclectic tastes."

The Man Who Couldn't Refuse

Peter Bennett's wide range of interests and abilities have served him just as poorly over the years. He studied economics as an undergraduate, and worked for the McGraw-Hill Publishing Company for a few years before returning to graduate school and taking an MBA. Although he wanted to run a company of his own, he decided to run everyone else's instead. "I hung up a shingle as a 'consultant,'" Peter said smiling, "and got a few accounts." His best one in the beginning was a plastics container company that he landed ten months after receiving his MBA. "One look at that place and I knew there was a market for my services."

But which services? Peter didn't want to be specific, and in fact he felt that it would limit the quantity of business he could do with each client. "I'm a grab bag of goodies," he joked at 32. "They can reach in and get anything they need. I can do it all." That was probably so. Our question was: could he do it all at the same time? Throughout his thirties and early forties, Peter certainly seemed to be trying.

He rarely said "no" to a customer request for consulting assistance, and he worked hard and long as part of his attempt to provide the right advice. A highly intelligent and indefatigable worker, he would respond quickly and fully to every problem he was asked to consider. And when he wasn't given a particular difficulty to remedy, he located ones that management at each firm hadn't yet seen. Some people labeled it make-work, yet he could always find something to do that *he* at least felt needed to be done.

Peter's hopes of playing his favorite sport, basketball, were dashed in high school when he stopped growing at 5'9". His interest in sports became sporadic after that, and his body, although not overweight, reflected the neglect. While his fair skin rarely tanned, his blond straight hair was streaked by the sun and flopped onto his forehead in a manner that suggested Peter was more casual than he in fact was. The same studied disarray was evidenced in his clothes, his tie always knotted just a bit too loosely around his open shirt collar.

For nearly two decades, from 32 to 50, Peter took delight in describing what he did for his clients by using a single word: troubleshooter. It was a grown man's version of the boy who wanted to be a fireman. A hot spot would develop in a firm's operations somewhere, an alarm would then sound, Peter would be called and he'd race excitedly to the rescue, every time in a different direction. The image acted as the foundation upon which his view of himself as a professional rested.

Listen to his comments during the two decades. "They can always depend on me to fix things up," he said at 34. At 36, "No matter what it is, any time of the day or night, I've got the cure—or can order one in." At 39, "I have a command of all of business; that's my business, if you know what I mean. Nothing escapes my attention." At 41, "I excel at taking a *total* look and finding the weak links in the chain." At 46, "I told them they don't need anyone else; I can cover the whole map." And at 49, "I'm the only one they need. If I can't put it [back] together [again], probably no one can."

It is easy to dismiss such comments as mild delusions of grandeur. Yet Peter's thoughts and actions during the period are typical of an important portion of the more than 350 MBAs we've been tracking for at least ten years: those who have gone into business for themselves— and not done well. Far from being an isolated and pathological instance, Peter's comments reverberate in this group. Most of the others echo his sentiments as often, if not more so, than he does. Images of omnipotence abound and must be taken into account before any of these individuals is hastily labeled as disturbed.

For the most part, they have simply allowed themselves to remain unspecialized masses of underdeveloped skills. When matched pairs of MBA-holders are monitored at regular intervals over the years from graduation on, a fascinating result emerges: those who have joined and remained at large firms become more focused in their approach; the area of expertise they develop remains relatively limited. On the other hand, those who go into business for themselves evidence significantly higher rates of spillover. No one confines them to a specific area of expertise, so they see little reason to stay there. The key point—and the self-employed are only too happy to state it—is this: they view that as cause for celebration. Be that as it may, our studies indicate that it is the most important cause of failure, not only among MBA-holders who are in business for themselves, but among those who are self-employed in other professions as well.

To see why required some patient, long-term digging. Over the years, we've interviewed all of Peter's old corporate customers without making direct reference to him. What we wanted to know was why they hadn't continued to retain his services. They thought well enough of Peter to hire him once, but something obviously had happened to prevent them from coming back for more.

Much to our surprise, not one of his past accounts had anything negative to say about him. "He was one of the better consultants we've had poking around here," said the president of the plastics company. The VP in charge of marketing at a chain of retail stores expressed a similar opinion. "Pete's a very helpful fellow; gave us a lot of good advice." So it went, at account after account. Where, then, was the problem? And there was indeed one, as Peter well realized. "My business hasn't been growing," he said offhandedly at 44. That meant new customers continually had to be found to replace the prior ones that hadn't renewed.

Peter viewed the unending search for new clients in as cheerful a manner as possible. He thought of it as par for the course ("Everyone has to do it, not just me") and attributed the need for it mainly to fickleness. "The managers of these companies aren't really sure what they want, so they try a little of this and a little of that." Meaning: having given him a chance, it was time to give one to somebody else.

That turned out to be a remarkably naive interpretation. Peter wasn't being replaced by a succession of people like him, each differing from the one before in name only. In the vast majority of instances, he was superseded by a person or firm that was equipped to offer a more specialized service than Peter could. For example, when we asked him at 43, "What areas of a firm's operations would you say you're most knowledgeable about?" his reply was, "I'm good at them all—finance, production, sales, inventory. The works."

Peter said pretty much the same thing a few days later to the owner of a sporting goods company that he had contacted. The pitch worked, and Peter managed to convince the firm to offer him a six-month consulting contract. When it expired, however, it wasn't renewed, much to Peter's dismay. Here, as before, no one at the company had anything negative to say about him afterward. "He did whatever he could," the owner of the firm said in an approving tone. Yet the next outside source of consulting help to which the firm turned four months later was one that specialized in inventory-control systems.

The switch was by no means a fickle one. The company merely needed assistance from people with better developed skills in this particular area than Peter could provide. At other companies, other areas of expertise were involved, but adjusting for that difference, the motive for the switch in each case was largely the same. It wasn't a vote *against* Peter—no one called him amateurish, a dilettante or jack-of-all-trades. It was a vote *for* hiring veteran professional experts. Over the years, Peter's naive, face-saving explanation for why he spent so much time seeking new clients, and why he had never really built a business at all, has cost him a small fortune.

Vera and Peter both understood clearly the need for self-discipline. "If I don't make myself do it, it doesn't get done," Vera commented more than once. Peter said, "I'm my own boss, so I have to watch myself [where slacking off is concerned] and stay on my toes. When I fall asleep on the job, I don't get paid." Like the majority of their self-employed peers, these two were proud of their ability to get themselves moving. They recognized that being self-propelled was essential—and claimed that this is one problem people working for large corporations don't have. "Someone tells them what to do each minute," Vera said confidently, "and then makes sure they actually do it."

That is nonsense. As people who've been employed at large firms for years are well aware, there is much less minute-to-minute supervision than most outsiders imagine. Two people who had positions of responsibility inside the firm comparable to the ones Vera and Peter had outside it would be largely on their own. No one would ride herd on them, and they would resent it if someone did. If they wanted to do next to nothing that day, they'd probably get away with it. Most know how, but they don't use the information. They are as big on self-discipline as their peers who are in business for themselves. This is *not* where the difference between the days and destinies of the two groups lies, regardless of the pats on the back the self-employed keep giving themselves in this department.

A different kind of self-discipline turned out to be crucial in order for people in business for themselves to succeed: the ability to stay in a particular area. No outside agency forced them to do it, and therefore in the vast majority of instances, they didn't. Being in charge of their own business lives afforded them a golden opportunity to try a variety of subjects and approaches. And that's as it should be—at least in the beginning. The entrepreneurial spirit that is essential for these people, and helps keep the nation competitive in world markets, requires that individuals be encouraged to find new and better ways to achieve old or changing goals.

But most of the self-employed people in our sample apparently found the process of experimentation intoxicating. As long as an area was new, it was exciting. Then, once it began to become even moderately familiar, they moved on. Impulsive pioneers, they never stayed any-where long enough to found a settlement, with the result that (1) they failed to develop a high level of expertise in any particular field, and (2) they didn't give the local business community a chance to get to know them *as* experts in that particular field.

In short, self-employment is free-form work. And those who were most successful at it over the years either consciously stayed with a specific area long enough to become outstanding in it or else achieved the same result unwittingly, because they came to love the area and didn't want to abandon it for extensive forays into closely allied fields.

Imaginary Conversations

There is an important psychological factor that makes it hard for people in business for themselves to concentrate on just one subject. The problem is similar to ones seen in sensory deprivation and isolation experiments. People need some kind of feedback from others around them. When it is absent for prolonged periods, they start to provide it themselves. Call it the hallucinatory factor in self-employment.

Bert Collins is very much like Peter. In fact, the two are as well matched as any pair of peers we could find in our sample, except that Bert works for one of the nation's 50 largest industrial concerns. Why bother following these two closely? For one thing, to see which talks to himself more often.

Bert really didn't have much chance to. He had his own office, but there were usually other people in it, either in person or talking to him on the phone. "I have to throw [one or another of my co-workers] out almost every day to get something done," Bert said with a smile. On the other hand, when he did want conversational contact with some-one, it could be done without effort. He would walk a few steps up the hall, stop in at someone else's office and plunk himself down. Most of the workers we monitored at this level proved themselves to be quite adept at getting such an interchange going.

If the two were friends, social topics typically served as the excuse for making contact. Sometimes humor was used. If the two were more acquaintances than friends, or the person sitting there was busy doing something, a work-related topic was more likely to serve as the opener instead. What is interesting is that very few people in our sample— less than 2 percent—who felt the need to make contact with a co-worker said voluntarily that they had ever "made up a question" to go ask the other person. Yet when asked about the practice, almost half— 46 percent—acknowledged that at one time or another, their social needs had motivated them to do just that. As we've said, they usually did it with enormous skill, using an unobtrusive approach that many admitted they had practiced and perfected while still in college. As Bert put it, "I used to 'slip into' the bull session going on up the hall [in the dorm]. And if there wasn't one in progress, I'd start one."

Peter's situation was very different. He certainly made regular contact with customers yet spent a significantly greater portion of his time alone than Bert did. Thoughts about his clients, their firms, and his own business may have wafted or raced through his mind while he worked or traveled, but there was no one of importance to his work around. It wasn't nearly as easy for him to rub shoulders whenever he wished to with a suitable co-worker. Peter made up the deficit by holding imaginary conversations in his head.

Not that he noticed it, mind you. He would simply be working away, trying to get something accomplished, and would populate the space nearby with invisible people who were at least as interested in what he was doing as he was. A head count showed that Bert and Peter talked to approximately the same number of individuals each day, only in Peter's case fewer of them could actually hear what he was saying.

Speaking to fictional or distant characters, who of course were always focused on what Peter was doing, not their own work, may have been a stopgap measure, but it didn't relieve him of the desire to speak to someone real. The desire intensified whenever he had a good idea. The length of time it took for him to find a receptive listener is one of the key variables that set Bert's and Peter's business lives apart. For Bert, the time that lapsed between the advent of an idea and a conversation about it was usually a matter of minutes. "How long did it take for me to tell someone?" Bert asked, repeating our question to him. "Two minutes, maybe. I just got up [after having the thought] and went across the hall."

For Peter, the time lapse was typically measured in hours and even days, not minutes. "I tried calling [the client] to let them know about my brainstorm, but they were having a meeting or something. I left my name and number. It's getting kind of late. I don't know if they'll be calling me back today."

The strong desire to share the idea, though, didn't disappear. Inside him, it hammered away, seeking release. Since it wasn't finding any, Peter was often a strange mixture of emotions: elation (about having the idea in the first place) and dejection (about not being able to tell it to anyone real). It didn't take many such episodes for him to become elated and dejected automatically, whenever a worthwhile thought occurred to him.

Peter was basically an upbeat sort who resisted depressions as unproductive. As he put it more than once, "I don't work well when I'm down." When a splendid idea therefore crossed his mind, most of the time he merely became excited. Happy, not sad. Until he could locate a qualified and willing ear to hear him out, however, he was in a pent-up, somewhat agitated state. Since a steady stream of what, to him, seemed like superb ideas flowed through his mind, he was frequently tense, eager to say something to everyone he encountered.

People who met him for the first time and sensed his inner enthusiasm and involvement concluded that that was the reason he had gone into business for himself to begin with. "He's bursting at the seams," said one. "He'd never make it at a large firm." Commented another, "Peter is like a big puppy that wants to jump on you." Said a third, "Once you get him started [about what he's working on], there's no stopping him."

When the same people met Bert, on the other hand, and noticed his usually calmer disposition, they quickly concluded that he was the perfect corporate type. There was no doubt in their minds that Bert's and Peter's personalities were perfectly matched to their respective business settings and, more important, that the difference in the personalities of the two came first and had caused them to follow such different routes.

That was false. What these observers were seeing were the consequences, not the causes of the business lives Bert and Peter respectively led. The personality differences weren't there in the beginning. They emerged slowly under contrasting pressures the two experienced over the years. More to the point, when the settings in which these two found themselves happened to change, so did their supposedly permanent personalities.

MBAs were in sufficiently great demand by business firms throughout the past two decades from the sixties to the eighties, to allow us to study them in both types of settings. Some started out self-employed and eventually joined large companies. Others took jobs at major firms right after graduation and only went into business for themselves a number of years later. The movement back and forth gave us a chance to study the same individuals in both contexts.

What we discovered can be stated simply: put Bert in Peter's position, leave him there for a few years, and he would have acted much like Peter—talking to himself because no one else was around. Conversely, put Peter in Bert's position and within a year he would have learned how to saunter down the hall, nonchalantly enter a co-worker's office and talk to his peers instead of an invisible audience that followed him around.

The same held true in other professions: those in engineering, sales, and design displayed a similar, long-term dependence on context. That's not to say that, for instance, extroverts became introverts and vice versa. Basic personality differences didn't vanish merely because two people who were well matched changed places, one becoming self-employed, the other joining a large firm. But the business setting in which people find themselves has a crucial effect on the way they think and behave.

Jack of All Trades, Master of None

What are the practical implications of these findings? More specifically, what do they indicate about the likelihood that people will succeed or fail if they go into business for themselves? When there is no one around with whom we can share work-related thoughts regularly, they pile up. That doesn't matter if our work doesn't matter to us. However, if we are serious about what we do for a living, the thoughts won't be ones that we will be content merely to throw away. When we finally do get some feedback from someone we talk to or hear from by mail, we are therefore likely to overreact to their words. Making careful note of our response to criticism is worthwhile, since we may find ourselves suddenly depressed in this situation by what seemed to be a not very weighty remark from a listener.

Even more important in the long run is the effect of each *positive* comment received by people who are self-employed. It is capable of swaying them first in one direction, then in another. The key point here is that, given the lonely context in which they are working, they are likely to be much hungrier for a personalized human voice than they realize. When they hear one at last, and their period of isolation temporarily ends, the voice may have much more of an impact than they imagine. Wanting more of whatever warmth and attention it appears to be showing them, they may unwittingly accord it great substance.

For instance, when Peter was working on a financial analysis for a client and received a phone call from someone asking him about shipping routes (via air and truck), he was thrilled. Having spent the entire morning poring over data sheets, cash flow projections, and unaudited quarterly figures given him by the firm's accountants, he wanted someone to talk to. It was a simple enough and normal need, but it produced major difficulties. Rather than treat the call as a welcome—and meaningless—break in the isolation he had been experiencing for hours, he did the reverse. Peter crammed the conversation full of all the good advice that he could give. He didn't know a great deal about shipping routes and schedules yet threw himself wholeheartedly into the conversation anyway.

He told us at the time that the reason he did it was, in his words, "I'm a troubleshooter. Got to handle everything." Our interpretation instead is that he had been isolated in his office at home too long and, therefore, was overly receptive to the opportunity for contact. Being a serious and hardworking professional, he didn't want to treat the conversation frivolously. That would have struck him as selfish and irresponsible.

Peter had a radio in his office which he played from time to time ("I've got to hear the news, you know"), and his wife or one of his children would call or stick their head in occasionally and say hello. But Peter was involved with his work and dedicated to achievement, and the diversion wasn't quite what he needed, though he found it pleasant enough in its own way. Above all, he wanted during the day to share his work-related thoughts with someone who knew something about them. As it turns out, he could do that only if he responded enthusiastically to their thoughts, not his own.

Without being aware of it, he was actually being dragged all over the map by his callers. They would get in touch with him because of a problem they had. Panting subconsciously for contact, he would then do his best to assist. Before he knew it, he had become caught up. Conscientious worker that he was, he would often stay that way after the call ended, resolving to learn more about the matter so that he would be better prepared the next time they called. The end result was predictable: this well-meaning and dedicated fellow never developed an area of expertise, one in which he so excelled that success was almost certain.

In fact, he was afraid to. Becoming highly expert at anything was a prospect that Peter secretly dreaded. For then the number and range of callers would have shrunk drastically, or so he feared. He wasn't afraid of success. Like most of the people to whom that label is applied, he was afraid instead of becoming a specialist.

Self-discipline plays a critical role in what happens to the self-employed. But being able to bully themselves into getting busy isn't the issue. Motivating oneself to work is essential to success whether one is employed at a huge firm or in business for oneself. The kind of discipline that will make or break one's career when one is self-employed is the ability to prevent oneself from roving around aimlessly. With no consistency to one's sense of direction, one doesn't build the momentum needed to propel one to the forefront of one's field.

In Peter's case, that meant treating the phone call he received in the appropriately lighthearted way. He would have been extremely reluctant to do that, since he always wanted to do his best. Here, however, the attempt backfired, because it wound up pulling him very far off course. Instead, he should have made himself aware of the fact that, after being alone all morning, working away, he was building an appetite for more than just lunch. His hunger for human companionship, in combination with a desire to share his work-related thoughts, was also growing.

Second, he needed to acknowledge to himself immediately when the question was asked, that he knew next to nothing about the topic. Had he been aware of the intense psychological needs that were accumulating within him, that would have been significantly easier to do. Not only would that have been more honest, it would have allowed him to blunt the threat those needs posed to his sense of direction.

As things stood, it was unlikely that Peter would level with the client and say, "It's nice to hear from you, and thanks for thinking of me, but I don't know much about the area." Or, "Here's the little I *do* know." Rather than make such a reply and seem flippant, Peter became quite revved up. He wanted desperately to help—and to keep the conversation going now that it had begun. Without his consciously recognizing it, the call was as welcome as a warm fire and hot drink would have been to someone who had been wandering around in the bitter cold. To let the caller go after a few friendly words would have seemed absurd.

Nonetheless, that is what he should have done. Both parties suffered needlessly as a result of Peter's actions. He frantically tried to sound well informed about the subject and led the client on a wild-goose chase as well. The advice he provided was nearly worthless, as the caller later discovered. Peter felt that he had no other choice. However that is exactly what is wrong with not being a specialist when one is self-employed; people who aren't truly expert in one area often feel compelled to pass themselves off as experts about everything.

Push-Pull Pressures

In sum, people can improve the odds significantly that they will succeed in their own business by not trying to be all things to all people. That may work well for them in their private lives, but it is lethal in the professional sphere.

Interestingly, it is individuals who are so multifaceted that they have been able to get away for years with wearing a variety of occupational hats who are most likely to start their own firms. As one put it, just before quitting, "I'm already a conglomerate, just ask my friends;

I help *everybody* with their work." The stereotype, the textbook version of the entrepreneur, is a person with one inspired idea who wants to pursue it at his own pace and in his own way, and therefore breaks away from a large firm in order to do so.

Our studies turned up a very different picture: men and women who go into business for themselves typically have a whole host of ideas and aren't sure what specific way they want to pursue them. Once they are on their own, they become even more versatile than they were before. A pulsating mass of promising possibilities, they unwittingly allow their customers to give them whatever professional definition they attain—until the next customer comes along and gives them yet another definition to live up to.

If that sounds remarkably like what happens to people in their twenties, that's because it is. As we saw in Chapter Two, by the time young adults enter the work world, many have become supremely confident of their ability to handle any situation thrown at them by using their personality. In fact, they have come to think of it by then as their strongest asset. "That and some fast thinking," they usually add.

Little happens right away to disabuse them of the notion. They encounter a variety of different events during the decade and find themselves able to meet almost every one by remaining "flexible." Nothing tells them in the early years that they are on the wrong road. If they stay at a large firm, however, someone eventually will. They are assigned a slot and expected to become ever more expert about that aspect of the firm's operation. Going into business for themselves brings the process of progressive narrowing, coupled with growing sophistication about the area ("knowing more and more about less and less"), to an abrupt halt. It often reverses it. For most of the people we studied, self-employment was the business version of a return to adolescence. Once there, it is apparently hard to leave, for they are still clinging to it, in many cases, decades later even though they have done poorly.

What is bizarre is that, as in Peter's case, they think they are only doing what is expected of them, given the route they have taken. Nevertheless, it is a recipe for disaster, for they are exposed now to the full force of the push-pull pressures that do the most harm to the self-employed. The push (from inside) is exerted by their own varied interests. The pull (from outside) is exerted by the varied needs of the people and firms with whom they do business.

Why are these pressures so dangerous when people are self-employed? Because at a firm that is even of moderate size, most of their interests as employees would lay fallow. They have been hired to do a particular kind of job, and their other areas of involvement are ruled out to prevent direct conflict with co-workers who would otherwise feel that someone is treading on their turf. Without being conscious of it, in such a setting people are likely to exercise quite a bit of self-restraint and remain within their own realm.

The flip side is even more important: someone at the firm is much less likely to ask *them* questions outside their field of expertise. The person would normally be aware that they probably don't know the answer and are merely trying to be helpful if they give one. In any event, the information the person obtains from them is viewed as temporary, until the final word can be gotten from the resident or outside expert. For instance, no one at Bert's firm would have asked him about shipping routes and schedules. Like Peter, he had concentrated on finance during his MBA program. But given the difference in their respective business lives now, if it made sense to ask either one such a question, it would have to have been Peter.

In short, thanks to his form of employment, Bert had most of the push-pull pressures that could have been lethal to his career handled for him. Peter on the other hand felt the full brunt of them—without realizing it. As with most of the people we've tracked who were self-employed, the forces that continually tugged at him shifted his orientation so often that the chances that he would ever do really well were radically reduced.

Making certain that the same thing doesn't happen to people who are or intend to be self-employed takes a bit of effort but is well worth the bother. To start, they need to keep track occasionally of the amount of time that they are spending alone. In a crowded world, it is easy to have a wrong impression of the accurate figure. The people one passes in the street, is jammed together with in an elevator, or who have an office up the hall, don't give one a chance to speak one's mind about one's work-related thoughts. The goals and important concerns that surround one's activities remain stored inside. Friends and family can help somewhat, but they aren't likely to serve the purpose either. People who are involved in their work need contact with other professionals in the same or allied fields. The amount of time they spend having relevant conversations with others, either in person, on the phone, or by mail, is the information we seek.

For most people who are self-employed, the figure is astonishingly low. More than 40 percent of the people in our sample who are in business for themselves spend less than 35 minutes per day on average engaged in such contact. Granted, some people need more interaction of the meaty sort we're discussing, and others less. Yet the typical figure seen is well below what anyone but a hostile hermit requires. For those who are serious about their work, people with whom to share thoughts aren't a convenience or a luxury; they are a necessity. Such people should find at least one colleague, and they should assume they will overreact to what that person says if that is the only such colleague they have. Keep in mind that social deprivation damages one's career not only because one feels lonely much of the time, but also because it can cost one one's sense of direction. When a person is emotionally needy, every business-related contact stands a good chance of spawning a new direction.

We know from our studies that deciding on a course and sticking with it is essential, but that doesn't mean one can't change it later. The world sorely requires the innovative ideas that come from a large number of people trying new approaches. Nevertheless, each path should be given a solid chance to pay off for them before it is abandoned. They will know how much self-knowledge they possess in this area when they can finally catch themselves confusing psychological hunger (for contact) with long-term professional interest in a subject; then they can do something about it before the confusion has carried them too far afield. In fact, it is worthwhile for the self-employed to pause regularly when they feel themselves becoming excitable and animated during a conversation with a client, and ask themselves, "Am I getting so caught up in this because I want to relieve my temporary state of loneliness *or* because I really am intrigued by the topic these people are asking me about and really want to become more involved in the field from now on?" The answer should provide the self-employed with a clearer picture of the area in which their basic long-term interests lie. That is important because they aren't likely to persist in areas of marginal interest; regardless of the field, persistence turns out to be crucial for success.

Juggler's Strain

Once the conversation is over and they are by themselves again, there is a valuable test that the self-employed can use to determine whether they are on their way to building or wrecking their careers. What they need to note is the amount of fatigue they feel when the conversation is through. If they were on ground that they are either knowledgeable about or enjoy, the interchange should leave them peaceful, not tense. On the other hand, if they wound up discussing— or worse, having to hold forth about—a topic that has only marginal appeal to them, they are more likely to feel wired and weary.

The underlying mechanism here is simple: people become exhausted much more quickly if they have to talk at length publicly about a subject they know little about. Conversely, the more they know about it, the calmer they're likely to be both during and after the period in which they speak. The words don't tire them. The accompanying nervousness, when they're on unfamiliar ground, does. In short, if the need for contact to break their isolation repeatedly nudges the self-employed onto unfamiliar ground, they are probably well on their way to destroying their careers. Each interchange will leave them feeling progressively more worn out instead of refreshed. After enough such episodes, they may find themselves feeling drained and, simultaneously, anxious before they even begin. Many who reach this position label themselves "burned-out."

A great deal of rubbish has been written in recent years about this subject. But let's make use of the term for the moment anyway, since so many of the people we've studied currently do. The first thing to note is that the self-employed in our sample were more than four times as likely to claim they were experiencing burn-out as were those who worked for someone else. Second, among the self-employed, it was almost exclusively people like Peter who were spread too thin, who burned out. Our results allow us to explain what burn-out really is. When used by employees, it is a face-saving synonym for failure to achieve the goals they have set for themselves. As used by the self-employed, it is a feeling of nervous fatigue that afflicts those who spend too much time discussing topics about which they know too little.

No matter what line of work people are in, they may find themselves feeling tired, even exhausted, if they have been working diligently, trying to do a good job. But that doesn't mean they are burned out. In all likelihood, they are merely weary and need some rest and recreation. It is also possible that they are bored. If that is frequently the case, instead of renewing their appetite for the kind of work they do, the vacation may increase their appetite for—well, more vacation. That indicates it is time for them to consider some other line of work.

It is easy to do too much of something one loves, but the high frequency with which people in our sample worked themselves into frazzled states was a surprise. Despite the many complaints we heard over the years about laziness, it turns out that there are a large number of dedicated workers in every field. Even more surprising was the fact that self-employed people did not work harder than those who were employed by large firms. They often boasted that they did (although the basis for the claim was nonexistent), yet the fact remains that both on average turned out the same quantity of work per week.

That should have made matched pairs such as Peter and Bert equally tired. They weren't; the people who were self-employed were significantly more so. As we said, it wasn't because they did more work. What produced the greater fatigue among the self-employed was the fact that they were spraying their energies in a wide variety of directions. Of necessity, that repeatedly brought them onto ground where they were tense and insecure, trying to make themselves sound as expert as possible. In light of the much greater portion of each day that they spent on thin ice, perhaps it isn't surprising that the slowly accumulating nervous fatigue finally took its toll.

Burn-out, which really ought to be called "juggler's strain in the haphazardly self-employed," is a term that people don't need, unless they are merely trying to communicate that they are very tired. When people are in business for themselves, however, one of their most crucial assets is energy. Anything which makes them *that* fatigued should be explored and understood, rather than labeled and forgotten. People who go into business for themselves and fail use as their most popular excuse undercapitalization. "I went down the tubes because I didn't have enough money," is a typical refrain. No doubt in some instances that is so, but in a larger proportion of cases, the most important capital the person possessed—time, energy, and brainpower—was simply squandered. Every contact with customers spawned a new "subsidiary" in the one-person firm. There wasn't enough capital to keep them all going and not enough real expertise in any field to justify its existence in the first place. The tiny firm badly needed pruning. Since it kept sprouting new branches instead of getting rid of marginal ones to fortify the trunk, it eventually collapsed under the weight of all the deadwood it was trying to carry.

There is an excellent rule of thumb that emerged during our study and can be used to prevent trouble here well before it arises. People who are discussing with a client a subject in which they are well versed should stay primarily serious. If the discussion turns to subjects that are outside their realm of expertise, they can lighten the tone of the conversation. It is a spectrum—the more they know, the more serious they can afford to be; the less, the more laughter is called for. Not only is this a satisfying form of interaction in and of itself, it will also help prevent them from unwittingly trying to use shaky grounds to maintain contact just because they feel isolated.

One important exception to the general rule emerged: There are occasions when it is appropriate to seek work with which one isn't familiar but wishes to be. Far from being a joking matter, this can at times be a good way of expanding one's area of competence. But note that in this case, it is done consciously and for professional reasons, rather than subconsciously and for psychological ones. Even in this case, the issues we have been discussing in this chapter need to be kept in mind to avoid self-deception. The question should still be asked from time to time: "Am I taking the work on because it makes sense in terms of my long-term career interests and goals, or am I mainly lonely and any work-related excuse for some social contact just now will do?"

In brief, versatility is a priceless possession, but it can readily get people into trouble at any stage of their lives when they are self-employed. A client, even a friend, who pierces their prolonged state of solitude may unwittingly exert great influence over them, forcing them to point in as many directions as a weather vane in a storm. If success matters to them and they want very much to be productive, it is essential for them to learn when it is appropriate to sit back a bit and laugh.

16

People Who Have Succeeded and Don't Know It

THERE ARE MANY outstanding individuals in our sample who have done well. No matter what measure of success one uses, they pass the test handily. The problem is that they don't know it. In spite of the enormous outpouring of ideas and energy, and their visible contributions to the firm's welfare, these dedicated workers remain oblivious to what they've accomplished.

There are two reasons why that is very strange. The first is that, in every other way, these people seem to be realists. For instance, they would rather hear the truth, no matter how unpleasant it is, than be lied to. Apparently, they can handle it, and in fact, are usually among the first to notice an unpleasant situation developing that others have overlooked. Then, instead of simply complaining about it as a way of calling attention to themselves, they are quick to remedy the deficiency, usually without fanfare. And yet, they are unable to see their own situation clearly. They seem so attuned to bad news that they can't appreciate the good that has come their way. To hear their assessment of what they have attained, one would think their attainments were nil.

The second odd aspect here follows from the first. The highly prized rewards that have come to them, mainly wealth and/or recognition, make little dent on their conscious thinking. As a result, they strive to achieve as if they are still in their twenties, though the majority of the people we are referring to are over 40. That is all to the good in some ways, since this group places a premium on staying lean and agile, which has an invigorating effect on the whole firm. Still, it seems strange that they act this way. The two features we have been discussing, that they are nearly blind to the results of their labors and therefore conduct their business lives as if no such results existed, are factors, but where does their misperception come from? More specifically, why are the most outstanding American workers usually so unaware of their own achievements? The answer has to do with the peculiar way in which they motivate themselves. Two representative examples highlight the underlying factors.

Humility or Amnesia?

No one told Ralph Powell to work, nor did they have to. He made the switch from biology to business with the same ease that he later undertook corporate projects and carried them through to completion. "Studying biochemistry was interesting and fun," he told us shortly after graduation, "but now the serious stuff begins." Ralph took a job in the specialty chemicals division of a major conglomerate.

The division was doing very well at the time, and there always seemed to be an endless amount of work to do. "It doesn't bother me," Ralph said in his second year on the job, and meant it. "I set my priorities and work my way down the list, one by one. They don't all get done, but anything that counts, does."

The fact that Ralph was organized was reflected not just in his work, but also in his clothes and manner. While never trendy, his clothes were up to date, chosen with taste and worn on a trim body. Ralph's neatly parted hair was cut frequently and he took pride in wearing the finest shoes.

Joyce Henley, like Ralph, didn't have to be pushed. She drove herself hard, too much so at times, and then became irritated or depressed that the people around her were unwilling to move at her pace. An economics major in college, she made the transition to the work world more smoothly than most because, as she put it at the time, "I want to *do* something with my life." The large state university she attended in the mid–1950s seemed to her mainly a way station. "There's too much fooling around," she commented as a junior. "Too many people who don't know why they're here." She did know, and couldn't wait for it to be over.

From her first week on the job, Joyce was certain that this was the arena in which she wanted to be. Her employer, a hospital-supplies firm, appealed to her, thanks to, in her words, "opportunity for advancement *and* lots of back and forth—good communication—with the people at the top. The outfit is small enough so you can get to know everybody." One of the women who worked there told that to Joyce during a tour of the firm as part of the interview, and it turned out to be true. "I really like it here," she said in her third year there.

Joyce had been athletic in college and still managed now to do some jogging at the end of her busy day. She resented the business attire forced on her by her job and claimed that she could get twice as much work done in her sneakers and a running suit. Nevertheless, she conformed without complaining. She bought minimum-care but expensive clothes and wore very little jewelry. The fact that she was unaware of her attractiveness to those around her, made her all the more so.

It is worthwhile for us to focus upon these two extremely bright people for three reasons: first, no one in our sample has worked harder year in and year out. There are others who are equally devoted to their work, but none is more so. Second, few people enjoy what they're doing each day nearly as much as these two do. Third, the rewards they've received during the last 24 years have been commensurate with the effort they've expended. The rub is this: they don't see it. "What I have here [in terms of salary and title] is nothing to write home about," Ralph commented recently. As Joyce put it a few days later, "My office is nice, and I earn enough to pay the bills, but I don't think I'm going to make the Guinness Book of Records [on either score]." It is tempting to interpret the casual manner in which they view their accomplishments as a subtle way of asking for still more. As if to say, "Don't hesitate to give me a raise; I'm not all that impressed by what I'm earning now." (In 1983, both earned six-figure incomes.) However, these two were not displeased on that score and actually complained very little about the subject of pay and promotions.

If we take a closer look at how they managed everyday situations, something fascinating emerges. Let's give it a name now and we'll see precisely how it works later. It should be called, "Deliberately bankrupting yourself every day."

The most important situation that Ralph had to handle when he was 34 was the expansion of one of the company's plants in Texas. The operation was sufficiently profitable to warrant tripling its capacity, and Ralph, together with three others, was given supervisory responsibility for the entire project once the initial funding had been approved. "The market is definitely there [for the products we'll be making]," he said enthusiastically. "We're running at full tilt now, selling everything we can produce." Ralph was thrilled to have been included at all, since he was at least 15 years younger than anyone else on the team.

It was a massive undertaking. There were some construction delays due to the temporary unavailability of certain parts, and cost overruns due to inflation, but as Ralph put it, "three months later—and a little more than we budgeted—the thing is cooking." Bringing the new facility up to full capacity added another six months to the two-year construction time. "Finding the right people [to staff the expanded operation] is a real pain in the neck. One of the new managers we hired showed up drunk the first day. Drunk! That's all we need—to have that shiny, new baby go up in flames."

There can be little doubt that the three years the project took represented a major chunk of Ralph's working life. But time alone doesn't tell the story. The project consumed him, costing him many a night's sleep and causing him to mobilize more of his abilities than he ever thought it would. As he put it gleefully near the end, "I learned about everything, from organic reaction mechanisms to return on total capital [debt plus equity] calculations." Yet as soon as the project was completed, Ralph went on to other things. He had other work to handle during the three years, since it was usually a full-time focus only for a few weeks at a time. Now, those activities as well as others, received more of his attention.

Five years later, when Ralph was 42, we asked him how he would assess his achievements thus far at the firm. "Who me?" he replied, buying some time to think about the matter. "Nothing much. I think there'll be some big ones in the next few years, maybe, but up to this point, there isn't anything I'd put on my resume except the title I got last month."

Was he being humble? Or did he have amnesia? If only this case had been examined, that is the kind of conclusion we might have reached. Ralph's colleagues certainly didn't agree with his self-assessment. In addition to the plant expansion, they were able to rattle off a list of over a dozen items that they felt were significant contributions that Ralph had already made. "And there'll be more," said the VP in charge of operations. "That much I'd bet my bottom dollar on."

Joyce reacted in the same way to her achievements. When she was 37, she happened to run into an old classmate of hers from high school. "What are you doing now?" she asked him. "I sell office supplies," he replied. They stood there and talked for about 20 minutes, while crowds swirled past them on the street during the lunch hour.

The conversation intrigued her because, as she put it, "It's nice to hear what the kids I grew up with are doing now. I've lost touch, but he knows the latest about all of them. He went to the class reunion; I didn't even realize they were holding one, and couldn't have gone [on that day] anyway." There was another reason the brief meeting caught Joyce's interest. In her words, "He talked about how important packaging is [in his business]—you know, the right number of units in each package, and all that." The sentence struck a responsive chord in her mind because she felt that too little consideration was being given the subject, not only at her firm, but in the industry generally. "The office supply companies—and the drug companies—are way ahead of us on this one. Either we sell bulk [to institutions] or individually wrapped [for retail]." The conversation, brief though it was, acted as a catalyst to convince her that the area in between, "small-quantity wrap," as she called it, deserved more attention.

During the next two years, she set herself the task of reviewing the company's products that were in her area. "Some are made for us by other companies under a private-label agreement," she said. But those over which her firm had direct manufacturing control were examined one at a time to see if there was room for improvement on this front. The firm's president had given the go-ahead, and the two people in charge of production worked with her on the assignment.

"It wasn't hard to do," she commented after the first idea had gone into effect. "We took 12 bottles and put them in a little cardboard tray—sort of a 12-pack, like soda bottles. The whole thing is only 3" × 5" × 12", but it looks neat and it's easier to store—and buy." Coming up with new packaging concepts may not have been difficult for Joyce, but waiting for the salesman to return with a broad sample of customer reactions was. "Maybe it was all for nothing," she said uneasily, a few hours before going into a meeting in which the order sheets from each region were to be reviewed.

As it turned out, the new format was a winner and remained so in the next few years. Joyce's fear that it would be a one-time thing, "a novelty that would soon be forgotten," or worse, would merely take business away from bulk sales, proved unfounded. "If anything," the sales manager mentioned at a subsequent meeting, "it's taking business from our competitors, since customers are now stocking *more* of our stuff than they were before." Top management was very pleased with the results and to this day remember who initiated the program.

The one person who seems to have forgotten about it is Joyce. Five years after the completion of the project, at which time the duties were assigned to a full-time design pro, we asked Joyce how she would assess her achievements thus far at the firm. "I've done a little of everything," she said thoughtfully, "putting my two cents in here and there. There hasn't been anything newsworthy. I've just kind of done my job."

Another brilliant amnesiac—or is it humble high achiever? The description fits Joyce every bit as poorly as it does Ralph. The essential aspects of what we are dealing with here can only be seen by sifting through a large number of cases. They fall into two, quite distinct groups.

"When Is It 'Miller Time'?"

Blue-collar work tends to be group-oriented and disjointed. That is, a group of manual laborers get together for a specific period of time to do a specific job; say, build a house or skyscraper. White-collar work, on the other hand, places much more emphasis on individual initiative. There is no group watching when people do this kind of work. Nor could there be. The work is largely mental, not manual. In many critical cases, there isn't much to see. Since each step of the activity isn't as visible as hammering nails, the actions can't be coordinated as well as they would be on an assembly line. Minds are more quirky than muscles and, although the work will get done, it is much harder to know exactly when.

There is significantly less camaraderie as well. Two people painting the side of a house together can joke to their heart's content. Their work requires them to use their hands, not their heads, which leaves them free to talk while they're busy. The more important varieties of office work rule out a similarly steady stream of banter. Continual conversation between two people whose desks are close together comes at the expense of their productivity. For them to work effectively and talk at the same time is usually impossible.

Finally, since office work involves individuals laboring away on their own as part of a loose confederation, there is more continuity than in the case of manual labor. There are separate projects to do in an office, but they tend to flow into one another, blurring the boundary between them. The beer drinkers in our sample characterized the difference vividly. "If I worked in an office," said a gardener, "I'd get confused. I mean, when is it 'Miller time'? I'd either have to drink all day [since so many little projects are being completed] or not at all [since each project overlaps and becomes part of another]." Doctors, dentists, lawyers, professionals of all sorts understand that attitude very well. They see a succession of cases, or handle a series of separate matters, yet each is part of a continuum, leading one into the other, connected in some way. Their profession overshadows any particular job.

That is a large part of what made Ralph and Joyce so oblivious to the distinction between one project and the next. They in essence had been trained not to celebrate after each piece of work was done, and therefore it was much more easily forgotten.

There is another, more important reason why these two, and the millions like them, think and behave in this manner. It has less to do with externals (recognizing achievement) and is more concerned with a key internal (maintaining motivation). Somehow, professional and managerial workers know that their ability to keep themselves motivated is absolutely essential to success. Once their interest flags, they know they are in trouble. "If I didn't give a damn about this place, I couldn't work," said Ralph. "The romance, the urgency would go out of it." In Joyce's words, "It would show if I stopped caring. The people here would pick up on it right away."

The crucial nature of the problem has made upwardly mobile white-collar workers invent a spectacularly effective way of keeping themselves motivated. Rather than just dismiss the importance of what they have achieved, they also dismiss the achievement itself. How? By banishing the memory? As we've seen in Ralph's and Joyce's cases, that is certainly what one might be tempted to conclude from their seeming amnesia. But wait a minute; it turns out that they haven't forgotten the acts. They remember participating in a plant expansion and repackaging program, respectively. However, they think those were minor accomplishments, not very important at all.

The sentences they use to embody their self-effacing approach are a stroke of sheer genius. "I'm only as good as what I do today." said Joyce. A good friend of hers who designs apparel said something similar. "I'm only as good as my *next* line. If it bombs, no one is going to want to hear about what I did in prior seasons." In Ralph's words, a comment he frequently repeated, "The real test of my ability will be the next quarter's earnings, not the last one." A journalist friend of his made a comparable remark. "I'm only as good as my next article."

Note well what these people are doing: they are using tomorrow to bludgeon yesterday into insignificance. More precisely, their view of the magnitude and importance of current and future tasks, yet undone, shrinks to nothingness the stature of past tasks, which they've successfully completed.

There can't be any doubt that the mechanism keeps them motivated, but it does so at an enormous price. In essence, on a daily basis, they deliberately go bankrupt. Past accomplishments are reduced to dust, and quickly at that. What happened yesterday is—well, yesterday. And the big question is, "What have I done today?"

Ralph and Joyce usually arrive at work in the morning carrying such things as reports, papers, or a newspaper. Yet when all is said and done, they come to the office each day empty-handed, with no laurels to rest on. The result is that they unwittingly apply a tremendous amount of pressure to themselves to accomplish something. After all, in their view, they have nothing. Their previous achievements having been stripped of significance, these two have no choice but to push themselves hard.

A critical part of the problem is that so little of what they do can be preserved on film. The end result of their work may ultimately be visible, but that is always the smallest part of the picture. The outcome of a battle misses the real story: the second-to-second struggle by each participant to do well against formidable odds. Where this group is concerned, that can't be put on film in any meaningful way. Too much of the work is internal.

Comparing established executives and well-known athletes makes the point clear. Youngsters who do well enough in the world of sports to become professionals will have miles of footage to examine if they wish. They will see not just the box score of each contest, but also the tension and involvement, the actual movements they made that helped bring their team or themselves victory or defeat. Also, if they so choose, and a growing number do, they can obtain pictures of themselves in practice, using movie cameras or videotape machines.

Executives have access to nothing similar. Whether they like it or not, the effort they pour into anything they tackle—the agonies, anxieties, and elation that surround the task—disappear immediately as soon as the day is done. The fact that on one of those days, the project is finally completed and a finished product is ready for display changes nothing. It is too small a vessel to hold all the emotions that have gone into it for months and perhaps years. The metal tubing in the plant that Ralph helped bring into existence and, even more so, the 12-pack that Joyce created were comically small containers for the abundant concern and intelligence that poured from them for a combined total of five years.

The upshot was that, unable to impress the right images on a piece of blank tape that they could have stored somewhere and treasured forever, they sometimes tried too hard to make a dent on subordinates. Both wanted to leave a mark in the world. When they were sufficiently frustrated with what they viewed as their lack of progress, the younger people with whom they worked became prime targets. This almost always backfired. Instead of building a lasting memorial to themselves in the minds of others, they bred resentment, which did indeed last.

Neither one was a bully, and they recoiled rapidly once the wave of annoyance passed from the harsh treatment they handed out. They may not have known why they were acting that way in the first place, but they didn't want it to continue. So in the next step, they cracked the whip on their own backs instead, trying to compel themselves to reach just a little further and seize at last what had always eluded their grasp: an undeniably great achievement. Then, they both insisted, they would rest.

The Ever-receding Finish Line

What they never realized is that the system was rigged, and that they are the ones who rigged it. Why would they do such an awful thing to themselves? To avoid a still more terrible fate, much like amputating a gangrenous limb. There was a horrifying prospect they didn't want to face, a nightmare that afflicted the majority of intelligent and industrious people we studied. They feared that they would finally achieve something so outstanding that they would no longer feel the need to continue the struggle to achieve. Nirvana? Not to people who have shaped their whole lives so that they can keep striving.

It is essential to get beneath the surface here since it is easy to be deceived by the deliberately casual remarks people make about this subject. "I want to hit it really big," said Joyce. As Ralph put it repeatedly, "More than anything, I want to do something *great*." They would have us believe that that is what drives them. They certainly believe it. Yet they are also terrified of the very thing they say they want most, because they fear that attaining it will bring them to a screeching halt. So they erase the finish line in order to keep themselves running. That serves their purpose admirably, for they can now say to themselves day after day, "How can I stop or even slow down? The race is far from being over."

Note well, however, that this is a strange kind of race: the farther one runs, the farther one still has to run. The more effort Ralph and Joyce expended, the more imperative they felt it was to keep on going. Or else, as Ralph commented, "all those years of education and experience will [instantly] go down the drain."

There is an illuminating way to look at the forces at work here. The idea of "making do with less," "diminishing expectations," and "a declining standard of living" has often been in the air in the past few years. The thorny problems experienced by the nation's economy have lent weight to the words. Yet such phrases do little more than obscure the underlying and more powerful trend: rising expectations. For instance, when Ralph and Joyce successfully accomplished something they were assigned to do or decided on their own to try, they merely set their sights higher. There was no longer any satisfaction to be derived from repeating a past achievement. Obsolescence anxieties alone would have made them move on as a way of keeping up. "Anything from yesterday is *old*," as Joyce put it at 45. "If you stand still while everyone else sprints," said Ralph at 44, "soon you won't even be seeing their dust. Got to stay in motion." However, we aren't talking about horizontal motion; what is at issue is vertical movement.

In their thirties, Ralph and Joyce wanted to top what they had done in their twenties. In their forties, they didn't want to look back at their thirties; they wanted to look down at it. So it went with each span of time. Any action they performed well in a previous decade therefore became not just obsolete but miniaturized, as if they were viewing it now from the roof of a tall building. Why were they so averse to repeating what had once provided such contentment? Their answer is the one voiced by the majority of highly motivated people. "Why would I want to do it again? I've already done it."

For others who feel the same way, and who have been using these mechanisms to keep themselves motivated, avoiding a major crisis as the years pass is nearly impossible. When we first began our study, we assumed that it was primarily the indifferent workers who would find themselves in deep trouble as the decades rolled by—and their more dedicated peers pulled ahead. The prediction was dead wrong. The indifferent developed their share of work-related problems, but since they didn't care much about their work or the firm to begin with, it irked them less than we thought it would when someone went roaring by them on the way up. Although they noticed it, they didn't consider the event something worth losing any sleep over.

Highly motivated workers, on the other hand, turned out to be the ones who were flirting with danger and, in more than 70 percent of the cases we monitored, it finally cost them dearly. By continually destroying their yesterdays as a way of keeping themselves interested in working hard today, they had nothing left to take with them into their tomorrows. When they were young, they could get away with doing this because their focus was single-mindedly on the future. However, in the middle and especially latter part of their work lives, it caught up with them. They had nothing to fall back on, nothing worthwhile to their credit. With each passing year the odds increased that they would become another statistic in our ongoing study, one more instance of what we have been discussing here: someone who has succeeded but doesn't know it.

The Thrill of Victory, the Agony of Defeat

The earlier people make a few changes in this area, the better. Nothing dramatic is called for, yet we have seen even minor modifications yield major benefits over the long run. To begin with, it is essential for such people to stop throwing away their past achievements one at a time. Once they have done this with any particular event, and allowed approximately eighteen months to pass, the process becomes irreversible. By then, they can no longer breathe vitality back into an accomplishment whose significance they removed as soon as the act was completed.

For instance, it was critical for Ralph to recognize the magnitude of what he had attained during the three years he devoted to the plant expansion project. Similarly, it was important for Joyce to spend a few moments reflecting upon what she had done, once the product repackaging program showed clear signs of being a success. But once they had shoved themselves onto other projects immediately, in order to compensate for the fear that they would loaf permanently after a victory celebration, it was too late. Remember, one can't resurrect a past achievement and see it as a triumph if one laid it to rest long ago as a nonentity.

It is worthwhile to understand why. How well one remembers an incident at all, and what it is specifically that one remembers, are greatly influenced by the emotions that surround it at the time of its occurrence. If the emotions are intense, one is more likely to be able to later recall both the episode and the feelings during it. On the other hand, if the event was one that caused neither joy nor sadness, but simply took place without arousing one's emotions in any way, it more easily disappears without a trace. Emotions help carve the event into one's memory.

Psychologists use the word "affects" as a synonym for "emotions." What Ralph, Joyce, and the majority of ambitious Americans in business who are intent upon keeping themselves highly motivated do, is to engage in "affect stripping." Basically, it is a subconscious form of self-suppression. That is, they strip away the emotions, especially elation, that would ordinarily be there near and at the end of a prolonged period of productive effort.

Anguish and ecstasy are permitted only prior to the completion of the event, not after it. Once it is done, the most permissible feeling is relief. And not too much of that either since, as good white-collar workers, these people know that one project should be followed almost immediately by another. If they want the thrill of victory and the agony of defeat, they are supposed to experience it vicariously, by viewing sports in a stadium or on TV. There, workers who are trying to stay highly motivated year round for four decades can attain temporary release from the strain of doing so by watching players who have to get "up" for one contest at a time—for only four months a year. Note also that when these workers themselves participate in athletics, it is endurance activity—endless running—that is held in highest regard. They can enjoy seeing someone else sprint or go out for a pass, but when they themselves run, the self-imposed rules dictate something more stringent: it must be a marathon.

The emotions connected with their work, then, don't disappear. They are merely moved forward in time. "Front-loading"—experiencing the bulk of the feelings before and during the project—is the standard operating style among outstanding business people in the United States. The evidence indicates overwhelmingly that it works.

However, displacing the emotions forward in time does serve to change them. At the conclusion of a project that one has successfully completed, joy is a natural emotion. One wouldn't expect to see people merry in the midst of a long and arduous task. The feelings more likely to be present would include courage, enthusiasm, annoyance, a spirit of determination, and at times, despair. These provide the act with a negative tinge and may therefore have an impact of their own upon one's memory of it. Pain associated with an event makes one more likely to forget it.

In short, if the positive emotions associated with one's work are experienced only anticipatorily—that is, solely *before* the event—they are modified greatly. In being shifted forward in time ("Boy, if I could just do that, I'd be so happy"), they first become muted and then unpleasant once the event is done ("What in the world am I going to do for an encore?"). In fact, as happens with an increasingly heavy load of weights being attached to a small floating object, they eventually sink it. When people who do this eventually look back at such a sea in their minds, nothing remains visible on the surface. They were never there.

Savoring One's Accomplishments

Leaving a trail behind them rich with vivid reminders of previous achievements requires two things: first, marking the spot well at the time, otherwise they won't even be able to locate it at a later date, much less dredge it up in all its glory. Second, they have to have confidence that celebrating past and present accomplishments won't distract them from future achievements. Let us look at the second topic first.

It is no exaggeration to say that the aspiring workers we studied, whether in business for themselves or working for someone else, were appalled at the prospect of doing too much reminiscing. It scared them. Musing about the past, reliving various moments from it, usually struck them as a useless activity, one that was suitable primarily for the elderly and inactive. An extensive review of souvenirs and memorabilia would be more appropriate, they felt, once they had retired. Right now, they were too busy to look back. In essence, their approach was, "I'm still *building* the monument that will be the consequence of my life's work. This is not the time for me to do a retrospective. It's premature." What they didn't realize is that when they got to the end of their careers and wanted to do one, there would be nothing left. They were destroying every meaningful souvenir at each stage.

Even had they realized that, they still might have chosen to push on rather than risk coming to an abrupt halt. Anything that jeopardized their ability to relentlessly pursue their goals was shunned. What needs to be said here is that pausing momentarily to mark the spot—at the time—helps rather than hinders their efforts to achieve. For it removes some of the self-imposed excess pressure, thereby allowing them to operate more efficiently. The fact that a moderate amount of something is good for people doesn't mean that more of it is better still. The classic example is vitamin A. We need some in order to avoid night blindness, but too much can cause bone disorders and death. Motivation has long been known to be subject to similar considerations. Some is necessary to get oneself moving, yet too much will bring one to a nervous standstill. A substantial portion of the people who think they are undermotivated are actually overmotivated. Naturally, their response is to push themselves still harder, which only makes the situation further deteriorate.

That is not a condition they can remedy as long as they regularly discard their past. With nothing to fall back on, they feel compelled to keep fleeing into the future; that is, until they run out of tomorrows as retirement approaches and they are suddenly confronted with a personal crisis for which there is no satisfactory solution. Then it is too late.

To make matters worse, they have taken the decades they devote to work and used them in a remarkably inefficient manner. The machine was belching smoke and fire constantly but barely moving. The pressure they applied to themselves continually made them less productive, not more.

Allowing themselves to enjoy what they have achieved can make a significant difference to future achievements. While they are laboring away at one project or another, it is appropriate for them to stay as absorbed as they are inclined to get. But as they near its completion, and even more so in the weeks and months following that date, it is important for them to devote a few moments to consciously savoring what they have accomplished. And if the project is an extensive or major one, it is worthwhile for them to do the same as various stages become complete. Handling it in the usual manner—stripping it of significance and nearly obliterating it from memory—will only make them desperate. The approach they take to their next task will then be that of a *kamikaze*, not a veteran professional with a growing number of successes.

Odd as it may sound, it is difficult for people who are accurately described as "driven" to know that they have accomplished anything. They have real trouble acknowledging, even to themselves, that they have just done something truly noteworthy. Ralph and Joyce, for instance, were typically blind to their own achivemeents. In fact, they were the only ones unable to see the steady stream of outstanding things they were doing. The people around them, sometimes green with envy, had little difficulty recognizing the undeniable contributions these two were regularly making.

It is precisely because of that envy, however, that one needs to be extremely careful about how one congratulates oneself on what has just been done. Competitive pressures in every field are now intense, and tooting one's own horn in public will only rile co-workers and superiors. They may think that one is demanding advancement and applause, things they want to give when, and if, they are ready. Praising oneself briefly in private as each phase of the project nears and then reaches its close is more effective. Spending a few moments from time to time in subsequent weeks or months doing the same is also important. After all, it is one's own memory, not that of others, which is most in need of modification here.

In sum, the majority of workers who are attempting to remain highly motivated can eventually expect to face a serious crisis. The problem is that in order to stay so motivated, they have been throwing their lives away one slice at a time. When they are young, they are able to erase the past by living in the future. In the middle and latter parts of their careers, they do it by downplaying and discarding the present. Instead of the passing decades making them feel increasingly accomplished, they end up feeling ever more empty; for they are running out of the time needed to finally make themselves overnight successes. The only effective solution is for them to start immediately to immortalize their feats one by one on career films in their minds, by pausing briefly each time to appreciate what they have done soon after doing it.

Postscript

Many Americans were able to succeed in past decades without really trying. The country was rich enough to carry even indifferent employees onward and upward. They may not have become millionaires or presidents of their companies, yet merely going through the motions got them surprisingly far.

Not anymore. Few workers are aware how drastically attitudes in the business world have shifted in recent years. The confidence, even smugness, that characterized many executives in the 1960s and 1970s is gone, replaced by a gnawing insecurity about competition and survival. Foreign rivals have put a major dent in a variety of our basic industries. Autos, shipbuilding, cameras, motorcycles, farm equipment machinery, steel, textiles, apparel, radios, TVs, stereos, and consumer electronics of all sorts have already felt the pressure. Domestic rivals too have learned how to be better competitors, each squeezing the others' profit margins in the process. The changed business climate demands a new look at the harsher realities of the work world, which has become, simultaneously, more high-tech and lean-and-mean. The conveyor belt of business will no longer carry everyone forward automatically. People have to make every year count now.

That means having a much clearer picture of the kinds of opportunities they will find and setbacks they are likely to sustain. Once they have already fallen victim to a situation that may have been many years in the making, it becomes much harder to escape unharmed, for public as well as private reasons. Co-workers and superiors remember failures as well as successes; in many instances, they remember failures better. In addition to the external factors in one's business life, connected with the economy's ups and downs, there are internal, psychological factors that are even more important. Most people create for themselves the wealth of renown they eventually gain. Fame and fortune don't become theirs just by luck. The same applies to people who do less well; their fruitless strivings, are to a large extent, the results of their own misguided approaches. Yet, it is possible to anticipate and overcome the hurdles that have brought many a budding career to a dead halt. As it turns out, the vast majority of situations we confront in the course of our business lives are not unique. Other men and women have remarkably similar experiences. We are not nearly as alone as it seems.

The problems people face each decade differ, in large part because they themselves have become different. The tactics they used in their twenties to get what they wanted usually have little in common with the approaches they take in their forties. Similarly, the words that pop out of their mouths in their thirties are another world when compared to the comments they make in their fifties. When they were given the chance to hear tapes of themselves in business on two days, twenty years apart, the vast majority didn't recognize themselves at all.

Not only do people change, decade by decade, so do their settings. The firm and, more important, the world around them undergoes subtle and not-so-subtle shifts. To them, caught up in their everyday activities, it may seem as though they are making very little career progress as the years pass but, like little changes in their personality and approach, important shifts steadily occur without being noticed.

In short, they may think that they are basically the same people now, operating each day in basically the same manner as they did years ago, yet that is not what the evidence we have collected indicates. They are indeed different—or should be—and will be still more so in the future. If they know more about how they and their work setting will vary as the years drift by, the major problems they face can be minimized. The people around them expect certain things from them at one stage in their careers, and altogether different ones at a later stage.

Being out of touch with either the shifts in their own personal direction, on the one hand, or professional demands they are supposed to be meeting now but aren't, on the other, is a recipe for trouble. In many cases, people are out of touch with both. Of the more than 5,000 people we have monitored for a quarter of a century, less than 3 percent had an *accurate* idea of the kinds of developments that would make or break their careers. What makes that particularly distressing is that the crises people face in the course of their business careers are largely predictable. Each person's experience of them will be unique; no two individuals react to the same event in exactly the same way. Nevertheless, there are enough similarities present to allow people in business to foresee and prevail over the most important obstacles they will encounter.

Let us review briefly some of the troublesome surprises that can be expected, decade by decade. One of the most dangerous—in fact, it is capable of undoing any success one has already attained—concerns the abundant theatrical abilities of young adults. The performances people stage in an office should stand in stark contrast to the ones they would be tempted to put on in a theater. Yet most of the ambitious workers we studied in their twenties seemed unable at times to make the distinction. A huge amount of research has been done in recent years to see what if any influence television exerts on the impressionable minds of young viewers. The concern of many of these investigations has been violence; namely, does watching destructive behavior make people want to imitate what they have just seen? However, there are other kinds of destructive behavior besides assaults against others or their property. People do violence to their own careers either by not even realizing that they are acting or, knowing it, but unwittingly overdoing it anyway. The dramatics often backfire, canceling the merits of one's job-related skills in the eyes of the business audience that witnesses the show. In Chapter Two we saw the harm people frequently do themselves in a media-crazed country when they can't distinguish between hard goods and Hollywood.

One's thirties are a time of great hope and expanding opportunity, and well they should be. But the rate at which one's own business grows or one advances in someone else's firm depends more each year of one's life on a critical factor: how well one can work with others. Teamwork is one of the most widely used and least understood words in American business. Yet it is simply too crucial to the firm and the individual to ignore. In Part Two we looked at intelligent and dedicated people whose undeniable talents might as well not have existed. Their picture of how a group of people in business behaves when functioning at its best as a team is so distorted, it is hardly surprising that they are nearly unable to participate productively.

The topic of job changes represents such an omnipresent facet of business life in the United States, it has been one focus of our research from the start, and was dealt with extensively in Part Three. Workers of every age, 21 and younger through 65 and older, are involved. Be that as it may, a seemingly simple switch from one firm to another can quickly turn elation today (about going) into depression tomorrow (once one is there). If one is working for a firm and doesn't like it or one's boss, this is a subject that needs more careful consideration than it typically receives before one leaves. Most people who are thinking of changing jobs are so repelled by their present positions that they rejoice at the mere thought of having another. That isn't enough. The hoped for results of a job change are too rarely realized. Trading a heachache for an upset stomach occurs far too often, yet this can be prevented by getting some answers to a few key questions that almost no one asks.

For instance, how many of the things that one needs in order to function at one's peak will be at the new firm? People don't ask this because only a small proportion have sat down and figured out what their current detestable company offers that has helped them get as far as they've gotten. The aspects they find obnoxious about the old place blind them to what may be essential—and missing—at the new. We looked at a number of representative cases, in which people who were prospering virtually destroyed the foundation upon which their success rested. Then, in a step-by-step manner, we saw how problems in this area can be drastically reduced.

In Part Four we saw that the forties is the most misinterpreted decade for people in business. They are continually told during these years that they are in their prime, and some of the time they believe it. More often, they feel lost and lonely, even if they have satisfying personal lives. Experience alone has taught them a considerable amount about their profession by this age, but the hard-won knowledge can suddenly seem very superficial and, worse, outdated. Workers in their twenties and thirties worry continually about keeping up, if they want to get ahead, and so do many in their fifties and sixties. But the brunt of the problem falls on those in their forties. To go wrong during the decade on this score is truly a tragedy because one has many years invested in a career at that point, and yet one still has many years left to go. This is no time to falter.

Making certain that one does well during that decade requires an examination of what is happening professionally not only to oneself, but to one's peers as well. One's relationship to them, and to subordinates, changes in what we now know to be a predictable manner, particularly if things start to go wrong. We saw how important it was to learn how to read and respond to signals indicating that an ominous loss of direction—and therefore, in many cases, a loss of self-control—is about to occur.

The fifties and sixties, the subject of Part Five, offer opportunities that are usually denied men and women of a younger age. People look at one differently during this period, a change that can be turned to one's advantage instead of detriment with surprising ease. The unparalleled stability that one is in a position to provide, however, must be based on the right attitude toward one's co-workers. We were surprised to find that not many people over 50, and even fewer over 60, possess it. Instead, they think they now have a license to sneer. Then, they are puzzled that the younger, more vigorous members of the firm are immensely eager to push them into early retirement. The final 10 to 15 years of one's career can be productive and deeply satisfying or one long, life-threatening crisis. We saw how remarkably minor an effort is required to tilt the situation one way or the other.

Part Six dealt first with self-employment, not only because this is an essential component of the American business scene, but also because people in business for themselves face special problems. To bring them into focus, our approach from the inception of our study has been to compare how well the self-employed do against one another and also how well they do when measured against their peers who work for someone else. For people who are self-employed or would like to be, there are some fascinating lessons to be learned from looking at the problems confronted by their twins employed at major firms in their field. The kinds of grief they and their double experience come from entirely different sources. We saw that the self-employed were able to convert an undeniable asset—their flexibility—into a damaging liability, by pursuing too many directions at once as a way of maintaining fleeting social contacts on the job.

The final chapter of Part Six, about people who have succeeded and don't know it, was a shock to us, and is one we never expected to write. In the late 1950s when we began our research, we would not have believed there were any such people. Checking their bank balance or net worth should have told them they were wealthy; beating away the crowds seeking their autographs should have given them a clue that they had become well known; and looking at the title on the door to their office or on their business card should have told them that they had arrived.

However, we now know that an important psychological factor blinds them to all that. It has to do with their expectations being raised as a result of an accomplishment. They live in a world that is dedicated to progress, so if they have already performed a particular feat, it is time to take the feat for granted instantly and go on from there. What hasn't yet been done receives enormously more attention than what has. Flying at the speed of sound, running a four-minute mile, and putting a man on the moon were thrillers—until they were attained. Then they became so totally accepted as to seem somewhat ordinary; certainly nothing to shout about.

Ambitious people are always looking for new mountains to climb, and they continually adjust their expectations upward right after each achievement. A special crisis awaits them just as their long and ostensibly rewarding careers come to a close. We saw exactly what it is, and what needs to be done about the perilous way they manage their motivations and memories, before they run out of time.

* * *

Before concluding, it is worth mentioning that the personal lives of people discussed in the book were downplayed only to keep the book from becoming too heavy to lift. We have accumulated a massive amount of material on the interplay of their personal and professional lives, and will treat this important subject in the near future. For the purpose, we have long since expanded the size of the sample to include the children's children, many of whom are now young adults. It will be interesting to see if they repeat their parents' mistakes. Our hope is that this book will help prevent them from doing so in their business lives.

Appendix on Methodology

The publication in the mid—1950s by the RAND Corporation of the first table of randomly generated numbers[1] allowed us to construct a sample of 2,000 investors, using the table and the five-digit account numbers of customers at nine brokerage firms; five national and four regional. Each was told that interviews at regular intervals would be required in addition to follow-up questionnaires. A mere record of purchases and sales, on the one hand, and data summarizing investor preferences (stocks versus bonds, long-term versus short-term, and NYSE versus Amex and OTC), on the other, would not be sufficient to permit detailed study of the decision-making process, and the subsequent re-actions and rationalizations surrounding each transaction.

Since this group tended to be significantly older (median age: 36) than employees accepting full-time, entry-level positions in industry, 1,500 students were also selected from 16 college and graduate schools that represented a cross section of United States institutions of higher education in 1958—59. A third sample consisted of 1,518 school-age children of the investor sample. The cost savings associated with clus-ter sampling were not the main reason for making our selections from a total of approximately two dozen brokerage firms and universities. Although we were aware that almost all varieties of clustering in sam-ple design decrease the precision of sample estimates since less new data about the population is obtained by selecting additional people from the same cluster than by taking people at random, background similarity was viewed as not necessarily a disadvantage in a long-term study emphasizing differential rates of promotion and pay increases. Initial differences among sample members, although smaller in some cases than we would have liked, soon widened, and in fact, facilitated the study of developmental changes by decade.

---

[1]RAND Corporation, *A Million Random Digits* (Glencoe: Free Press, 1955).

Nevertheless, attention was given throughout to inter-, as well as intra-group differences. Repeated comparisons, at least on an annual basis, were made between sample means and population means, by utilizing College Placement Council, *Salary Surveys*; Endicott, *Trends in Employment of College and University Graduates in Business and Industry*; U.S. Bureau of Labor Statistics, *Employment of Recent College Graduates*; National Science Foundation, *Two Years after the College Degree*; data on "Consumer Income" and "Educational Attainment" from U.S. Bureau of the Census, *Current Population Reports* on mean earnings of four-year college graduates; U.S. Bureau of the Census, 1960, 1970 and 1980 Census of Population, *Occupational Characteristics, Earnings by Occupation and Education* and *Occupations of Persons with High Earnings*; U.S. Department of Labor, *Employment and Earnings*; and American Council on Education/UCLA, *National Norms for Entering College Freshmen* (various years), for shifts in career plans in response to job-market changes.

Although the initial series of questions were intended to elicit information about annual earnings (from employment and/or investment) and growth in company size (among the self-employed) or promotions (among employees), the respondents themselves were the first to volunteer this information in career contexts. For example, respondents were seeking to justify what, in certain instances, were substantial pay decreases, on the grounds that it heightened the chances of later advancement at another firm or their own. The number of respondent references to occupation was so much higher than anticipated in these early interviews, it was clear that this factor could not be omitted from any serious investigation of financial success or failure that resulted from employment or investment. The careers of these individuals provided the backgrounds against which financially related activities of every sort were interpreted.

To ensure consistent data coverage in this area, each sample member was asked to provide a list of the half-dozen co-workers with whom the frequency of on-the-job interaction was highest and/or of greatest importance. The explanation offered for the request was that, as part of the dimension of job satisfaction, brief reviews emphasizing positive or negative features of each co-worker would be useful. Highly critical comments across the board, with no co-workers excepted, did indeed serve to indicate an elevated level of job dissatisfaction as measured by the differential rate of subsequent job change. Nevertheless, the lists turned out to be of great utility in maintaining continuous contact with each member. In fact, the sample size would have suffered significantly more attrition (18.4 percent; 924 out of 5,018, as of February 1984), had it not been for the lists, which were updated annually if the same employment position obtained, or within four months after each employment shift.[2] In hundreds of instances, when post office, phone company, or residential neighbors were unable to specify the new address, phone number, or institutional affiliation if any of a sample member who had moved to an unknown location and thus threatened to become lost to follow-up inquiries, the inner circle of co-workers in each case was able to help us restore contact by offering the name and location of the new employer and/or place of residence.

Close co-workers—in addition to being what were often the only knowledgeable link between past and present varieties of employment of sample members—also provided valuable information about factors involved in the move, a subject they were more willing to discuss freely now that the person in question was no longer with the firm. Considerable care was exercised to make certain that the inquiries appeared to be off-the-record probes about the firm rather than about any specific individual who was no longer employed there. That was necessary since it was not uncommon for sample members to once again find positions at prior employers at future dates. Moreover, the information gathered from co-workers of sample members assisted us in determining what the overall rate of turnover was at the firm during the period under examination, a critical reference level against which to measure the frequency of job changes by sample members in that particular industry or company.

Similar considerations applied to changing levels of demand within each occupation, as monitored on a current basis using monthly indices such as the *Engineer/Scientist Demand Index* by Deutsch, Shea, and Evans, Inc., calculated from want-ad placements. The expansion and contraction of employment demand within any given occupation had a calculable effect on the individuals whose cases are discussed in this work, but we have given prominence to predictable, age-related, and internal factors in career development, as opposed to hasty reactions necessitated by external factors, particularly by rapidly shrinking demand, such as that which teachers at all levels faced in the early 1970s. The statistical basis for the decision was that the proportion of career shifts undertaken by members of our sample three or more years after graduation from college or graduate school which were not responses to changing job-market conditions far exceeded those that were.

A concerted effort was made throughout the study to obtain reliable

---

[2]The peak attrition rate, 29.5 percent, was experienced with the student sample, with 443 out of 1,500 missing or deceased in December 1979. Stepped-up funding by a corporate sponsor, which began on January 1, 1980, allowed us to locate and again continue monitoring 142 of the 443 (median lapse of monitoring times of the 142 was 15 months).

data on consumption expenditures by sample members, to assess their impact on career development. Again, sample and stratum means, on the one hand, and population means, on the other, were compared annually; for instance, during the 1970s, as a national average, 2.6 and 8.2 (versus our 1.7 and 12.8) percent of consumption outlays were devoted to alcohol and tobacco, and recreation, respectively, with consistent decreases in the case of the former commodities as income rose above $7,000 (3 percent of $7–7,999; 2.7 percent of $12–14,999; 2 percent of $25,000 +), and consistent increases in outlays for recreation (6 percent, 7.8 percent and 11.3 percent in the three income categories cited above). For further details, see U.S. Department of Labor, Bureau of Labor Statistics. *Average Annual Expenditures for Commodity and Service Groups Classified by Nine Family Characteristics, 1972 and 1973*, Consumer Expenditure Survey Series: Interview Survey, 1972 and 1973, Report 455-3, 1976. One of many conclusions to emerge from our data was that, using constant-dollar three-year income averaging as a standard, more than 58% of the sample slipped to a lower income level briefly (seven months, on average) at least once during the period under study, and were significantly more likely to maintain the consumption pattern established in the previous income span than to decrease expenditures to bring them more into line with reduced earnings. This imbalance had the effect of compelling the individual to shelve temporarily career plans in exchange for an income matched to current consumption outlays. Nonetheless, as was clear from repeated comparisons of the results obtained from comprehensive questionnaires administrated to all three samples at three-year intervals— in which information about psychological, economic, and social attitudes, group affiliation and identification, as well as more standard data on income, education, and marital status, was collected and assessed with respect to background information and biographical factors—a prolonged period of reduced earnings (on the order of 50 months) was usually required for a significant modification of previously stated career objectives.

One effective way to get beyond some of the limitations associated with the combination of stratified and cluster sampling we employed was to regularly test the tentative conclusions arrived at by using interested self-employed, employee, and managerial volunteers. Although here too self-selection introduces distortions of its own—which are then frequently compounded by researcher bias—we believe that much invaluable information of a practical nature was obtained by proceeding carefully and remaining mindful of the work by R. Rosenthal, *Experimenter Effects in Behavior Research* (New York: Irvington Publishers, 1976); R.A. Jones, *Self-Fulfilling Prophecies: Social, Psy-*

chological and Physiological Effects of Expectancies, (Hillsdale, New Jersey: L. Erlbaum Associates, Publishers, 1977); as well as J. Cohen, *Statistical Power Analysis for the Behavioral Sciences* (New York: Academic Press, 1977) on effect size.

Index

A

adolescence, changes during, 45
Ages of Man, 199
aging and irritability, 207
alienation, 4, 37
ambivalence toward subordinates, 169–170
American Express, 38
anonymity, fear of, 82
anti-business sentiments, 3
anti-democratic dimensions of work, 74
anxiety
  emergence of, 55
  suppression of, 14
Architectural Digest, 235
attitudes toward the elderly, 211

B

baby-boom generation, 195
Battle of the Bulge, 203
Belgium, 203
Broadway shows, 233
Burger King, 139
burn-out, 249

C

California, 31, 122
career specialization, 30–31, 42
Chicago, commodities firms in, 122
clones, 164
Cohen, Jacob, 279
college diplomas, 57

college graduates, numbers of, 29
competition among employees, 208, 225, 266
compliments
  artificial, 193
  varying with age of recipient, 165, 192
compulsive socializing, 34
computers, 9, 176, 185–191
concern about grades, 30, 32
corporate acquisition activity, 18, 22, 74, 214
corporate bankruptcy rates, 183–184
Coser, L. A., 140n
Cuban missile crisis, 30
culture shock, 57

D

Data General, 187
deception
  by employees, 17
  by executives, 115–116
Depression, the Great, 5, 184
Deutsch, Shea and Evans, Inc., 277
Digital Equipment, 187
distrust, 99–101, 219

E

Einstein, Albert, 76
employee timidity, 123
Erikson, Erik, 199–201
Europe, 42
executive recruiters, 93